The
Web
Library

The
Web
Library

Building a World Class Personal Library with Free Web Resources

Nicholas G. Tomaiuolo
Edited by Barbara Quint

 Information Today, Inc.

Medford, New Jersey

First printing, 2004

The Web Library: Building a World Class Personal Library with Free Web Resources

Copyright © 2004 by Nicholas G. Tomaiuolo

Publisher's Note: The author and publisher have taken care in preparation of this book but make no expressed or implied warranty of any kind and assume no responsibility for errors or omissions. No liability is assumed for incidental or consequential damages in connection with or arising out of the use of the information or programs contained herein.

Many of the designations used by manufacturers and sellers to distinguish their products are claimed as trademarks. Where those designations appear in this book and Information Today, Inc. was aware of a trademark claim, the designations have been printed with initial capital letters.

Library of Congress Cataloging-in Publication Data

Tomaiuolo, Nicholas G., 1955–
    The Web library : building a world class personal library with free Web resources / Nicholas G. Tomaiuolo ; edited by Barbara Quint.
       p. cm.
Includes bibliographical references and index.
    ISBN 0-910965-67-6
    1. Computer network resources. 2. Online information services. 3. Digital libraries. 4. Internet searching. 5. Web sites--Directories. 6. Internet addresses--Directories. I. Quint, Barbara. II. Title.

    ZA4150.T66 2003
    025.04--dc22

                                                                2003015424

Printed and bound in the United States of America.

Publisher: Thomas H. Hogan, Sr.
Editor-in-Chief: John B. Bryans
Managing Editor: Deborah R. Poulson
Editorial Services Manager: Lauree Padgett
Copy Editor: Pat Hadley-Miller
Graphics Department Director: M. Heide Dengler
Book Designer: Kara Mia Jalkowski
Cover Designer: Ashlee Caruolo
Indexer: Enid Zafran

Dedication

For Kristin, Ben, Vicki, and Carmen.
With love and thankfulness.

Contents

Chapter Two

Chapter Three

Chapter Four

Chapter Five

Chapter Six

Chapter Seven

Pixels at an Exhibition 293

Figures

Tables

About the Web Page

Your Key to Building a World Class Personal Library

As the philosopher Heraclitus adroitly observed, "it is not possible to stand in the same river twice." This is true, in spades, when considering the World Wide Web. That's the reason the author has placed all the Web sites discussed in *The Web Library* at http://library.ccsu.edu/library/tomaiuolon/theweblibrary.htm. With the book in hand, readers are encouraged to use the links on the page to reach valuable content. Furthermore, the author will monitor the appearance, disappearance, and reappearance of resources as they evolve.

The companion Web page for this book was created to help you, the information seeker. Bookmark it and use it whenever you wish to view the current status of free content on the Web. Visit it often; it's not only your portal to the sites listed in the book, it is also your gateway to updated links and new resources.

Disclaimer:
Neither publisher nor author makes any claim as to the results that may be obtained through the use of http://library.ccsu.edu/library/tomaiuolon/theweb library.htm or of any of the resources it references or links to. Neither publisher nor author will be held liable for any results, or lack thereof, obtained by the use of this site or any of its links; for any third-party charges; or for any hardware, software, or other problems that may occur as a result of using it. http://library.ccsu.edu/library/ tomaiuolon/theweblibrary.htm is subject to change or discontinuation without notice at the discretion of the publisher or author.

Foreword

by Steve Coffman

"I can get it for you wholesale." Those are some of the most seductive works in the English language. And in *The Web Library: Building a World Class Personal Library with Free Web Resources*, Nicholas G. Tomaiuolo goes them one better. He promises to get them for you free. Magazine subscriptions, journal articles, reference works, online indexes and databases, books, newspapers, broadcast archives, images, special collections. You name it. All free for the taking on the Web.

It wasn't all that long ago that the only place you could come close to finding such a collection of content at such a good price was at the library—and even the largest libraries could not have provided access to everything Nick has collected.

But today, all of that has changed. The development of the Web has provided us with a distribution channel that makes it cheap and easy to share information with others. And the Web, in turn, has attracted legions of individuals and organizations with information to share. Some of them do it for purely altruistic reasons, like the hundreds of volunteers on Project Gutenberg, typing their fingers to the bone to get yet another book online. Many are universities, government agencies, associations, and other authoritative sources that have discovered that the Internet is simply a cheaper and more effective way of disseminating their information than print on paper. And many are commercial publishers and Web content producers who are willing to risk giving some of their content away for free on the Web, in hopes they will be able to entice you into a subscription or at least make you stick around long enough to see some of the ads on their sites. Whatever their reasons, the end result is the same. Lots and lots of information you previously would have had to pay for is now available for the taking to anyone who wants it.

Anyone willing to take the time and trouble to find it, that is. And therein lies the crux of the problem. While there have been many wonderful and useful resources added to the Web in the past few years, there has been much more trash, junk, and just plain schlock. Finding the good stuff among all of the garbage takes time, effort, and a good deal of skill. That's time, energy, and skill that most of us don't have. So, even though there is a virtual cornucopia of free, high-quality information now available on the Web, few of us have ever taken advantage of more than a tiny percentage of it, because we lack the time and knowledge to track it down. Poverty in the midst of plenty.

Nick has radically changed that equation. He's done the legwork to track down the good stuff, and in *The Web Library* he has drawn a road map showing exactly where to find it. Want access to a rich periodical collection without the high subscription costs? Nick guides you to dozens of sources, like FindArticles, MagPortal, and others that provide full-text articles from hundreds of titles that would cost thousands of dollars if you subscribed to the print editions. But he doesn't stop there; he tracks down similar sources for research journals, compares content available on periodical Web sites, such as Atlantic Unbound and Time.com, with the content that appears in the print versions, and points the way to the thousands of full-text titles available through subscription databases on many library Web sites. Of course, with such a massive collection, you've got to have ways of finding the articles you want within it, so Nick points out free indexes, abstracts, and specially designed search engines like ARC, the Cross Archive Searching service that will locate research articles on preprint servers. And if what you want is not available for free, Nick compares prices and delivery options from many of the key pay-per-view services. Finally, when you are working with free resources, it is just as important that you know what you are *not* getting in the bargain, and Nick is careful to point out the limitations of the sources he recommends. Follow the instructions in *The Web Library* and for very little effort you can build yourself a periodical collection that would be the envy of many libraries, for next to nothing. And Nick gives similar treatment to online books, reference works, image files, news sites, and "AskA" reference services.

Nick's primary purpose in writing *The Web Library* was to show how individuals could take advantage of free or low-cost resources to build their own personal libraries online. The real irony here is that in these tight economic times, it is libraries themselves that may be one of the best markets for this information. One of the key functions of a library is to assure that its patrons get the best information at the best price. And when money is so tight for libraries, it is just professionally irresponsible to pay for resources that are otherwise available for free. So, I would highly recommend that all libraries carefully evaluate their current collections and acquisitions policies in light of the resources Nick describes in *The Web Library*. And I'll wager there are few libraries that won't find ways to stretch their limited acquisitions budgets a good deal further within these pages.

It is also important to note that building your Web library is not a one-time effort. There's plenty more great content out there that nobody has found and documented yet. New resources come onto the Web all the time. Existing sites change their coverage or features, and recently many sites have withered or closed down entirely, as Internet advertising revenues have dried up. So the Web is a moving target. In *The Web Library*, Nick has taken a snapshot of the Web at a particular point in time, but somebody has to take responsibility for keeping up with it.

That job is bigger than any one person or any one book. But it might be just the right size for libraries. As *The Web Library* points out, we have now reached a point where many of the information resources—once the exclusive province of libraries—are now available to anybody on the Web. It is simply ludicrous for libraries to continue to purchase things that everybody else can get for free. It is high time we re-evaluated our traditional collections and roles in light of the changing reality of the Web. It may be too early yet to come up with a definitive understanding of the roles the library might play in this brave new information marketplace. But we can certainly start by taking up where Nick has left off and helping each of our patrons build and maintain their own Web libraries— both by helping them select and keep track of the best free content on the Web, and by purchasing databases, periodicals, and other resources. The exact details still need to be worked out, but clearly the traditional library could play a critical role in continuing the work started here.

Steve Coffman is Vice President for Product Development, Library Systems and Services, Inc. (LSSI), Germantown, Maryland.

Acknowledgments

The author wishes to acknowledge the following people who were instrumental in helping research and write this book:

Barbara Quint for her ideas, patience, guidance, and encouragement.

Maggie Ducharme for her patience and generous moral support.

Katie Bacon, Paula Berinstein, Allegra Burnette, Michael Calia, Tara Calishain, Steve Coffman, Brian Coutts, Bill Dimm, Gary Duchane, Lisa Guernsey, Richard Hanley, Michael Hart, Péter Jacsó, Paul Katcher, William Katz, Simon Kirwan, Susan McGlamery, Patricia Memmott, Eric Lease Morgan, David Moynihan, Greg Newby, John Mark Ockerbloom, Joan Packer, Edward Picot, Diane Shaw, Bernie Sloan, Patti Tuohy, and Eva Wolynska for shared time, expertise, perspectives, creativity, cooperation, and wit.

All the talented publishing professionals at Information Today, Inc., especially John Bryans, Deborah Poulson, Lauree Padgett, Heide Dengler, Kara Jalkowski, Ashlee Caruolo, Pat Hadley-Miller, Tom Hogan, Jr., Lisa Wrigley, and Thomas H. Hogan.

The faculty and administration of Central Connecticut State University and the Board of Trustees of the Connecticut State University for their support of the project.

Introduction

In the best economic times, smart people still want to know how they can "get the most bang for their buck." Even when you have a wallet full of bills, it makes no sense to walk away from a deal that saves money. Yet it makes no sense to shop for bargains that are poorly made and are of no use. This book is not only about finding resources that save money, but finding resources that are valuable and can be put to practical use. Librarians and individual information seekers should be interested in discovering these sites, because despite the resources they may already be paying for, they will be surprised to learn that countless sites are providing the same information (or in some cases nearly the same information) without charge.

A physical library houses books, periodicals, reference materials including indexes and abstracts, and special collections. The Web Library is similar. It offers digital books, journal sites, search engines that identify articles, and often free articles. Then it goes farther. Live chat and expert sites exist for reference. Electronic archives of images, unpublished materials, etc., exist for special collections. This book will show you where to look for electronic versions of items that, if translated into physical items that would sit on library shelves, would cost considerable money. Whether you're accessing the full text of journals from a Web site and saving thousands of dollars in subscriptions, downloading hundreds of novels at no charge, inspecting a rare book valued at $5 million, or visiting a scientific preprint site where information is being distributed prior to being published in a printed version, you will recognize the value of *The Web Library* as each chapter unfolds.

Moreover, some of the information that can be acquired on the World Wide Web is even more valuable because it doesn't have a physical counterpart.

What Was and What Is

When I began working at a medical library, most of my time was dedicated to searching clinical databases for information to assist physicians and medical/dental educators. Although the information retrieved from these searches included only the bare bones (i.e., bibliographic citations and abstracts) required to determine the value of reading the actual research papers, the searches were not free. Database vendors charged varying prices for access to this important literature. The library paid a fee to the vendors, then added a surcharge and passed the cost to the requestor of the information. Back in 1989 even searches of the publicly supported National Library of Medicine's MEDLINE database, which carried only bibliographic citations and abstracts, ranged in cost from under a dollar to several dollars to search depending on the information vendor that supplied the database. Now anyone can search that same database for free at http://www4.ncbi.nlm.nih.gov/PubMed.

As time progressed and individuals became more adept at searching CD-ROMs and the World Wide Web, I noticed that the cost to access to these materials had actually begun to drop! Subscription services that ran automatic searches of the literature of interest to individuals (called Current Awareness or Selective Dissemination of Information services) began to yield to people performing their own searches. Librarian-mediated computer database searching at many libraries began to decline also. Librarians who once performed thousands of searches a year for their clients reported that requests had diminished to a fraction of their old business. Searches that would once have cost from $5 to

$300 can now be performed free and, in many cases, retrieve not merely bibliographic but full-text or full-image results. Some database producers began to put portions of their databases on the Web at no charge, and entrepreneurs found other strategies for providing free access to materials that once required payment.

Many of the materials that once cost considerable sums of money to access in either electronic (online or CD-ROM) or print form have actually become less expensive to obtain via the World Wide Web, and are sometimes absolutely free. One of the strings attached, however, is that you need to know where to look to find the free materials. I use the Web every day to find books, magazine articles, documents not published elsewhere, news, images, and answers to questions. This book aims to show readers where to find these sites and how to use them to save time and money.

This doesn't mean people won't be visiting libraries. Librarians are on the leading edge of helping individuals find information. Nor does this mean that people should always opt for the least expensive resource. A free or inexpensive resource may be adequate or identical to a resource that is also for sale. Conversely, the resource may not do the job so well. You must also understand that many types of information will never be free. Among resources that you will still need to pay for or, at the very least, make a trip to your local library to use, are sensitive company information, the newest bestsellers, and periodical articles that never make it to the Web. Each library collection offers something slightly different from the next, as will your own Web Library.

It is unwise for individuals to trust everything they unearth on the Web. This is where a librarian's knowledge and judgment become crucial. Historically, librarians were the custodians of books. Learning about books and the classification of knowledge was their charge. Later, librarians became the database experts. In the 1980s any librarian with a good book collection and a subscription to a database vendor was at the top of the game. Books, journals, and databases are no longer the only information sources the librarian needs to know. A librarian's mandate now goes beyond simply guaranteeing access to information—librarians must distill information, recognizing value and separating it from dross. Librarians have always done this by evaluating sources and applying rigorous criteria to what they have put on their shelves and, more recently, the vendors to which they have entrusted their clients. Now that the ultimate self-publishing medium, the Web, exists, the mandate becomes even more important, though not necessarily more difficult to achieve. To help librarians and individuals gain insight into the Web, this book contains interviews with more than a dozen Web information experts—the people behind the content (my notes are included in brackets in italic text). From the Internet Public Library to the Museum of Modern Art, from the *Atlantic Monthly* and Time.com to Project Gutenberg, from academics to aggregators, these individuals let readers know what shapes their decisions and what goes on at their Web sites. Their comments will enlighten you.

Welcome to the Web Library

The Web Library is arranged into nine chapters providing examples, alternatives, and strategies for building a personal collection of free (or at least, low-cost) virtual resources and services matching those usually found in a physical library. Most chapters discuss a library service or resource and tell you where you can find equivalents on the Web. The remaining chapters discuss related issues such as where to store the information and what software will facilitate viewing the collection you make.

Because both timely and retrospective information from magazines is so important to the public, especially professionals and students, we begin with a chapter on finding free magazine articles. Magazine subscribers, whether librarians or individuals, understand that periodical subscriptions are expensive and continue to increase in cost. Imagine the amount of money that a small library with just 200 subscriptions or a large library with 8,000 dedicates each year to magazine and journal subscriptions! If you know where to look, however, you can often find magazine and journal literature online for free. The content ranges from entertainment to scholarly tracts. The same goes for indexing and abstracting tools. Chapter One provides many starting points.

I have to smile whenever another newspaper's circulation department telemarketer offers me a deal on delivery. Apparently, many individuals still do not know that hundreds of papers operate excellent Web sites that not only rival but in many cases expand the coverage of their hard copy publications. Combine this with the other comprehensive and breaking news sites profiled in Chapter Two and you will not only be on top of the news, but you will also be able to appreciate it from multiple perspectives.

Chapter Three, Ready or Not, discusses free reference works. Beginning with a listing of core reference works and their hard copy costs or online costs, Chapter Three explores free or low-cost versions of those works as well as comparable free electronic resources. Everyone knows how busy reference librarians are, and rightfully so, since they command knowledge of thousands of essential resources. This chapter will help you take command of those resources from your computer.

Chapter Four continues our consideration of reference information by introducing numerous "Expert" and "AskA" sites that may help answer a broad range of questions. Chapter Four also discusses online 24 hour a day/7 day a week (24/7) reference and other forms and sources of virtual expertise, including library programs. It may also help answer the question: "How much does it cost to answer a reference question?"

Chapter Five, Books in the Web Library, provides information on the number of books at various libraries, costs of acquisition, cataloging, maintenance, and circulation. The cost and availability of some retail books are contrasted with their virtual equivalents. For example, what percentage of a benchmark anthology of literature, such as that offered by the Encyclopedia Britannica's *Great Books of the Western World*, is available as free electronic text? The chapter also describes some of the limitations of electronic book archives and discusses some of the major electronic text sites such as Project Gutenberg and the University of Pennsylvania's On-Line Books.

Web browsers—Netscape, Internet Explorer, and Opera, for example—provide our graphical means of exploring information on the Internet. The term "Web browser" implies we will encounter images—graphics—at the Web sites we visit. Chapter Six, When Image Is Everything, discusses strategies for locating images and digital image collections. But not all images are free, so be prepared for a primer on copyright issues that govern downloading these files from the Web.

Special collections: Not all physical libraries have them, but your Web Library does. From Dr. Seuss to quilts to fine arts and Web-only exhibitions, Chapter Seven helps put museum and exhibition goers into the present, past, and future of galleries in cyberspace.

Many books published by Information Today, Inc. offer companion Web sites that link to the resources they discuss. Creating the Web page that accompanies this book located at http://library.ccsu.edu/library/tomaiuolon/theweblibrary.htm proved to be one of the most enjoyable experiences I have had using computers. That is where readers will find links to the sites profiled in this book. (For more information, see "About the Web Page.") "Software Keys to the Web Library" provides practical suggestions for creating a personal Web page so you can link to free Web sites that provide library-quality material. It also supplies information about the plugs-in required to manage a Web library and some of the "cool tools" from which you can benefit. Once you've decided which components of your library are most important, you can customize your own Web page and use it as your portal to the Internet.

We may need to put our Web library into perspective: What does it hold; what might it never have? How much have we saved and what have we learned? All World Wide Web users should be aware of the incredible pace at which things change—including Web site content and addresses. Chapter Nine, Final Considerations, discusses effectively using the Web to ensure you will be able to add to your personal Web library in the years to come.

While attending library school, I recall a classmate who created an impressive slide presentation on the subject of personal libraries. One of the slides showed that the student's basement contained library shelving packed with books. I was impressed not only because my friend had obviously read (or at least collected) a large number of books, but also because the books and shelving appeared so expansive. Individuals should relish the size of their personal libraries and display them with pride. We should recognize, however, that the information we may require for academic and business assignments, as well as personal enjoyment, need no longer occupy row upon row of bookcases. Nor should this information push your entire credit card limit, for that matter. There's plenty of valuable, free information in the Web library. (Should you doubt the value of free information, such as public domain books, take a look through the titles in a Disney film and feature-length cartoon catalog!)

Are you ready for a healthy dose of insider information combined with a thorough exploration of many of the Web's most valuable sites? I promise you will be astonished by how much you can save and what you will learn. Read on!

Chapter One

Free Articles and Indexes: Can You Afford Not to Use Them?

Two important resources that every library offers are periodical literature (e.g., magazines, scholarly journals) and indexes and abstracts (the tools traditionally used to access the information in periodicals). Casual readers, consumers, businesspeople, health professionals, teachers, and students frequently turn to periodicals not only for entertainment, but also for product evaluations, management data, research concerning medical treatments, lesson plans, and subject background information. Even younger pupils in primary grades are often expected to locate periodical articles to complement their budding research projects on volcanoes, the rainforest, and endangered species, for example. Although libraries are repositories of the materials required to fill these information needs, many librarians find it difficult to sustain collections that satisfy all their users' expectations.

Budgets for periodical and index subscriptions have tried to maintain the status quo at a time when costs for such materials increase steadily. The results of price surveys appear in both *American Libraries* and on the American Library Association Web site. The results indicate that while overall percentages of price increases stayed at under double digits for 2002, the average price for the sample of 3,919 periodicals rose from $261.56 to $282.31, translating into a 7.9 percent increase. That's a very slight decrease over the 2000–2001 increase rate of 8.3 percent, but in 1999 the rate jumped by 10.4 percent and then 9 percent more in 2000.[1,2]

In one case the problem of overpriced periodicals was perceived as so severe that Dr. Mark Riley, a professor at Florida State University, resigned as an unpaid referee for a nuclear physics peer-reviewed publication in 1999. His action protested the rising cost of journals published by Elsevier Science. Charles Miller, dean of libraries at Riley's institution, applauded the protest, citing that journal subscriptions accounted for 75 percent of the libraries' spending.[3] In many cases libraries cancel journal subscriptions in order to maintain fiscal balance, but this strategy has its pitfalls. Journal publishers may increase prices to replace the revenue lost due to cancellations.

The phenomenon is not limited to scientific journals. The cost of magazines that consumers take for granted has risen also. Simply look through and compare some of the issues from the 1970s, '80s, '90s, and today. The cover prices and subscription prices will quickly illustrate the point.

Nor do indexes and abstracts come cheaply. Setting aside the scientific services where *Chemical Abstracts* commands $23,000 a year or the considerably less expensive *Engineering Index,* which fetches $4,000 annually, even basic indexing tools can add up. The public library's standard print resource for locating articles is the H.W. Wilson Company's *Reader's Guide to Periodical Literature.* It costs a minimum of $310, and if the librarian opts for a more timely edition of the *Guide* (nine per year), the price increases. Placing a few more standard resources from Wilson such as the

Humanities Index, Social Sciences Index, Education Index, and *Applied Science and Technology Index* onto the shelves requires a modest library to invest at least $2,000 each year to access simple bibliographic information—author, title, source—for periodical literature. Definite costs for some of these resources cannot be directly ascertained for our purposes because the publisher prices them according to the Service Basis (a sum calculated as a function of "the degree of service or use the index provides the particular library that subscribes to it"). If librarians purchase the CD-ROM versions, the charge can easily triple or more.

Online databases that provide not only indexing, but also summaries (and in some cases full text), cost even more. Because subscriptions to these services are often configured using many variables, specific costs cannot be stated here. You can safely surmise, however, that individual consumers would not choose to foot bills that could range from $2,000 to $10,000 and higher. These products are valuable resources for many libraries and their users, but they take a considerable chunk of an institution's budget.

Despite the financial picture portrayed in the previous paragraphs, the good news is that the Web offers several viable alternatives. Where at one time, perhaps in a past too distant for some readers to recall, each and every fragment of information provided by indexes was exquisitely valuable and for sale, a number of access points to the periodical literature exist gratis on the Web. Moreover, an appreciable amount of the full text of magazine literature itself is free.

Why It Pays to Listen to Mother
Subscription Options

Soulful vocalist Smokey Robinson said it in 1961, and it's still true today: "You better shop around!" Although the most comprehensive indexing and full-text Web-based services will never be inexpensive, you should look closely at those that are free. Often individuals need to know about only a handful of Web sites to optimize their general research and recreational reading. Many individuals may choose to subscribe to a service that offers an easy search and document delivery mechanism. eLibrary heads this list. eLibrary, which offers the full text of more than 600 periodicals (not counting other matter such as television and radio show transcripts), costs $19.95 per month or $99.95 per year. Questia (http://www.questia.com), a company that markets to college students and their parents, offers a virtual library including approximately 150 journals; access costs are $19.95 per month or $44.95 for three months with the annual subscription priced at $119.95 in 2003. XanEdu (http://www.xanedu.com), another product aimed at college students, offers thousands of full-text periodicals priced at $19.90 for three months, $29.90 for six months, and $49.90 for a year. Another option is Infotrieve's ArticleFinder priced at $99 per year.

Pay-Per-View

Another popular option is using pay-per-view services. Ingenta at http://www.ingenta.com (approximately 28,000 publications), Elsevier's ScienceDirect (scholarly journal articles), and HighWire Press at http://highwire.stanford.edu are among the resources offering this arrangement. Note, however, that occasionally these services may offer some journals, especially back issues, for free. For example, out of a total of 342 HighWire hosted journals, 254 are pay-per-view. When choosing the pay-per-view option, the information consumer needs to become a savvy shopper. Prices of individual articles can be tolerable or terrible, depending on the service. Example: Let's say you're a college student enrolled in a distance education English composition course and studying author Tom Wolfe. You need to locate three background sources for a short research paper. You have several options even if you haven't

Table 1.1   Typical article retrieval from full-text journal services, including cost

Article information	Services where located	Full text delivery cost
"The End of the Ectomorph" by John Derbyshire. *National Review,* November 20, 2000	Ingenta	$22.25
"Hooking Up" by Midge Decter. *Commentary,* January 1, 2001	Ingenta	$21.50
"Material Boy" by Rand Richards Cooper. *Commonweal,* May 7, 1999	Ingenta	$18.32

subscribed to the monthly or annual services. The professor has recommended using Ingenta because you can search it without charge and view full-text on a pay-per-view basis. The type of retrieval you can expect is shown in Table 1.1.

The total cost to view all these articles is $62.07. But if the objective is to locate three full-text articles about Tom Wolfe, you should know that you could find the three articles previously listed for free using a Web site called FindArticles. Unfortunately, no single resource will have the answer to all of your information questions, but it pays to know which tool to consult for free information.

FindArticles is the best resource for entirely free periodical articles. Its publication list hovers around 500. Because it has been available for several years, it appears to have a degree of durability. Librarians have observed, however, that some journal titles are dropped without notice. So if you become dependent on FindArticles for reading a specific magazine, you may not always find that title the next time you search the resource.

A Note on Article Formatting

When you use a free resource such as FindArticles, you should not expect too many frills. The strength of a free resource lies in its provision of the verbal content of articles. A value-added, pay-per-view or subscription service may often produce the same full-text content and add the images from the original article.

On the other hand, many of the articles offered by the pay-per-view and subscription services, particularly older archives, omit images. For example, LexisNexis Academic Universe, a powerful full-text database service focused on newspaper and journal articles and commanding a high subscription price, does not include the photographs that run with the original material. Whether you choose a pricey database with full images, a pricey database without images, or a free resource without images, depends on your own requirements. Is it important to see another still photograph of Alan Greenspan as he testifies before the United States Congress or will reading his comments suffice? Is it sufficient to read about the latest oil spill off the coast of Spain or do you need to view the damage?

Depth of Coverage

Regarding FindArticles, one issue that I needed to explore was the depth of coverage of each periodical. Associates at the Gale Group, the company that supplies the full-text content for FindArticles, state that the coverage for the majority of the publications extends back to 1998 and is continuous. They are quick to add that as new publications come on board, however, coverage begins at that point (there is no retrospective coverage of new periodicals). But could a free resource really include all the articles from the publications it covers?

I performed a few test searches and learned that every article from the March 2002 issue of one of my favorite magazines (*Searcher: The Magazine for Database Professionals*) was available free. I checked this by looking at the print copy and comparing it with my search results from FindArticles. If you wanted a print copy of *Searcher* to read and file away, the cover price was $8.95. If you had deep pockets, you could get the full text of the articles by paying over $20 for each article at Ingenta (including the service charge and copyright charge). Regarding that specific issue of *Searcher*, FindArticles passed my test.

The very popular *Psychology Today* is among the hundreds of other periodicals FindArticles covers. Again I wanted to verify that every article from this publication was available. For *Psychology Today's* January/February 2001 issue, I noted that 39 articles (from very brief to moderately long) were published in the print magazine. I found all the articles free online via FindArticles with the exception of one.

Still skeptical, I explored one additional title: a scholarly, peer-reviewed journal published by Cornell University called *Administrative Science Quarterly*. In my test of its volume 45, issue 4 (2000) contents, all the printed articles were available free at FindArticles.

FindArticles has one major problem. The user *must* read the "Search Tips" to effectively locate information. Failing to execute a query as the Web site specifies will retrieve hundreds of irrelevant documents. Unlike Google or other resources we may be accustomed to, this database requires some training for successful usage. Nonetheless, as the list at Table 1.2 shows, if you use just six percent of FindArticle's periodicals, you save over $2,000 per year.

Other publications available in FindArticles include *American Forests, American Journal of Sports Medicine, ArtForum, Harper's Magazine, Hearing Journal, Macworld, Pediatrics, Saturday Evening Post, Sex Roles: A Journal of Research, The Sporting News,* and *Wines & Vines.* (The full title list is available at http://www.find articles.com/cf_0/PI/name.jhtml.)

Was the Tom Wolfe search too offbeat? A more topical search that may demonstrate the benefit of using FindArticles over a pay-per-view service, shown in Table 1.3, concerns the collapse of Enron and the impact its demise had on investors. The three articles referenced in the table appear free at FindArticles.

Table 1.2   Random sample of publications, representing 6 percent of the periodicals covered free by FindArticles, and their actual subscription costs to individuals in paper copy

Periodical Title	Minimum cost of personal annual subscription rounded to nearest dollar (Source: actual publication or *Ulrich's International Periodicals Directory*)
Academy of Management Review	$105
American Political Science Review	$25
Black Enterprise	$22
Business Horizons	$96
College Student Journal	$24
Commonweal	$47
Dance Magazine	$35
Down Beat	$35
English Historical Review	$120
Film Comment	$25
Film Quarterly	$27
Gifted Child Today Magazine	$35
Golf Digest	$48
History Today	$62
HR Magazine	$70
Humanist	$25
Industry Week	$55
Journal of Law, Medicine, and Ethics	$110
Magazine Antiques	$40
Mergers & Acquisitions	$595
National Review	$59
Psychology Today	$16
School Library Journal	$98
Sloan Management Review	$99
Soccer Digest	$24
Social Research	$30
Twentieth Century Literature	$30
U.S. Banker	$52
Vegetarian Times	$24
Women's Quarterly	$20
30 titles	Minimum total cost of personal print subscriptions: $2,053

An Illustrative Comparison

Let's discuss three different types of full-text services. I performed 20 searches using FindArticles (free), Ingenta (pay-per-view), and the XanEdu Research Engine (subscription). Each search used a strategy constructed to maximize relevant retrieval from each service. If you wish to replicate these results, you will need to read the

Table 1.3   Additional typical retrieval from full-text journal services, including cost

Article information	Services where located	Full text delivery cost
"What Investors Can Learn from the Enron Mess" by Matthew S. Scott. *Black Enterprise*, April 1, 2002	Ingenta	$13.07
"Beyond Enron" by Ronald Fink. *CFO*, February 1, 2002	Ingenta	$19.24
"Enron's Bastard Children" by Ramesh Ponnuru. *National Review*, May 6, 2002	Ingenta	$19.97

Help and Tips at each site as well as become conversant with a number of other options that vary among the services. These searches were performed in early 2003. Table 1.4 shows features of each service and the number of hits returned from each service for each query.

For most of the searches, FindArticles seems to be the best choice. But consider that Ingenta covers more than 27,000 titles and often locates information in more scholarly sources as well as magazines such as *Martha Stewart Living, Maclean's,* and *Time.* Any of the three is worth exploring; FindArticles provides the most value as a free full-text source, and Ingenta is a praiseworthy free indexing database. When evaluating the raw results, note that the number of hits does not necessarily increase with the number of journals covered by each resource. For example, FindArticles indexes and provides full text for more than 500 journals; a search within its collection for Shakespeare and Hamlet yields 212 articles. Ingenta, a much larger database in terms of the number of journals covered, offers only five articles. XanEdu's retrieval tops out at 50 articles. According to a XanEdu customer service associate, this limit was determined by XanEdu's programmers. Neither subscribers nor free trial searchers can get beyond the first 50 retrieved articles. Note also that I used XanEdu's free trials, which allow searching of just one subset of its total periodical list, therefore

Table 1.4   Comparison of free and fee services including selected
service features

Features	FindArticles	Ingenta	XanEdu
number of sources =	500	27,500	?
list of journals available?	yes	yes	no
service terms	free	pay-per-view	subscribe
full text	yes	yes	yes
free searching and citation info?	yes	yes	no
Subject Areas and Topics			
Arts & Humanites			
"Eyes Wide Shut" and Traumnovelle	13	2	8
Film noir	512	97	50
Funding for the arts	44	84	50
Moai	12	5	9
Ship of Theseus	6	2	3
Shakespeare and Hamlet	212	5	50
Science			
Airbags and death	46	8	7
Drilling and ANWR	90	4	50
Methylphenidate and ADDH	19	4	50
Needlestick accidents	40	28	15
Cell phones and cancer	743	10	50
Shuttle Challenger / responsibility	13	2	17
Social Sciences			
Andrew Johnson's Impeachment	47	7	50
Classroom activities for gifted children	12	7	12
Online shopping and privacy	623	4	50
Whistleblowing	38	137	50
Grade inflation in higher education	36	5	11
Slavery / reparations	181	25	50
Domestic violence and alcohol	280	65	50
Axis of evil	290	36	50

even though the topic "Shuttle Challenger/Responsibility" retrieved only 17 hits in XanEdu's Science subset, other articles may have been available in the Social Sciences subset. Subscribers would have access to all the subsets and, theoretically, retrieve more information.

Another limitation affecting the number of retrieved articles is the number of fields designated as searchable. For example, although Ingenta's database contains the authors, titles, summaries, and full text for the majority of the archived articles, only the titles, authors, and summaries are easily searchable. By contrast, FindArticles automatically searches the full text and yields, in most instances, many additional hits. While Ingenta is a powerful database with much more content than FindArticles, the searcher needs to spend more time massaging the Ingenta database to produce comparable results. Professional searchers realize that bibliographic searching requires a certain amount of tap dancing when trying to extract content from any database, but end-users may not necessarily be so persnickety about their retrievals.

In case you are wondering how FindArticles can offer free content, consider this simple explanation. For a fee the Gale Group supplies full text (i.e., the FindArticles database) to Looksmart, the well-known Internet search engine. Looksmart partners with other businesses; these businesses may pay Looksmart to appear as "Sponsored Listings" or "Related Sponsor Sites" when certain types of searches are performed. For example, an individual begins a search at http://www.looksmart.com. If the search was for the keyword "antidepressants," Looksmart provides Web results and offers the option to "Find news and magazine articles on 'antidepressants' at FindArticles.com." If the individual follows the link, full text articles are retrieved and Sponsored Listings (links to sponsors) are shown. As you may have deduced from this example, going directly to http://www.findarticles.com is really using the back door, though this probably doesn't matter to Looksmart or its FindArticles' sponsors, as long as the user sees the Sponsored Listings.

More for Free

BioMed Central
http://www.biomedcentral.com

BioMed Central (BMC) is a Web publisher of biology and medical research. Since the site launched in 2000, more than 102 free, peer-reviewed BMC journals have come online. The full text of these publications is accessible without charge to registered site visitors.

In 2002 BioMed Central began charging authors a processing fee for publishing their articles. One may suspect that a publisher who charges a writer $500 to publish a work might be running a vanity press; however, this is apparently not the case. Some authors who contribute to BMC journals are affiliated with esteemed private institutions such as Harvard, Yale, Duke, Stanford, New York University, and Johns Hopkins. Upper tier public institutions such as U.C.L.A., Rutgers, and the University of Connecticut are also represented. I cross-referenced some BMC authors and their affiliations to entries in more traditional journals indexed by the National Library of Medicine's MEDLINE database.

The publisher, writers, and other individuals who use BioMed Central are interested in credible research that can be accessed in a timely way. Since BioMed Central does not print physical journals, it can immediately publish articles that have passed the scrutiny of peer-reviewers.

Dissertation Abstracts
http://wwwlib.umi.com/dissertations/search

You may search for relatively new (current year plus a one year backfile) dissertations and theses on the University Microfilms Database without charge. The full file, available on commercial services, extends back over 140 years to 1861. Keyword searches, author searches, advisor searches, plus school and degree name searches are all available. The great feature about this point of access is that for all listed documents you can get a 24-page preview (in addition to the citation and the abstract). If the information in the extended excerpt appeals to you, order a PDF copy of the entire document for under $30.

HighWire Press
http://highwire.stanford.edu/lists/freeart.dtl

This Web site specializes in disseminating science and medical information and allows free access to approximately 500,000 articles from over 340 journals. Free journals include the *British Medical Journal, Clinical Diabetes, Injury Prevention,* and the *Journal of Psychotherapy Practice and Research.* (Annual subscriptions to these four journals alone totals $500.)

Science Direct

http://www.sciencedirect.com

This subscription/pay-per-view full-text journal database from Elsevier can also be of use to nonsubscribers who are interested in the sciences and social sciences. Guests can go to http://www.sciencedirect.com and browse the tables of contents of 1,700 journals. Free full-text exists but is spotty, unfortunately, with only a single issue of some journals (e.g., *International Journal of Accounting, The Lancet*), or entire runs of others (e.g., *Accident and Emergency Nursing, Midwifery*) being available. The free full text is a huge money saver (Elsevier's journals are expensive), and the user may also browse journal tables of contents and abstracts without charge. Regrettably, the journals cannot be searched. Guests may also set up journal alerts and have tables of contents e-mailed to them when designated journals are published—a service that libraries furnish by subscribing to *Current Contents,* another relatively pricey product, or by tediously photocopying the information for clients.

All Academic

http://www.allacademic.com

Search Google for the phrase "academic journal search engine" and your first hit will be "All Academic," which was founded in 1999 by faculty members at the University of Oregon. Journals accessible through this site must be available at no charge. All Academic offers direct access to the sites of approximately 370 high quality publications (e.g., *American Psychologist, American School Board Journal, Conservation Ecology, Essays in Philosophy,* and the *Stanford Humanities Review*). Basic and advanced search functions are available. A great feature of this site is that retrieved source citations can be automatically formatted in APA, MLA, or Chicago Manual style.

Selected Collections of Digitized Journals

Internet Library of Early Journals
http://www.bodley.ox.ac.uk/ilej

This collection is based on a project undertaken at the Universities of Birmingham, Leeds, Manchester, and Oxford. It allows access to only six journals, but it constitutes an important collection because it carries some of the older online periodical titles on the Web. Its digitized images of the pages from the *Annual Register*, for example, date back to 1758.

MOA Journals
http://www.hti.umich.edu/m/moajrnl
http://cdl. library.cornell.edu/moa

Both the University of Michigan and Cornell University maintain archives of selected periodicals as part of the Making of America project under a grant from the Andrew W. Mellon Foundation. As access points to older magazines, both sites bear investigation.

Electronic Journals from the Digital Library and Archives,
University Libraries, Virginia Polytechnic Institute and
State University
http://scholar.lib.vt.edu/ejournals

Virginia Tech provides access to 18 electronic journals. Although most are scientific, it also presents a few social science and humanities titles.

Pointers to Online Collections

The following sites successfully accomplish the task of scouring the Web and gleaning links to collections of full-text periodicals. The collections to which these three sites refer contain thousands of free articles.

Online Books Serials Page
http://onlinebooks.library.upenn.edu/serials.html

This portal page leads to external archives that contain 90 periodicals dating back to the mid-1700s, but include some titles from the present. For example, some of the links will bring the user to the Making of America archives, while others lead to the University of Virginia or other individual magazine Web sites.

Resources for Research Periodicals
http://home.earthlink.net/~ellengarvey/rsapresource1.html

Ellen Garvey's links to online journal collections as well as individual journal archives is most impressive. It is well designed and helps the user go directly to sites offering free access to full text. Important collections such as the University of Michigan's and Cornell University's Making of America journals are accessible from Garvey's page, as well as magazines from the present (*Salon Magazine*) and those that allow the reader to peer into the past (*Godey's Lady's Book*).

A Word to the Wise (Librarian)

Instead of lugging out *Ulrich's International Periodicals Directory* to learn which database covers a particular periodical, why not acquaint yourself with JAKE—the Jointly Administered Knowledge Environment? JAKE is a fairly new development that allows users to enter a journal title and discover if it is indexed by a subscription database. Sure, you all know that the top garden variety databases are going to offer access to *Newsweek* and *Rolling Stone*. But *Maledicta* may be more difficult to track down! JAKE will tell you that it is covered by the MLA Bibliography. Don't have access to the MLA Bib? Take heart, because it is also covered by Sociological Abstracts. Search JAKE at http://jake. med.yale.edu.

Online Magazines: A Close Read

While the sites previously under discussion will help you find articles within specific sets of journals included in a database, there are several other ways to access periodical information in the cyber magazine/journal environment. Some of the numerous magazines and journals on the Web are complete duplicates of their print counterparts. Others are merely persuasive pages that beckon individuals to subscribe to a print magazine. Some are Web-only publications that have never existed as a print magazine. But many are committed to republishing much of the content from print issues, while going beyond the paper copy to enrich the reader's experience. Falling into the latter category of online magazines are Time.com (see Figure 1.1) and Atlantic Unbound. I had the privilege of discussing those Web sites with principals from both publications and have included some of their comments in the two sidebars that follow.

Figure 1.1 Many magazine Web sites offer content that updates on a daily basis. Courtesy of *Time*, copyright 2003.

INSIDER'S VIEWPOINT FROM YOUR WEB LIBRARY PROFESSIONAL: PAUL KATCHER, TIME.COM

Side-by-Side: *Time* Magazine and Time.com

Averaging 10 million page views a week, Time.com ranks high as one of the most popular sites on the Web. *Time* magazine, a publication that has been a favorite with people since its birth in 1923, has a subscription readership of 4,056,150. But with such a successful print magazine, why would the publisher indulge in a freely accessible Web site that might rival the original periodical and, in the view of some, jeopardize its existence?

Paul Katcher, Senior Producer at Time.com, noted that, although the Web site is extremely popular, no "cannibalization" of the printed magazine's market has been perceived. People are not canceling their *Time* magazine subscriptions and viewing it exclusively on the Web. The Web site actually increases subscriptions through online offers of four trial issues of the magazine. (Advantages to subscribing include a Sunday night e-mail newsletter featuring an in-depth preview of what to expect from that week's paper copy, including a Q&A with the author of the cover story and inside information on how the stories were reported and produced. Magazine subscribers also get access, without charge, to the last 52 weeks worth of magazine articles on Time.com. Nonsubscribers get only the last two weeks free.)

The Web site, however, has significant value beyond the hard copy. Although Katcher estimated that they reprint only 50 percent of the hard copy's articles on the site, he also indicated that unlike the newsstand issue, the Web site has no limit on the number of pages, so the work of good authors is "never left on the cutting room floor." And if only 50 percent of the magazine makes it to the Web site (and that *always* includes the cover story), it leaves unlimited space for authors to participate in other projects. For example, in June 2002, 12 writers from bureaus all over the world contributed to the World Cup Soccer Weblog, an ambitious project for Time.com. Mr. Katcher added, "This same kind of participation, with no such thing as running out of space, was a tremendous asset to Time.com during the hectic news months after 9/11. And it will continue to be through the 2002 elections and beyond."

What is the goal of a magazine's Web presence? In *Time*'s case, it is to be everyone's daily destination: ready for them in the morning and in the afternoon with the top stories refreshed whenever appropriate. What is its value for the site visitor? Read important articles from the magazine and have it complemented with additional information on a daily basis. All without spending a dime.

Yet the site makes money. First, sponsors, as with the print magazine, pay to advertise their goods and services. From an information perspective the site also serves readers and itself by making its archive of articles available for searching (free) and the articles themselves available for purchase at $2.50 each or with a $4.95 day pass, $7.95 monthly subscription, or an annual fee of $49.95.

The *Atlantic Monthly* is an attractive magazine that has contained articles on a variety of interesting subjects, written by renowned authors, since its inception in November 1857. Featuring travel writing, fiction, poetry, the arts, and commentary on politics, science, language, and even food, the print edition is a bargain at the newsstand price of $3.95. But if you don't mind reading off the computer screen, you can enjoy almost every bit of the magazine and much more free at the Atlantic Unbound (http://www.theatlantic.com).

The Atlantic Unbound, the online publication, goes well beyond what fits between the covers of the print *Atlantic Monthly*. Besides providing a complete archive of issues back to September 1995, special feature articles augment and edify the content of items from the current issue and enrich the backfile with essays that put older stories into perspective. Sidebars and links take readers to interviews with authors, Web-only columns by *Atlantic* editors, and multimedia items. Cheryl LaGuardia, writer of *Magazines for Libraries,* calls the site "a sophisticated and scintillating choice for any electronic magazine collection." Katie Bacon, the executive editor of the Atlantic's Web site, and I discussed the content of the Atlantic Unbound.

INSIDER'S VIEWPOINT FROM YOUR WEB LIBRARY PROFESSIONAL: KATIE BACON, THE ATLANTIC UNBOUND

NT: Has the *Atlantic Monthly's* Web site articulated a mission? This might help readers and Web surfers more fully understand why magazines appear on the Internet.

KB: The Atlantic Online has a two-fold mission: first, to serve as the *Atlantic Monthly's* home on the Internet, delivering the magazine's digital edition and continually building a useful online archive; second, to present an original online publication, Atlantic Unbound, that is an extension of the magazine. The Atlantic Online strives to use the medium in ways that enhance the print magazine for its readers who use the Web, and at the same time to offer compelling content (both repurposed and Web-only) to online readers who may or may not subscribe to the print edition.

NT: The *Atlantic Monthly* is a popular print magazine. Could you elaborate on the Web site, perhaps comparing it to the news-stand edition?

KB: Each month the Atlantic Online offers the contents of the *Atlantic's* print edition (augmented with links to related articles, other Web sites, and/or special online sidebars) alongside a weekly update of original Web-only features in Atlantic Unbound. These Web-only features include interviews and dialogues with leading writers; timely essays and reviews on books and culture; commentary on politics; essays tying together articles from the *Atlantic Monthly's* archive that have become newly relevant; streaming-audio poetry readings; cartoons; and more. The Atlantic Online offers free access to back issues of the

Atlantic from November 1995 (when the magazine first appeared on the Web) to the present, as well as hundreds of articles selected from the magazine's 143-year archive. In addition, The Atlantic Online has recently added a premium archive, which offers the full text of the *Atlantic Monthly* from its founding, in 1857, to the present (due to copyright issues, about 30 years are not available). Readers may purchase individual articles as they originally appeared in the magazine, or purchase a monthly pass. The Atlantic Online also hosts a reader forum, Post & Riposte, in which *Atlantic Monthly* authors at times appear to discuss their articles with readers.

NT: Are the Atlantic Online and the Atlantic Unbound interchangeable as far as what the site is called?

KB: The Atlantic Online is the overall umbrella name of the site. Atlantic Unbound applies to those articles that only appear on the Web. I should also say that all the content we put up in Atlantic Unbound is designed to somehow supplement the magazine—either interviews with authors of *Atlantic* articles, interviews with authors of books that are somehow connected to or complement the magazine, flashbacks highlighting old *Atlantic* articles, and columns by *Atlantic Monthly* editors.

NT: Could you tell me about more about Post & Riposte? I believe it's an online forum for readers and that it is an added feature that is unique to the Web site.

KB: You can see all the different conferences that exist at http://www.theatlantic.com/pr. The staff decides which folders to create (though we occasionally respond to requests, as with the "Writer's Workshop" and the "Sports and Leisure" folders. A whole range of people participate, though we haven't done any specific surveys on them. I would guess that many of the people on the message boards are not *Atlantic Monthly* readers, though we do seed the message board with discussions about *Atlantic* articles, *Atlantic* authors sometimes appear on the message board, and some readers start their own discussions about *Atlantic* articles. I'm not sure about the genesis of "Religion and Spirituality," but we started "Word Court" and "Word Fugitives" to go along with the columns by the same name in the magazine.

NT: Can you tell who is using the Atlantic Online?

KB: Visitors to the site come from all corners of the globe, and range in occupation from business executives and professionals to journalists and members of the academic community. Students and teachers make up approximately 25 percent of the Atlantic Online's visitors. Only about 20 percent of the site's visitors subscribe to the print magazine.

NT: According to a standard library reference book, *Magazines for Libraries*, the Atlantic Unbound has *all* the articles from the print *Atlantic Monthly*. Is this true?

KB: In general, all articles from 1995 on are online, except in those cases when the author does not grant us rights. When we post the current issue, we only provide half of the articles for free; the rest can usually be found in our premium archive. Once that issue is off the newsstand, all of the articles become available for free. Our "flashbacks" feature highlights articles from 1857 onward that have become newly relevant, and those highlights are also available for free.

NT: If a site visitor can get most—or even all—of the magazine online, plus access special features such as back issues and contribute Post & Riposte forum, doesn't the Web site jeopardize its subscriber readership?

KB: This is why we only provide half of the current issue on the Web site (and never the cover story). Also, we don't include any graphics from the magazine online. It's true that we may lose some people who figure they can get a good chunk for free. But our thinking is that we gain more people who come to the site, see what we have to offer, become familiar with the magazine, and then decide to subscribe. Incidentally, over a thousand people a month subscribe to the magazine via the Web site, which is quite an impressive number in the industry.

NT: A quick search located several interviews that you have conducted with authors such as Studs Turkel, Jane Smiley, and Chinua Achebe; have you formed any overall impression of how authors perceive the Web, especially as it relates to the dissemination of their works?

KB: I think that at this point they see it as just another way to promote their books— but I don't get the sense that many of them think about the Web in any larger way. Most of them seem to think it's par for the course these days—we rarely have people who refuse us online rights. In fact, some people seem eager to have their articles online so that they can e-mail them to friends, etc.

NT: As an editor at a functional, attractive, and informative Web site, do you have any other electronic magazines that you personally or professionally enjoy or use for research or other purposes?

KB: I read Slate [*Slate, a Microsoft partner, offers commentary on topics of current interest; http://slate.msn.com*]; I used to read Salon before they started charging. [*Salon, http://www. salon.com, which describes itself as "independent, original, and intrepid online journalism" moved its News and Politics links to a premium archive in 2002. Site visitors may read Salon without subscribing, but premium content, as well as the option to read the online magazine without advertisements, is restricted to paying customers.*] I use Encyclopedia Britannica. And I often go to the *New York Times* Web site, as well as CNN's.

As Katie Bacon said, the Atlantic's Web site allows readers access to eight years of the print publication's articles without charge. It is interesting to note that one of the Web resources we've discussed (Time.com) always includes the cover story, while the other (the Atlantic Online) never includes the cover story. Yet this demonstrates that both strategies succeed for publications and readers.

Time and the *Atlantic Monthly* are only two of many magazines that you can find on the Web that provide free content. To locate your favorite magazine, try using a Web site that lists and links to periodicals (see later in this chapter under "Other Aggregators and Portals for Online Magazines and Journals"). A simple Google search for the publication's title generally works, too. These links in the Google directory also display lists of online magazine sites:

http://directory.google.com/Top/Shopping/Publications/Magazines

http://directory.google.com/Top/News/Magazines_and_E-zines/E-zines/Directories

http://directory.google.com/Top/Arts/Online_Writing/
E-zines/Directories

Another alternative is to access an aggregator's Web site or a magazine portal where you will not only find links to online publications, but may find some added features. One prominent aggregator—MagPortal (http://www.magportal.com)—offers several additional options for individual site users.

MagPortal.com:
An Aggregator at Your Service

Individuals visiting the MagPortal site may access recent articles of interest by either browsing categories (12 including Business, Health, Education & Reference, Finance & Investment, Pets, and Science & Technology; each category has subcategories) or by entering a keyword search. Help is available for searching, but you won't have to strain yourself with its easy-to-use search engine. Since the database is updated each day, it's an excellent place to stay on top of a favorite subject or to retrieve freshly published information. Short summaries accompany the article information, and clicking on the article's title takes you to the magazine or journal site to get a free read or printout of the article. Another feature is the option to find similar articles by clicking on an icon to the left of the parent article's title.

To illustrate MagPortal's usefulness, I performed a search on the keywords "health maintenance organizations." The day I searched the database, it located 190 items, as illustrated in Figure 1.2. The first 10 articles are listed on the left along with the name of the journal, the author, and the date. Although an excellent tool for current awareness, MagPortal also archives articles so users may perform a relatively thorough review of the literature on their topics. Most of the publications have been covered since 2000, but some go back to 1998 (173 titles and counting). A complete list of publications indexed appears at http://magportal.com/help/user/which_mags.html.

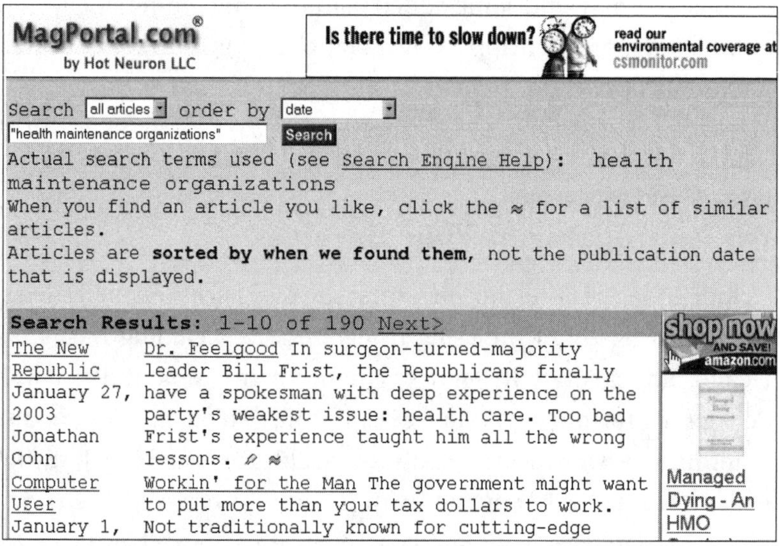

Figure 1.2   MagPortal's retrieval for a keyword search on "health maintenance organizations." The title of each article is linked to the Web site where you can read it. Courtesy Hot Neuron, copyright 2003.

INSIDER'S VIEWPOINT FROM YOUR WEB LIBRARY PROFESSIONAL: BILL DIMM, MAGPORTAL

Bill Dimm, MagPortal's CEO, holds a doctorate in theoretical elementary particle physics from Cornell University. Luckily for librarians and Web surfers, he has also been involved in mathematical modeling and computer programming. His company,

Hot Neuron, has been facilitating access to free content since 1999.

NT: For the benefit of readers who may not know some of the publishing jargon: I've read in several journal articles that MagPortal is an "aggregator." Can you help define aggregator in a way that will help them understand the site's role as it relates to the individual reader?

BD: An aggregator collects together content from disparate sources in some organized way. For example, if you wanted to find the most recent articles on search engines, you could visit the Web sites of a half dozen publications on that topic, or you could just go to the appropriate category on MagPortal.com (http://magportal.com/c/edu/research) and find links to all recent articles in a single location. Not only would you find articles on search engines from publications dedicated to that topic through MagPortal.com, but you would also find articles on search engines from publications (like *PC World*) that only write about search engines occasionally.

NT: Bill, I have found many Web sites that list links to magazines and journals. What's different about MagPortal?

BD: Unlike Web sites that provide a directory of links to magazine Web sites, we provide links directly to the individual articles. When you are trying to find an article on something specific, we take you straight to it instead of leaving you to hunt through the publications individually.

NT: Using Google, I see that at least 2,500 Web pages are linked to MagPortal. Many of them are public libraries, but many are pages on freelance writing ("Beginner's Guide to Freelancing" at http://www.poewar.com/articles/beginner.htm), and others include helpful pages about how to build one's own Web site (for example, "Library Support Staff" at http://www.librarysupport staff.com/webpubhelp.html). I have also read articles about MagPortal that state it is helpful to put a link on a business site to MagPortal to facilitate access to current information. It's obvious how the individual gains from these links to you, but how does MagPortal benefit?

BD: Links to MagPortal.com bring more users to our site, which means more ad impressions and the opportunity to make more people aware of our premium feed offering.

NT: MagPortal isn't just a set of links to online magazines and journals. Isn't it an engine to help users find exactly what they want from publications with free content on the Web?

BD: MagPortal.com provides several ways to find articles. First, we have over 200 categories that our human editors populate with articles. New articles are normally added within one business day of the publisher putting them on the Web, so you can easily browse the most recent articles on a topic if we've created a category for it. Second, we provide a full-text search engine. Our search engine is more current than the generic search engines, and it has some features that generic search engines often lack. For example, in addition to sorting results by quality-of-match, you can also sort by date, and you can restrict the search to a particular category or publication. Finally, we provide "similar articles" links next to the articles (represented on the screen by wavy orange equal signs) that use our Hot Neuron Similarity software to provide listings of articles that our proprietary algorithm determines to be similar to that article. Once you find an article you like, you can click the yellow highlighter pen next to it to mark the article so that you can easily find it later. Unlike a bookmark, this feature allows you to add your own annotation, and we will take care of fixing the URL if the publisher moves the article whenever possible.

NT: At the MagPortal site there is information about AmSouth Bank using MagPortal for fresh content. I believe these are called "feeds." What is the site's feed component all about?

BD: The premium feeds allow other companies to embed a mini MagPortal.com in their Web site that uses a subset of our data. They get the article listings, search engine, and similar articles, restricted to the particular topics that they license. We provide them with a small piece of software to install on their Web server that automatically pulls any necessary data from MagPortal.com and displays it directly on their site to match the site's look and feel. The article links take the user to the publisher's site, as on MagPortal.com. We customize the datasets for the premium feeds to exactly match the client's area of interest. Web sites using the service range from a very narrow focus like nursing, marketing, law, etc. to more broadly focused like AmSouth Bank's site, which displays all of our business and Internet topics in its small business section.

NT: From a practical point of view, can you explain the process of indexing the free online content so that it is searchable for the general reader? For example, I enter "bin laden" and retrieve 608 hits—that's a lot better than browsing to find articles about him. I'm hypothesizing that you have to take the raw data and feed it through an engine. How is this achieved?

BD: Like any search engine, we have a piece of software, called a "spider" that hunts through pages on the Web. Our spider has been tailored for each of the publications that we cover, so it heads immediately to the table of contents page for the current issue of the publication to see if there is anything new. It also knows how to follow the "next page" links within an article and recognize that all of these pages are part of the same article (generic search engines index pages rather than articles, so they don't have to collect things together this way). We then run the HTML for the pages through our parser, which attempts to extract the title, author, date, and body of the article. A human reviews the result for accuracy, writes or clips a very brief summary, and categorizes the article.

To put this into the search engine, we cut each article down into words and discard any unimportant ones like "the" (called "stop words"). We count the number of times each word appears in the article, and we normalize by the length of the article. This information goes into a database. Much as the index at the back of a book helps you to easily find the pages a word occurs on without searching each page one by one, this database allows our search engine to quickly find out which articles contain a particular word. It also tells us how important that word is in each of the articles (i.e., how many times the word appears in the article relative to the total number of words in the article), which allows us to sort the search results by quality of match.

NT: What topics seem to interest site visitors the most?

BD: We have a very broad user base ranging from students doing schoolwork to professional searchers to people who are just browsing for articles on their favorite pastime. We do notice surges in traffic from people hunting for reviews of hot new electronics products or car models. We usually have such things in our index long before the generic search engines do.

Other Aggregators and Portals for Online Magazines and Journals

Business.com's Publications Lists

http://www.business.com

Although its interface is similar to Yahoo!, this portal focuses in human resources, management, industry, and all business topics. To get to its lists of periodicals you must begin at a directory heading or subheading (e.g., "Energy & Environment" or its subheading "Coal"). Select the "Reference" link and the select the "Publications" link. By "drilling" through the category you will discover links to magazines, journals, and newsletters including *Coal Age*, *Coal People*, and *Coal Week* (or, in other categories, *Fast Company.com*, *Directorship Magazine*, *Electronic Journal of Radical Organisation Theory*, *BrownPaperBag Journal*, and *The Entrepreneur's Mind*).

Electronic Journal Miner

http://ejournal.coalliance.org

More of a library catalog than simply a list of Web sites, this product of the Colorado Alliance of Research Libraries assigns Library of Congress Subject Headings to its listings and provides comprehensive annotations to each electronic journal in the catalog along with a link to the journal's site. Note: Use this link off the Electronic Journal Miner's page to retrieve more lists of electronic periodicals: http://ejournal.coalliance.org/info/other.html.

Famous Magazines

http://magazineworld.spedia.net

This site is a curious but functional collection of links to online magazines. Be prepared for a crudely constructed home page, occasional pop-up advertisements, and a few dead links. Users, however, will be able to locate dozens of specialty magazines here such as *Cat Fancy, Scuba Diving, TrailerLife, DollReader, Climbing,* and *Vibe.*

Free Medical Journals Database
http://www.freemedicaljournals.com

Free Medical Journals provides links to 1,020 periodicals. Although you cannot search the site, you can look for journals by specialty or alphabetically.

According to the home page, "Over the next few years, many important medical journals will be available online, free and in full-text. The access to free scientific knowledge will have a major impact on medical practice and attract Internet visitors to these journals. Journals that restrict access to their Web sites will lose popularity."

That's a brave hypothesis; we will have to wait and see.

Headline Spot
http://www.headlinespot.com/type/magazines

Headline Spot links to 200 magazines. A visually appealing page lists the periodicals filed under one of 18 categories.

Internet Public Library Serials
http://www.ipl.org/div/serials

A well-ordered list of annotated links to online periodicals grouped by subject.

Librarians' Index to the Internet: Magazines by Topic
http://www.lii.org/search/file/magazines

By accessing the Librarian's Index to the Internet's magazine topics links, the user may access journals by one of 54 subject categories. Clicking on "Literature" for example yields five journal titles; clicking on "Science" yields eight, and so on. The links for each title go to the publication's site.

Librarians' Index to the Internet: Periodicals
http://www.lii.org/ search?query=Periodicals;searchtype=
subject;view_all=Please

This page displays annotations and links to 285 online periodicals.

Magatopia
http://www.magatopia.com

Magatopia provides links to 1,000 online magazines with a very basic search mechanism.

Magazine Directory
http://magazine-directory.com

A basic and unadorned alphabetical list of hundreds of magazines with a Web presence.

Magazines A to Z
http://www.magazinesatoz.com

Another handy list of links to magazine Web sites. Incidentally, don't be fooled by the "Search for Articles" option—it just sends your request to FindArticles; it does not search for articles in the manner of a value-added aggregator such as MagPortal.com

magOmania
http://www.magomania.com

A portal to 300 Canadian magazines, which allows you to search through its database by keyword, subject author, title, date, or phrase. magOmania searches through recent tables of contents and online articles (and retrieves the full text). The site also offers "Ask An Expert" search help for magazine articles as well as several other features including "A Mania Minute" (a guide to hot topics).

Newsdirectory List of Magazines
http://www.newsdirectory.com/ news/magazine

The home page offers access to the Web sites of electronic periodicals by subject category. The user may also search for a magazine title or browse for publications by geographical region or country. The range of periodicals listed is impressive. It includes numerous foreign magazines as well as the typical Western newsstand titles.

Primedia Business Magazines
http://industryclick.com/icmagazines.asp

Primedia is a publisher of trade magazines as well as a provider of other business services. Its site provides searchable access to selected content from approximately 100 of the company's publications. The site also links to publications so the user is only one click away from the magazine's own site.

Locating Additional Aggregators, Portals, and Individual Magazines

Use these directory pages to find more free periodical content:

Google
http://directory.google.com/Top/News/Magazines_ and_ E-zines/Directories

Open Directory Project
http://search.dmoz.org/cgi-bin/search?search=magazines

Just Help Me Find It!

A standard index to magazines and journals, which is used by many libraries, is the *Reader's Guide*. This print index costs about $310 a year. If you are a customer of a commercial online database vendor such as DIALOG, a search in file 141 "Reader's Guide Abstracts with Full Text" costs 67 cents per minute and $1.50 per citation. Shall we consider a frugal alternative?

Launched in May 1998, Ingenta enjoys strong alliances with the Gale Group and a retinue of other leading publishers that supply it with a steady and reliable stream of content. The company purchased UnCover (a freely accessible bibliographic database with pay-per-view features that was a favorite with librarians) in 2000. Ingenta picked up Catchword, a British document delivery competitor, in 2001. The current service is an amalgamation of these content-rich entities. Although Ingenta is in the business of marketing full-text to libraries and other institutions, anyone may search it for free and locate bibliographic information from thousands of periodicals. If your search succeeds and you locate resources, Ingenta will display a summary and a citation (with enough information to facilitate acquiring the resource from a library or other information outlet).

But providing article information is what the *Reader's Guide* does isn't it? Yes, but not for free. And the *Reader's Guide* covers over 300 publications, which librarians help choose for indexing. True, but Ingenta, a healthy service in terms of longevity and publisher relationships, covers about 30,000. But the latter list does not entirely overlap with the *Reader's Guide*. The question is how well does the freely accessible Ingenta publication list stack up to the librarian-accepted *Reader's Guide* list of publications indexed?

Ingenta covers 242 of the publications (i.e., 80 percent) indexed by the *Reader's Guide* list. Furthermore, of two other heavily used H.W. Wilson sources, the *Social Sciences Index* and the *Humanities Index,* Ingenta also overlaps significantly. These three highly regarded Wilson indexes cover approximately 1,344 periodicals. Ingenta allows searches of author, article title, keyword, journal title, and International Standard Serial Number (ISSN) for the majority of them. No charge. Of course, if you like what you find, Ingenta can almost always fax, e-mail, or deliver the material online for a fee.

During this comparison of Ingenta and these Wilson indexes, it became apparent that even though Ingenta didn't duplicate the legacy indexes under discussion, it indexed so many publications that, indeed, it probably overlapped significantly with other

Wilson titles. For example, Ingenta's coverage of the IEEE was extensive. Similarly, its coverage of scientific, medical, financial, and education topics is excellent. Searching Ingenta in lieu of buying indexes or compact discs that merely include citations and abstracts, therefore, saves not only the amount spent on just a few Wilson products, but many of them. Using Ingenta, the general public index user will locate articles in *AARP Modern Maturity*, *American Heritage*, *Car and Driver*, *Commonweal*, *Ebony*, *Ladies' Home Journal*, and information from the *Canadian Journal of Physics*, *Circuit World*, and the *ABA Banking Journal*.

Ingenta does not employ the most user-friendly search interface, so the best strategy is to proceed directly to the advanced search interface and, if comprehensiveness is a factor, be sure to perform your search over the maximum number of years. The default search is 1997 to the present, but I have always selected 1988 to the present. You should also be aware that there are actually two Ingenta periodical databases. One is called "Online Articles" and offers over 5,000 full-text publications for immediate online delivery. An even larger database is called "Fax/Ariel Articles" (sometimes Ingenta also calls this file "Uncover Plus") and covers more than 26,000 publications. There is overlap, but you need to perform your search twice to get a true picture of the literature on your subject. (Hopefully, Ingenta site developers will merge these two files to facilitate searching.) This is a simple matter; selecting an alternate tab at the top of your retrieval page will automatically rerun your search in the other database (Figure 1.3).

In Figure 1.3, the searcher seeks articles about "aboriginal art." Note that the searcher is not interested in book reviews. The search locates 60 items meeting the search criteria. Also note that the search was run in the Fax/Ariel database, but can be rerun in the Online Articles database for possible additional retrieval. Additional options include viewing a summary of the article and its terms of availability. The searcher can purchase the article or pursue a number of other

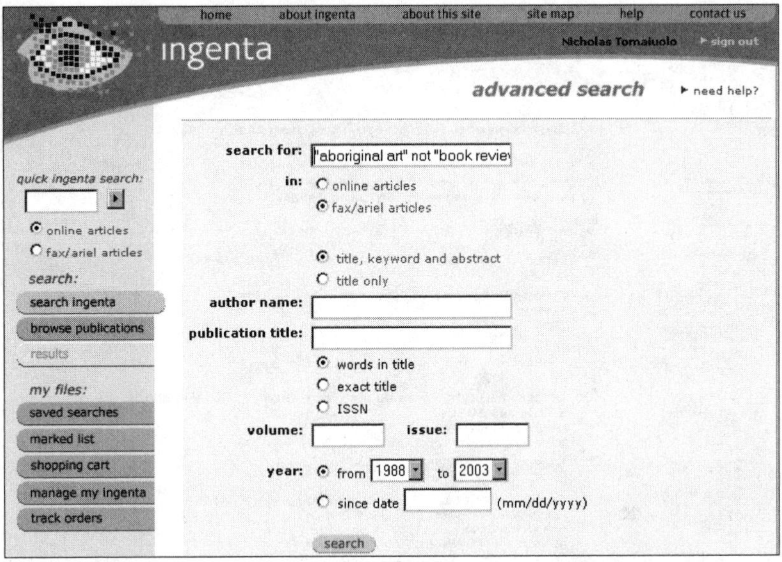

Figure 1.3   Ingenta provides flexible searching for more than 27,000 periodical titles—it's a free database for locating bibliographic information! Courtesy Ingenta, copyright 2003.

ways to obtain it without charge, including an affiliated library or interlibrary loan. The bibliographic information, shown in Figure 1.4, is sufficient for these two latter options.

Because Ingenta covers so many publications, you can expect to find information of interest on almost any subject. (For example, an Ingenta keyword search on "Lakers" locates articles in *Sports Illustrated, TV Guide, Newsweek, Sport,* and *People Weekly.*)

Other Free Indexes to Help You Locate Periodical Articles

Ask ERIC
http://www.askeric.org/Eric

Teachers and administrators know the Educational Resources Information Center (ERIC) database as the foremost resource for

Figure 1.4   BINGO! This is as good as a bibliographic database can get!
Courtesy Ingenta, copyright 2003.

accessing literature in the field of education. The database, updated monthly, indexes about 1,000 journals, plus other documents submitted and accepted by ERIC (lesson plans, conference papers, guides, speeches, and more) including some full text called "ERIC Digests." More than 1 million items dating from 1966 to the present are available for searching.

What you get from the free AskERIC service:

- Free access to bibliographic citations for use in conjunction with a document delivery outlet

- Free ERIC Digests

- No subscription fees

Many commercial database vendors license the database and offer it to libraries by subscription. Regardless of the apparent inexpensiveness of the database, it is more prudent to access it without charge, especially for individual end-users. An ERIC search done by a subscriber using a top vendor (DIALOG) costs 58 cents per minute and 80 cents for each citation. An ERIC Digest document in full text also costs 80 cents. A quick search on the topic "Suzuki musical instruction" limited to journal articles yields four items in AskERIC's free service. For each I can read the bibliographic information without charge. Using DIALOG's subscription service, the same search costs approximately $7. This may not seem like much, but a thorough literature review or sequence of search requests executed by an "information intermediary" could add up.

ERIC is a bibliographic database. Users receive the information required to seek the text of an item from another source. Many of the items in the ERIC database may be purchased from ERIC, but the journal articles found in the database must, in general, be obtained from libraries or other outlets. ERIC Digests are the exception. ERIC produces the digests internally; the digests synthesize selected research and usually run two pages in length; 2,200 digests are available free at AskERIC.

MEDLINE/PubMed
http://www.ncbi.nlm.nih.gov/PubMed

MEDLINE—PubMed—what's the difference? For the end-user the difference is hardly worth discussing. PubMed contains all of MEDLINE's citations plus additional citations from literature somewhat peripheral to MEDLINE. The contrast is thoroughly explained at http://www.nlm.nih.gov/pubs/factsheets/dif_med _pub.html.

MEDLINE is also a bibliographic database. Although it will occasionally link to free full-text documents, its primary function is to allow the user to search through the literature, determine what is of interest, and use the information to secure important documents from other resources.

You could choose to pay for your access to MEDLINE from vendors that license the database, but why would you? It's free at the National Library of Medicine's Web site. MEDLINE consists of three subset indexes: *Index Medicus*, the *International Nursing Index*, and the *Index to Dental Literature*. These indexes cover 4,600 journals published in the United States and more than 70 other countries.

Hundreds of thousands of articles are added to the medical, dental, and nursing literature each year. Since 1966, the database has totaled 11 million citations. Even if some of them are dross, consumers and health professionals should not overlook the literature on their topic. PubMed is the one-stop searching source for finding the literature in these fields.

PubMed is relatively easy to search, but users should read the help found by clicking "Index/Preview" when they first visit the site. Keywords can be used, though many professional biomedical searchers adhere to the Medical Subject Headings (MeSH).

MEDLINE for the Consumer:
Reality Database Searching

In 1990, a mother and father were alarmed by the number and frequency of ear infections suffered by their toddler. The pediatrician recommended evaluation by an otolaryngologist. After a physical examination, the verdict was that tympanostomy tubes would need to be inserted to help drain the child's ears. Although the physician was forthcoming concerning the possible complications and relative efficacy of the procedure, a certain diagnostic test had not been performed.

Just prior to the scheduled surgery, the parents asked a medical librarian to perform a MEDLINE database search. The parents agreed to pay the $30 cost recovery fee. The search yielded several citations that indicated one further test that could rule out the surgery.

The parents returned to the specialist and requested the additional test. The physician complied; the results were negative, and the procedure was cancelled. The child's ears and hearing are perfect today. Without knowledge of the test acquired from the MEDLINE search, the child may have undergone unnecessary surgery. (See "Objective diagnosis of otitis media in early infancy by tympanometry and ipsilateral acoustic reflex thresholds," by C. D. Marchant in the *Journal of Pediatrics*, Volume 109, pages 590–595, October 1986).

Thirty dollars is negligible when health and peace of mind is at stake. In 1990 the parents could not have accessed MEDLINE and performed the search themselves. Now consumers are empowered to do so, and at no cost.

National Criminal Justice Reference Service (NCJRS)
http://www.ncjrs.org/search.html

The NCJRS offers two great services for site visitors seeking criminal justice information from books, pamphlets, government reports, unpublished research reports, and journal articles. You may search either the "Abstracts Database" for citations or the "Online Full Text" database. Periodicals indexed include *Prison Journal, Justice Quarterly, Journal of Research in Crime and Delinquency, Police Chief,* and *Crime & Delinquency.* Approximately 100 journals are scanned for inclusion in the searchable database.

Staying Alert Without Caffeine, Exercise, or Meditation

Before the advent of the Web and the subsequent "democratization of information dissemination," individuals determined to maintain the leading edge on certain topics sought information specialists who subscribed to expensive databases for current awareness services (CAS) and selective dissemination of information (SDI) services.

A typical SDI involves taking a topic, working it into an efficient search strategy, and entering it into a database for storing and rerunning on a periodic basis (usually monthly). The search results are then delivered to the subscriber, who evaluates the results and decides whether to obtain the original articles to which the SDI refers. The benefit of SDIs and CASs is the updating function they offer through automatic notices to subscribers.

Another form of current awareness involves a less sophisticated approach, but many readers find it still works. In this service only the tables of contents from the newest issues of selected periodicals go to subscribers.

Many people admit that information overload has all but paralyzed them, but staying on top of topics of importance continues to be a priority. Many of these same people have SDIs performed by research librarians at their companies, academic librarians at their institutions, or execute their own SDIs, usually on subscription databases. It should come as no surprise that several valid free Web databases offer users the opportunity to stay on top of their searches without charge.

Databases for Free Alert Services

Ingenta: A registered user (registration is free) may request up to five tables of contents from over 5,000 online periodicals. Alerts are e-mailed whenever the journals publish a new issue. Keyword search alerts, called "Research Alerts," are only available to users who have purchased a license. The Research Alerts cover more than 20,000 additional print journals.

- Begin at the home page (http://www.ingenta.com) and register.

- Click "Manage My Ingenta" on the left of the screen.

- Choose "my e-journal alerts."

- Click "create a new alerting profile" and add up to five journal titles.

- Note: A related alert service from the commercial database vendor DIALOG costs approximately $11.75 per month based on charges for file 141—Reader's Guide Abstracts Full Text.

HighWire Press: Five thousand science and medical journals, including MEDLINE and 342 free HighWire-based publications.

- Begin at http://highwire.stanford.edu and click "Register" (free).

- Once you have registered, begin at the HighWire Press Home Page, sign in, and click "My Email Alerts."

- Click "Add a new eTOC alert" or "Add a new CiteTrack alert." You may create alerts for tables of contents of selected journals (eTOC Alerts) and/or create customized alerts using authors or keywords (CiteTrack Alerts).

- You will receive e-mail concerning relevant articles and specified tables of contents.

Infotrieve: Select from 20,000 journals for tables of contents alerts.

- Begin at http://www4.infotrieve.com and "Register" (free).

- On subsequent logons:

    - On the right-hand side of the Infotrieve home page click "Tables of Contents."

- Locate the journal you want and click "Add to TOC alert profile."

- Infotrieve will notify you when a new table of contents for your periodical(s) becomes available.

PubMed: Articles from thousands of biomedical journals.

- Begin at PubMed: http://www.ncbi.nlm.nih.gov/PubMed

- Looking to the left of the screen, scroll down and click "Cubby."

- Register (free) to save search(es) in your Cubby.

- Enter your search terms and click "Go."

- After your search is run (you may or may not have retrieved any articles), click "Cubby" on the left and store your search.

- Whenever you return to PubMed, you may go to your Cubby, select the saved search you want to run, and click "What's New for Selected."

- Follow your usual procedure for obtaining the full text of important items.

- Note: A related alert service from the commercial database vendor DIALOG costs approximately $6.40 per month based on charges for file 154, 155 MEDLINE. However, DIALOG will e-mail you the results without requiring you to remember to return to the service.

STM—Scientific, Technical, and Medical Literature: Whither Free Content?

The beginning of this chapter mentioned the resignation of a scholar, Professor Mark Riley, as an unpaid peer reviewer for Elsevier Science. It also mentioned the vote of confidence he got from Charles Miller, a librarian colleague, on his campus. The scholar left because he felt the publisher charged too much for its science journals; the librarian applauded the move because he agreed.

Web publishers of medical literature such as BioMed Central have intrepidly begun offering electronic journals for free. FreeMedicalJournals.com is a dedicated gatekeeper site of links to more than 900 free biomedical journals, mostly from traditional publishers. And individuals seeking to identify important biomedical articles need search no further than the free PubMed database.

There is probably no category of periodical literature generally more expensive to access than the scientific, technical, and medical (STM) literature. Ironically, there is probably no greater need for inexpensive access to a category of literature than STM. In order to promote health, treat diseases, and make informed administrative, research, and clinical decisions, medical researchers generally agree that the dissemination of this literature should be rapid and free. The British Medical Journal Publishing Group has recognized this priority and announced that it will disseminate 23 of its specialist journals without cost to 100 developing countries.[4]

Another resource in the STM researcher's toolbox is "preprint servers." What is a preprint? Several professional organizations and government departments have defined them. The United States Department of Energy, Office of Scientific and Technical Information defines a preprint as "a document in pre-publication status, particularly an article submitted to a journal for publication."[5] The American Physical Society expands this by stating that the concept of e-prints includes any electronic work circulated by the author outside of the traditional publishing environment.[6] The American Chemical Society, which does not accept manuscripts previously posted online, defines preprints as "a draft of a scholarly paper that has not yet been formally peer-reviewed."[7] In some subject fields, where rapid transmission of knowledge is critical, electronic dissemination of preprints is an absolute necessity;

subsequent traditional publication is a formality. In mathematics and physics, for example, formal publication provides archiving and serves more as a notice to the scholarly community reminding it of the paper's initial appearance and, ultimately, as a vehicle to support the standing of the author.[8]

Not long ago, scholarly communication involved mail, fax, or, more recently, anonymous FTP, gopher, and electronic mail. Although these methods of sharing information are still used, it is easier, quicker, and less expensive to post papers on the World Wide Web for reference, review, and comments. While traditionally producing and publishing a document requires a significant investment of time, materials, and money, placing a preprint on the World Wide Web involves no printing costs and practically no distribution costs. Access to an HTML program and a Web server are usually all that is required. Paul Ginsparg, a renowned physicist formerly at the Los Alamos National Laboratory and presently at Cornell University, developed the first preprint archive in August 1991. Originally dedicated to papers in high-energy theoretical physics, the "arXiv.org e-Print Archive" at http://xxx.arxiv.cornell.edu initially attracted 1,000 users, but, after a few months, reported from 35,000 to 150,000 visits per day.

Professional societies, government sites, and universities often host preprint servers. Disciplines such as astronomy, chemistry, computer science, mathematics, and physics have been on the leading edge of preprint distribution. The vast majority of preprint servers contain scientific information. Fields in the humanities and social sciences have recently followed the trend, but significantly lag behind in terms of servers. CogPrints (http://cogprints. soton.ac.uk) offers preprints in psychology, anthropology, philosophy, and linguistics.

Many preprint servers contain links to other preprint servers, as well as being searchable themselves. Here are some notable preprint sites:

e-Print archive
http://xxx.arxiv.cornell.edu

Begun in 1991 at the Los Alamos National Laboratory and moved in December 2001 to a server at the Cornell University Library, this well-organized, if somewhat user-unfriendly server, covers physics, mathematics, nonlinear science, and computer science. Full text is available in various electronic formats.

CERN Document Server: Preprints
http://preprints.cern.ch

Full text is usually provided; coverage extends back to 1994 and includes links to other preprint servers.

SLAC SPIRES-HEP (Stanford Public Information Retrieval System —High Energy Physics)
http://www-slac.slac.stanford.edu/find/spires.html

Containing over 500,000 entries with full text from various other sites, the scope of this Web site includes preprints, journal articles, theses, technical reports, and other documents.

American Physical Society E-Prints
http://publish.aps.org/eprint

This server began in 1996 and, although a searchable archive, it was closed to submissions on May 31, 2000. It now redirects authors to Ginsparg's site at Cornell University or to the American Physical Society's journals.

Clinmed Netprints
http://clinmed.netprints.org

Launched by the *British Medical Journal* and HighWire Press, this site provides a place for authors to archive their completed studies before, during, or after peer review by other agencies. It covers original research in clinical medicine and health and includes a warning that articles posted "have not yet been accepted for publication by a peer reviewed journal. ... Casual readers should not act on their findings, and journalists should be wary of reporting them." It also has a list under Journal Policies of journals that will and will not accept submissions that have appeared on preprint servers.

Social Science Research Network (SSRN)
http://www.ssrn.com

SSRN is a database of working papers in accounting, economics, finance, and law. This server helps users identify papers and authors, but charges to view them.

E-Math
http://www.ams.org/preprints

The American Mathematical Society maintains this preprint server for mathematicians. The mission of the server is to make available the current home page URLs and e-mail contacts of all mathematical preprint and e-print servers throughout the world. The server itself does not offer full text, but it may be used as a tool to link to servers that include text.

Chemical Physics Preprint Database
http://www.chem.brown.edu/chem-ph.html

A joint project of the Los Alamos National Laboratory and Brown University's Chemistry Department, this archive hosts full-text documents for the international theoretical chemistry community.

ChemWeb
http://www.chemweb.com

Launched in July 2000, this site allows free searching of chemistry journals as well as reviewed chemistry Web sites. Citations and abstracts are free, but full text is by subscription or "pay as you go."

NCSTRL (Networked Computer Science
Technical Reference Library)
http://www.ncstrl.org

Online since 1995, this server distributes technical reports in computer science. Searching and online access to full text are free.

PrePrint Network
http://www.osti.gov/preprint

Sponsored by the U.S. Department of Energy, this searchable gateway links to preprint servers that deal with scientific and technical disciplines of concern to DOE, including scientific and technical disciplines such as physics, materials, and chemistry, "as well as portions of biology, environmental sciences and nuclear medicine." Users can search across the gateway by author, title, full record, date, and collection, or browse the databases alphabetically or by subject pathway. Search returns include title, author, source, number of pages, and a link to an abstract, which then links to the full text. The format of the full-text papers can vary considerably.

Preprints and the Future

Some searchers may find that pinpointing the best preprint server for their search is a challenge, but scholars in the scientific disciplines are working on a solution in real time. Imagine a scenario in which any researcher quickly accesses any preprint from any archive. Librarians, publishers, researchers, and computer scientists met in Santa Fe, New Mexico, in October 1999 where their unifying goal was the establishment of such a universal preprint archive. Laying the foundation for the resolution of technical challenges such as archive maintenance, accessibility, and interoperability, the project was called the "Open Archives Initiative." The database is now called "ARC: A Cross Archive Search Service."[9] (Search the service at http://arc.cs.odu.edu.) Searching the open archives is exciting because it offers metasearches of important

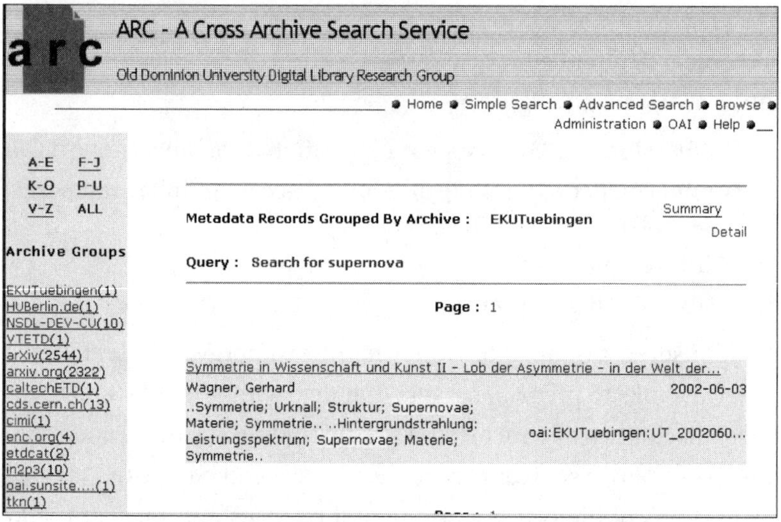

Figure 1.5   The ARC Advanced Search Form. Courtesy ARC, Old Dominion
University, copyright 2003.

preprint servers and then delivers the information in a clear manner using user-selected sorting (Figure 1.5).

For Web surfers as well as Web researchers, preprint information
may play a role in freely locating and accessing the full text of
important papers that may never appear in a journal.

Great Things Ahead

Although certain specific resources have disappeared from the
free content toolbox (e.g., the U.S. Government's Office of
Scientific and Technical Information discontinued the popular
PubScience on November 4, 2002, despite the protestations of
librarians, researchers, and information specialists. OSTI now
refers PubScience users to commercial Web resources), others are
emerging. As readers may judge from the comments about
preprint servers, individuals are dedicating effort to making free
resources available.

Péter Jacsó, professor in the Department of Information and Computer Sciences at the University of Hawaii's Library of Information Science Program, has embarked on providing a suite of resources that allows powerful searching of publicly available information in several disciplines. "Peter's PolySearch Engines," located at http://www2.hawaii.edu/~jacso/extra/poly-page.html, includes metasearch access to science, biography, dictionary, and encyclopedia information with additional subject area poly-searches under development. Dr. Jacsó selects the databases to query, writes the software, and offers the interface to Web users, all at no charge.

Use Your Library Card

While learning about independent resources on the Web that provide free information, don't forget about the physical libraries with which you are affiliated. At last count, 46 states had contracted with information vendors to make periodical databases, including full text, available to residents with library cards. Under names like "Badgerlink," "SLED," "InfoNet," "TexShare," "iConn," "Magnolia," "Powerlibrary," "SILO," "ODIN," and "Inspire," various statewide library systems from Maine to Alaska help their users get valuable information on their computers.[10]

The majority of states have allocated funds allowing students and residents to search various databases from their offices and homes away from the actual libraries. Alabama's state legislature, for example, appropriated $3 million in 2000 for the Alabama Virtual Library System.[11] Libraries around the world are moving toward public access to subscription databases. If you have not explored whether your library offers this service, it makes sense to check it out. Simply inquire at the public library in your community.

Table 1.5   A table to help readers locate free articles

Mission: Using Your Web Library to Find Journal and Magazine Articles

When You Need Full Text Articles
 	
FindArticles, http://www.findarticles.com
BioMed Central, http://www.biomedcentral.com
Britannica.com, http://www.britannica.com
HighWire Press, http://highwire.stanford.edu/lists/freeart.dtl
Internet Library of Early Journals, http://www.bodley.ox.ac.uk/ilej
MagPortal, http://www.magportal.com
Making of America at University of Michigan, http://www.hti.umich.edu/m/moajrnl
Making of America at Cornell University, http://cdl.library.cornell.edu/moa
Digital Library and Archives, Virginia Polytechnic Institute and State University,
    http://scholar.lib.vt.edu/ejournals
Online Books Serials Page, http://onlinebooks.library.upenn.edu/serials.html
Resources for Research Periodicals,
    http://home.earthlink.net/~ellengarvey/rsapresource1.html

Online Magazines Themselves (e.g., Time.com, Atlantic Unbound, and others) Electronic Journal Miner, http://ejournal.coalliance.org Famous Magazines, http://magazineworld.spedia.net Free Medical Journals Database, http://www.freemedicaljournals.com Internet Public Library Serials, http://www.ipl.org/div/serials Librarians' Index to the Internet: Periodicals, http://www.lii.org/search/file/magazines Magatopia, http://www.magatopia.com Magazine Directory, http://consumer-news.com/magazine Magazines A to Z, http://www.magazinesatoz.com Note: Check the library with which you are affiliated for information about accessing full-text magazines from your home or office.
When You Will Settle for Bibliographic Information AskERIC, http://www.askeric.org/Eric Infotrieve, http://www4.infotrieve.com (DocSource and Medline only) Ingenta, http://www.ingenta.com MEDLINE/PubMed, http://www.ncbi.nlm.nih.gov/PubMed National Criminal Justice Reference Service, http://www.ncjrs.org/search.html
What to Do with Bibliographic Information Request articles at your affiliated library (you may be able to do this on the Web). Check individual magazine Web sites.

Conclusion

Anyone can create what may appear to be a periodical article and post it on the Internet; it should be comforting that many credible publishers are making the contents of their periodicals available. This chapter detailed resources for gaining value from a considerable number of those publications. We also discovered that bibliophiles and information specialists are very busy digitizing and presenting collections of fascinating old periodicals and that any magazine desiring the consumer's attention works diligently to get visitors to its site. Scholars are also making their work appear more quickly and without charge by circumventing print publication; this may constitute the forerunner of a trend. Imagine! Your public library may only subscribe to a few hundred magazines, but your Web library can deliver thousands. See Table 1.5 for more information.

SAMPLE ANNUAL SAVINGS

Britannica.com	=	$2,000
FindArticles.com	=	$20,000
HighWire Press	=	$1,000
Ingenta	=	$4,500
MagPortal	=	$2,000
PubMed, ERIC	=	$1,500
UPenn electronic journals	=	$1,000
Individual Magazine sites	=	$1,000s
Free e-mail article and TOC alerts	=	$100s
Scientific, medical preprints	=	priceless

Endnotes

1. "Surveys Show Periodical, Serials Prices Remaining Steady." *American Libraries*. May 2002. Volume 33. Issue 5. p. 75.

2. "U.S. Periodical Prices—2002. Chart A: Price Index Comparison." American Library Association. http://www.ala.org/alonline/ archive/periodicals02/2002perpricescharta.html. June 11, 2002.

3. Declan Butler. "Referee Quits Journal Over Price Rise as Library Faces Cutbacks." *Nature.* June 17, 1999. Volume 399. Issue 6737. p. 623.

4. Richard Smith and Alex Williamson. "BMJ Journals Free to Developing World." *BMJ: The British Medical Journal.* February 16, 2002. Volume 324. Issue 7334. p. 380.

5. Sharon M. Jordan. "Preprint Servers: Status, Challenges, and Opportunities of the New Digital Publishing Paradigm." *InForum '99.* May 5, 1999. http://www.osti.gov/inforum99/papers/jordan.html. July 24, 2002.

6. American Physical Society. "What are Eprints?" January 7, 1998. http:// publish.aps.org/eprint/docs/faq.html. July 25, 2002.

7. Sophie Wilkinson. "Preprint Policy: ACS Journals Won't Accept Manuscripts Previously Posted Online." *Chemical & Engineering News.* January 15, 2001. Volume 79. Issue 3. p. 10.

8. Edward Lim. "Preprint Servers: A New Model for Scholarly Publishing?" *Australian Academic and Research Libraries.* March 1996. Volume 27. Issue 1. pp. 21–30.

9. Herbert Van de Sompel and Carl Lagoze. "The Santa Fe Convention of the Open Archives Initiative." *D-Lib Magazine.* February 2000. Volume 6. Issue 2. http://www.dlib.org/dlib/february00/ vandesompel-oai/ 02vandesompel-oai.htm. July 23, 2002.

10. Rita Barsun. "Statewide Access to Databases." *The Tenth Off-Campus Library Services Conference 2002.* Bloomington: Indiana University. http://www.lib.waldenu.edu/conferences/MLA_Conf/statewide.html. June 28, 2002.

11. Josie Morgan. "Turning a Dream into a Virtual Reality of Statewide Information Sharing." *Computers in Libraries.* January 2001. Volume. 21. Issue 1. p. 50.

Chapter Two

All the News that Fits and a Few Gigs More

You've seen them. They appear in small boxes near the masthead of your newspaper or sidebars on the front page. They can occasionally run for a column or two. Your newspaper is notifying you that the price of newsprint has gone up and, consequently, you must now pay more to stay in touch with the world, your community, your favorite sports teams, and your stock portfolio. A description of the publisher's strategy to "hold the line" occasionally accompanies the announcement: "Beginning today the pages of your paper will become slightly smaller. This change will yield savings that will enable us to keep bringing you quality news coverage. For some readers, the trimmer width will make your daily paper easier to handle."

The cost of newspapers depends on many variables, but the fluctuation in the cost of the actual paper publishers need to buy in great quantity is a direct factor. It is not an element we think about every day, but this factor will keep resurfacing as long as there are trees and printing presses. On July 8, 2002 five top North American newsprint producers lined up for a $50-a-ton hike invoked on August 1.[1] (The price on July 9, 2002 was $430 per ton.) Yet four months earlier, sources at the trade magazine *Editor & Publisher* stated, on the basis of a forecast by Merrill Lynch, the average annual price per metric ton would decrease by 10–15 percent in 2002. With the downturn in the United States economy, it was thought that producers would have to keep prices stable until the economic picture brightened.[2] In developing countries the problem is much worse. The cost of newsprint can rise more than 30 percent with little notice.[3] Some publishers worry that such hikes could make news unaffordable for most people in countries such as Zimbabwe. The worst-case scenario is that publishers may simply shut down.

Even when times are good and people are spending (which leads to increases in newspaper advertising and thicker papers with more advertisements), the price of newsprint increases due to "supply and demand." Publishers often move to stockpile paper before the prices go up—but this, inevitably, leads to even higher prices in the end. As newsprint prices climb, so does the cost to subscribe. My last bill from the *Hartford Courant*—"America's Oldest Continuously Published Newspaper"—increased from $38.87 for 13 weeks to $45. When the cost of newsprint finally stabilizes or goes down, as it has been known to do, the event is never accompanied by a decrease in the newspaper price.

The obvious alternative is online news, and research shows that not only will readers accept it, but that it may even displace the physical newspaper in the future.

Here's the Scoop on Newspaper Reading

Begin by looking at some of the market research. The Newspaper Association of America found that, although in the 18-to-24-year-old age bracket physical newspaper reading and online newspaper reading was the same (14 percent of the sample read both), the figures changed in older age brackets. Among 25-to-35-year-olds, 25 percent read the online paper and 19 percent read the hard copy. The 35-to-44 age group also skewed slightly in favor of online newspapers (28 percent to 25 percent for print).

The NAA's report revealed other interesting facts. While 57 percent of adults read a daily newspaper, 67 percent read a daily paper online; and while 67 percent read a Sunday paper, 78 percent read a Sunday paper online. The report, called "Synergize for Success," was based on 3,693 interviews with adults (aged 18 and over).[4]

Another study, commissioned by the Internet service provider Freeserve, stated that the Web placed third in terms of where people get their news—behind television and radio, but before newspapers.[5]

There are, however, conflicting reports. In July 2002, a study by the Pew Research Center for People and the Press reported only 25 percent of Americans go online for news at least three times per week. The report, based on interviews with 3,000 adults, hinted that perhaps "news" doesn't stand out as a category because of its ubiquity.[6] Forrester Research, a well-respected market analysis firm, concluded that just 23 percent of Internet users say the Web is where they get their news. Television is the preferred source.[7]

Other polls show Web news use going mainstream and rising, with 80 percent of Web surfers trusting Web news providers and 7 percent of that number saying that online news was more reliable than any other media![8,9] Concerning the future, Forrester concluded in a separate study that 57 percent of children aged 6 to 15 believe that they will get the majority of their daily news from the Internet.[10]

What Online News Consumers Want

Historically, the strength of newspapers has lain in their timeliness. The era of waiting for the newspaper carrier to stop by or, in cases where the mail carries news from "home" through an out-of-state paper, has ended. Web surfers want their news whenever they are ready to read it, and the Internet affords this advantage.

A joint study by Stanford University and the Poynter Institute for Media Studies concluded that when individuals go to a news Web site, they go there to gather information. This may seem obvious, but the study showed that when online, Web surfers read about 75 percent of the articles they look at, while people who read hard copy magazines and newspapers read around 30 percent of each article.[11] The study also found that photos and other graphics are, by far, of secondary concern.

The conclusions seem to contradict the experience of Mike Wendland, a journalist who covers the Internet and is a fellow at the Poynter Institute. In a *New York Times* essay, Mr. Wendland described personal research where he went without the physical newspaper for five months. He wrote, "I surfed the Web several times a day, reading the electronic editions of my regular papers and several others. Let me tell you: for a guy who has devoted the last few years of his professional life preaching new media and the Internet, I am amazed at how frustrated I was without my printed newspaper. I missed it."[12]

Mr. Wendland stated he could not find much local news; he also missed leisurely turning the pages and the serendipity of fascinating articles that waited. But he also concluded throughout the five months of monitoring the Web sites of the *New York Times*, the *Washington Post*, CNN.com, ABCNews.com, the *Detroit Free Press*, and the *Detroit News* that, overall, he didn't miss much news.

Pay for Online News? I Think Not

The top five daily newspapers by circulation are the *Wall Street Journal*, *USA Today*, the *New York Times*, the *Los Angeles Times*, and the *Washington Post*. Four of these publications are free to read, almost in their entirety, on the Web. Only the *Wall Street Journal* has maintained a subscription model for access to its site.

This has not always been the case; in the future it may not continue to be the case. In the early days of Web news, some publishers attempted to charge for access to their papers' sites. In 1997, *Editor & Publisher* reported that the *San Antonio Express-News* site (http://www.mysanantonio.com) was charging for most of its content—and turning a profit.[13] Today it no longer charges. Similarly, the *San Jose Mercury News* at http://www.bayarea.com/mld/mercurynews, which had charged a subscription to its site beginning in April 1995, dropped its fees by June 1998.[14]

The reasoning behind free access to newspaper sites is based on the realization that news can be readily obtained via thousands of providers. You can turn on the television or radio and get basic news free. If a Web site charges for its content, it alienates readers who will simply go to another site that does not. If a site invokes fees, it may engage some diehard readers, but it will drive away a million others. Is it more effective to expose millions of site visitors to the Web site's sponsors through banner advertisements and co-branded services and products, or simply hope that subscription revenue will sustain the site?

Recent trends indicate that Web users are more willing to pay for certain products. Subscriptions to e-greeting card services is an example. But with innumerable news sites available, many of which will probably never introduce fees, such as the BBC in the United Kingdom, it remains difficult for publishers to charge. One strategy that some Web sites use involves a tiered subscription model. The *Financial Times* (http://www.ft.com) from London, for instance, has three tiers. Site visitors have free access to the latest news and business data. Subscription level #1 allows full access to the news including search and retrieval of five years of the paper, plus access to surveys of business trends. Level #2 subscribers receive, in addition, world company financial information for 18,000 businesses plus access to World Press Monitor's 500 media sources. The hypothesis is that no one will be driven away by the fees because they can still access the mainstream news, and truly interested parties will pay for the value-added content.

Some players have made the fee-based model work: The *Wall Street Journal Online* had 200,000 paying subscribers in 1998 and 591,000 in June 2001. The *WSJ* even raised its online subscription rate from $59 to $79 in July 2002.[15] Boasting 646,000 subscriptions, the news and financial Web site has proved that charging for access can work. The *WSJ* takes a completely different approach when contrasted with the *Financial Times*. All the information from the *WSJ* is "behind the veil," accessible only to subscribers. Everything but the skeletal headlines requires a subscriber login. It works because its readers have well-defined interests that only the *WSJ* can satisfy. But few news Web sites that charge have been successful.

Once in awhile, albeit infrequently, Web surfers will come upon the odd news site that requires a subscription. The *Chanute Tribune* (based in Kansas) at http://www.dailynews.net/chanute offers free online content, but turned to password-protected subscription access for most of its news. Moreover, the paper not only charges $4 per month for Web access to people outside its local delivery area, it charges $6 per month to people who live nearby. But when the fee was imposed, site traffic that had averaged 600 hits per day dropped by 50 percent.[16]

Almost all newspapers with a Web presence are free. The *Wall Street Journal Online* and the *Chanute Tribune* are conspicuous exceptions. Newspapers on the Web reason that they can provide free content, and not rely on subscriptions, because they do not have to run advertisements that people may only happen to be interested in, but can show site visitors advertisements that will appeal to viewer interests by using various Web tools.

Typical Newspaper Expenditures by Libraries and Information Professionals

Purchasing decisions for news change when the shopper is a librarian or information professional. Consider the invoice a hypothetical library pays for print subscriptions to a varied list of newspapers. In an effort to provide a wide variety of news for a diverse readership, this hypothetical library subscribes to 22 papers: some dailies, some weeklies, some with Sunday editions. The standards include the *New York Times*, the *Manchester Guardian*, the *Washington Post*, the *Wall Street Journal*, and the *Christian Science Monitor*. A couple of local dailies are represented. The library also receives *Barron's*, *Variety*, the *New York Review of Books*, and *The Times Literary Supplement*. A smattering of other newspapers may reflect the interests of certain ethnic groups in the community, e.g., the *Moskovskie Novosti* (the Moscow News), the *India News*, the *Polish-American Journal*, Italy's *America Oggi*, *La Prensa*, *The Brasilians*, *China Daily*, *Gazeta Wyborcza* (the "Election Gazette").

The pricier titles include the *New York Times* at $586, the *Washington Post* at $871, and the *Gazeta* at $504, and, at the low end, the *Polish-American Journal* at $18 and *The Brasilians* at $20. The annual subscription charges for this collection total $4,757—perhaps not all that much when we consider the information it offers and the people it serves, but a substantial investment nonetheless, and certainly nothing in which even the most ardent and voracious news junkie would indulge.

Librarians and other information specialists have traditionally used subscription database aggregators in their searches for newspaper articles. The cost of documents through these vendors can quickly deplete one's financial resources. By using subscription databases, information professionals gain access to a deeper backfile of documents, and they can usually search and retrieve the documents quickly and be assured of high relevancy. In a corporate environment, these charges can be tolerated; they may be written off as expenses or absorbed in other ways. Also, users who access a news database (such as LexisNexis) through a local public or academic library may not realize the high price the library has paid to provide that database. The average individual, however, should not expect to use these vendors without paying a high price. It makes sense to turn to the free news sites.

Newspaper Web sites are not affected by the cost of newsprint. They are not constrained by the print medium. Their stories can provide more depth. They link to related articles. They can employ multimedia. They are usually searchable. They can provide e-mailed updates. They refresh their stories as appropriate. They are dynamic. Most importantly, newspaper sites are, much more often than not, free.

Free Model Is an International Model

Research scholars are savvy to the benefits of accessing the news they need from global resources. For example, one Polish language periodical that the Central Connecticut State University Elihu Burritt Library *does not* subscribe to is *Rzeczpospolita* (Poland's *Wall Street Journal*). Situated in New Britain, Connecticut, the university serves a community with a large Polish population and the library maintains a Polish Heritage Archive under the supervision of its archivist Eva Wolynska. But Ms. Wolynska, a native of Poland, forgoes *Rzeczpospolita*'s $864 annual subscription, preferring to consult it for news and research purposes without charge on the Web at http://www.rzecpospolita.pl. She still occasionally reads the hard copy, but notes that the Web content is as comprehensive as the newsprint edition and allows her to maneuver throughout the site for added features.

So what will it be? Forty-five dollars for 13 weeks of your favorite daily and Sunday newspaper? Sixty-five cents per day for the New York Times Electronic Edition—"An exact digital replica of the New York edition of the Times"—at http://nytimes.com/ee? (Note: The *New York Times* is free on the Web at http://nyt.com, but it isn't an "exact digital replica.") Or reading the best reporting from the best papers at their respective Web sites for free?

What's Online?

According to an *Editor & Publisher* survey, all of America's largest newspapers have Web sites. Out of the top 150 newspapers, 148 offer all or most of the news stories that appear in their print editions. Many smaller, local papers are also online. Newslink.org, a site that links to newspapers around the country and the world, reports that there are over 4,000 newspapers online from the United States alone. Which newspaper sites should you consult?

The publishing industry and individual entities present awards to the best news sites on the Web. *PC World* named the *New York Times* at nyt.com as the top site in 2002. The site, free to access with registration, received the honor because "When the most important news story in decades changed our lives overnight, nothing mattered more than expert reporting and analysis."[17] Of course, opinions vary. In the same year the Newspaper Association of America awarded the *Washington Post* at http://www.washington post.com its highest honors in its annual "Digital Edge Awards" for best news presentation for a paper with over 250,000 circulation.[18] *Editor & Publisher* magazine gave its "EPpy" awards to the *Los Angeles Times* (http://www.latimes.com) for "Best Overall U.S. Newspaper Online Service in the national with daily circulation over 250,000 category." Individuals in search of excellence in online news may wish to look at the entire EPpy list at http://www.editorandpublisher.com/editorandpublisher/ eppys/index.jsp. Earlier winners of the EPpy are also good bets. They include the *Washington Post* and the *Chicago Tribune* (http://www.chicagotribune.com). Other news Web sites frequently mentioned at award ceremonies include Kansas's the *Topeka Capital-Journal* (http://www.CJOnline.com) and the

Christian Science Monitor's Electronic Edition (http://www.cs
monitor.com).

Free Sites with High Standards

The New York Times
http://www.nyt.com

Winner: 1998 "EPpy" Best Overall Online Newspaper Service
(100,000+ circulation). *Editor & Publisher* magazine.

1998 "Digital Edge Award" Outstanding Achievement in
Interactive Newsgathering. Newspaper Association of America.

The *NYT* site offers incisive coverage of world and national news
plus its renowned *New York Times Magazine*. A remarkable site, it
excels in its use of the Web's ability to blend text, sound, video, and
graphics. For example, a retrospective on Stanley Kubrick's film
"The Shining" included high-quality video of scenes relevant to
the article, along with links to other pertinent information about
the movie. A relatively new "Multimedia" section on the site features Pulitzer Prize winning photographs, audio interviews, news
videos, slide shows, and interactive music videos. Once you have
registered, you can access book reviews, search for news and
reviews from 1996 to the present, and receive free e-mailed
newsletters on "Your Money," "Circuits" (the technology section of
the *NYT*), "Movies," "Vital Signs" (health), and several others. The
daily Web-based *NYT* is free. Articles a week old and less are free.
Articles from the archives, except reviews, are available for purchase. The cost is nominal, and different types of premium content
passes are available. The famous *NYT* crossword puzzle is a premium (pay) feature available for $19.95 a year.

The Washington Post
http://www.washingtonpost.com

Winner: 2002 "Digital Edge Award" Best News Presentation
(250,000+ circulation). Newspaper Association of America.

2001 "EPpy" Best Overall U.S. Newspaper Online Service (250,000+ circulation). *Editor & Publisher* magazine.

The *Washington Post* is 125 years old, but its site is as current as any on the Web. Use of the site is free; registration is required for some extras. Extras include "MyWashingtonPost" where users can personalize the online paper. The personalization process—not unique to the *Post,* many other sites offer it—allows registered users to choose the types of news they want to view upon accessing the site. For example, if you just want the sports and weather, those items will display first. The "Live Online" section features live Webcasts on various topics and maintains a video archive of past "Live Online" presentations. Discussion forums are also available; individuals interact via message boards on various topics based on the content of the news on the Web site. Free newsletters on sports, politics, travel, home, entertainment, and others are available to registered members via e-mail. Articles from the most recent 14 days are free, and you can search the archives back to 1977. Articles older than two weeks are available for purchase.

The Los Angeles Times
http://www.latimes.com

Winner: 2002 EPpy Best Overall U.S. Newspaper Online Service (250,000+ circulation). *Editor & Publisher* magazine.

Part of the Tribune Company, which also publishes the *Chicago Tribune, Newsday* (New York), the *Hartford Courant,* and *Hoy* (a Spanish-language newspaper based in New York), the *LA Times* Web site offers almost all the same content as the paper with the exception of some copyrighted photos, cartoons, syndicated columns, and some tables in very small fonts. Conversely, the Web site provides free material not in the paper, including Web-only entertainment coverage, specially organized special reports, searchable classifieds, and audio and video content. Articles are available for seven days, after which they are archived and require payment for access. To read most current articles, users must register, but registration is free. Registered members may also personalize their news, receive focused newsletters on topics of interest, and share opinions on the site's Discussion Boards.

Wait—There's More

To access other newspaper sites, try these sites. Each consolidates links to all types of news publications:

American Journalism Review
http://www.ajr.org/Newspapers.asp?MediaType=1

Based at the Merrill College of Journalism at the University of Maryland, the site links to 1,024 dailies, 1,188 nondailies, 322 campus newspapers, 69 major metropolitan newspapers, 163 papers from the alternative press, and 77 specialty publications. All the Web sites are from the United States. For newspapers from other countries, go to AJR's alternate link, http://www.ajr.org/News papers.asp?MediaType=1&Type=ForeignNews.

NewsDirectory
http://www.newsdirectory.com

This page links to 3,600 newspapers and, for good measure, 4,800 magazines. It may be searched by the publication's title, but geographical breakdown works better. For instance, choose "United States," choose a specific state, and the resulting page lists links to the daily and nondaily papers in specified state. Pickings aren't limited to the U.S.—Asian papers, African papers, European papers, and papers from Oceania and South America are also represented. So there is an opportunity to read non-English language newspapers. Oddly, Italy is missing.

NewsLink

http://newslink.org

Offering roughly the same number of links as NewsDirectory, NewsLink is also broken down geographically. Links to campus newspapers and television news sites also appear. A "Resources" link (http://newslink.org/spec.html) takes the user to journalism Web sites, online newsletters, and access to wire services.

NewsLink also keeps statistics on the sites most visited through its links. You will notice that the *Wall Street Journal* did not make this list of frequently accessed sites. *WSJ* ranks 69th overall in terms of how often it is accessed via NewsLink's pages. My hypothesis is that charging for access deters site visitors. According to NewsLink's reports, based on 8,347,600 reader accesses, the top 25 newspaper sites in the United States are as follows:

1. Washington Post
    http://www.washingtonpost.com

2. Los Angeles Times
    http://www.latimes.com

3. New York Times
    http://www.nyt.com

4. Miami Herald
    http://www.miami.com/mld/miamiherald

5. USA Today
    http://www.usatoday.com

6. New York Post
    http://www.nypost.com

7. New York Daily News
    http://www.nydailynews.com

8. Atlanta Journal-Constitution
    http://www.accessatlanta.com/ajc

9. Dallas Morning News
   http://www.dallasnews.com

10. Washington Times
    http:/www.washtimes.com

11. Philadelphia Inquirer
    http://www.philly.com/mld/inquirer

12. Boston Globe
    http://www.boston.com/globe

13. Chicago Tribune
    http://www.chicagotribune.com

14. Detroit Free Press
    http://www.freep.com

15. Phoenix Arizona Republic
    http://www.arizonarepublic.com

16. San Francisco Chronicle
    http://www.sfchron.com

17. Tampa Tribune
    http://www.tampatrib.com

18. Orlando Sentinel
    http://www.orlandosentinel.com

19. Baltimore Sun
    http://www.baltimoresun.com

20. Charlotte Observer
    http://www.charlotte.com/mld/observer

21. Chicago Sun-Times
    http://www.suntimes.com

22. Cleveland Plain Dealer
    http://www.plaindealer.com

23. St. Louis Post-Dispatch
    http://home.post-dispatch.com

24. Indianapolis Star
    http://www.indystar.com

25. Fort Lauderdale Sun-Sentinel
    http://www.sun-sentinel.com

You may also look for links to newspapers using major directory utilities. The Open Directory Project, Google, RefDesk, and Yahoo! maintain good lists. Check out:

http://dmoz.org/News/Newspapers

http://directory.google.com/Top/News/Newspapers/ Directories

http://dir.yahoo.com/News_and_Media/Newspapers

http://www.refdesk.com/paper.html

For additional newspapers by country refer to:

http://directory.google.com/Top/News/Newspapers/ Regional

http://dir.yahoo.com/News_and_Media/Newspapers/ By_Region/Countries

Foreign Language Newspaper Directories

While I have not successfully located any comprehensive directories pointing to newspapers by language, the libraries at the Massachusetts Institute of Technology have tried to bridge the gap at http://libraries.mit.edu/guides/types/flnews. Newspapers, magazines, and electronic journals written in Chinese, French, German, Italian, Japanese, Portuguese, Russian, and Spanish are listed on the MIT page.

Behind the Scenes at a Newspaper Web Site

Journalists have reputations for being high-energy. The imme-
diacy of online news probably compounds this. A Connecticut resident, I read the *Hartford Courant* and also regularly visit its Web
site at http://www.ctnow.com. A venerable paper with a long history, its masthead proclaims it "America's Oldest Continuously
Published Newspaper" (Figure 2.1). This newspaper's site gives me
the majority of the newsprint edition's content and, with no space
restrictions, many of the site's stories provide more depth than the
paper; the site even offers the coupons that come with the print
edition (I asked).

Hoping to learn what happens behind the scenes and to discover what strategies dictate the content, I contacted the site's editor, Mr. Gary Duchane. My interview with him follows.

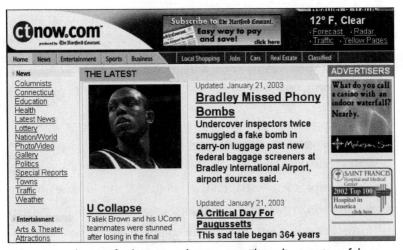

Figure 2.1   The *Hartford Courant's* home page. The online version of the
"oldest continuously published newspaper in America" features
in-depth stories that go beyond what had appeared in the
newsprint edition. Courtesy of CTNOW.COM, copyright 2003.

INSIDER'S VIEWPOINT FROM YOUR WEB LIBRARY PROFESSIONAL: GARY DUCHANE, *HARTFORD COURANT*

NT: Your title at the *Hartford Courant* is Online Editor; what are your responsibilities in connection with the *Hartford Courant's* CTNOW Web site?

GD: I am responsible for all news and entertainment content posted online from the *Hartford Courant*, its affiliated Tribune sister Web sites, and from our 20 content affiliates, which include Fox 61 WTIC-TV, Connecticut Public Television and National Public Radio WNPR, the *Hartford Advocate*, the *Yale Daily News*, the *Fairfield County Weekly*, the *New Haven Advocate*, and the *East Haven Courier* among others.

I am also responsible for developing Web-only content, bringing newsroom projects onto the Web site in a form that makes sense for the medium, and a host of technical duties relating to the platform itself—one shared by all Tribune Web sites.

NT: How many people, with what types of backgrounds, work at the electronic version of the *Hartford Courant*? What are the different roles being carried out? What is it like "behind the scenes?"

GD: The staff numbers 18 people. A general manager, online editor, three producers, a site developer, a sales manager, three sales people, several classified folks, and a few other ancillary positions. Most, if not all of us, came from the newspaper.

Behind the scenes, it's nonstop action. We are all working extremely hard to make this a profitable business both for the *Hartford Courant*, and our parent company The Tribune. On the content side and the advertising side we work closely with the newspaper. In addition, we work with our TV partners Fox 61— a Tribune-owned station, and NECN (a cable station) in terms of moving video content to the partners and online.

NT: I am a *Hartford Courant* subscriber and I read most of your newspaper every day. When I visit the CTNOW Web site I have noticed that the site offers the reader a great deal of flexibility to search for current as well as older news stories, to look for specific goods and services via the classifieds, and to find obituaries and town news. As I browse the site I think one of its strengths is that it offers a great deal of regional and town news. For example, it appears as though I can look at the town news from other editions of the paper whereas my subscription to the physical paper only includes a few towns in close proximity to me. CTNOW also has links to town information that sometimes rivals the actual town's Web sites. What are some other areas of the Web site that offer this type of comprehensive coverage?

GD: Our town story galleries are probably our most broad areas of content, and of the greatest interest to the largest number of users. In the area of entertainment, we offer the ability to read reviews from the *Courant* and our affiliates, then check out venues for upcoming shows in our entertainment databases, and buy tickets, too. We have databases online, for many things, including current census data, an Internet directory, elections information and results. Further, we carry multimedia content, extensive photo and video galleries, and special project reports. A recent special project discusses Puerto Rico's 50 years of commonwealth status at http://www.ctnow.com/news/nation world/hc-pr50-sp.special.

NT: Although there's plenty of timely news available at CTNOW, the *Courant's* Web site does not run the columns by many of the syndicated writers, which appear in the print newspaper. While Ellen Goodman's columns and George Will's items are available for example, John Rosemond's parental advice is not. I realize I can find them at other Web sites, but I miss the one-stop reading convenience I get with the physical paper. Why aren't some syndicated columnists present at CTNOW?

GD: We don't have Web rights to publish certain wire-service stories and photographs. At this point, we have determined that the cost of adding these would not necessarily translate into substantial increases in site traffic or advertising sales.

NT: So the decisions seem to be mainly related to profit. Is that also the reason I haven't been able to find many of my favorite features such as the crossword puzzle, the comics, the editorial cartoons, as well as some of the other items that really complement the paper for me? I realize the serious news seeker will get most of what is needed at the Web site, but speaking for those of us who enjoy the more recreational aspects of the newspaper, may I ask if these items are omitted for any particular reason?

GD: We don't see our mission as one to duplicate the newspaper. We complement the print product, choosing carefully the products that add value at a premium cost to us. Given a choice between adding a crossword puzzle or increasing Web-only content, or local stories, the choice is clear—we choose what is of most interest to the greatest number of users. Metrics data has shown us the traffic for these extras is limited.

NT: I see; the decisions are not arbitrary. How does the *Courant's* Web site work with its partners to bring added value to the reader that is not present in the physical newspaper?

GD: We place their content on our site, giving us added depth. In return, they are associated with one of the biggest and best Web sites in the state. The affiliate content is clearly marked, and a link back to the affiliates' sites, giving them an opportunity for expanded traffic. As I noted earlier, we work closely with our television partners, too.

NT: In addition to complementing the physical paper, do any aspects of the Web site go far beyond what is possible in newsprint? Are you especially pleased with any particular parts of the Web site?

GD: The "Special Reports" page (http://www.ctnow.com/news/specials) showcases the best work of our content team that enhances the print projects in an online format. We take great pride in improving on what the newspaper has done, in our own medium.

NT: Newspapers take up a lot of space and I don't always have time to read every story. One of the useful aspects about the *Courant's* site is that special materials are archived. Your photo galleries for instance. I can use them to go back in the news to 2001 if I wish. The Special Reports link you mentioned features some stories back to 1998. I don't keep more than a week's worth of the actual newspaper, so how far back in time does free content like this extend? Besides the photo gallery and the Special Reports, can the reader find other sections of the Web site that archive materials? What are some of the alternatives for readers who need older news?

GD: Most stories are available for two weeks. In many cases the producers can set individual stories and galleries to live indefinitely. The users won't be able to tell what lives beyond two weeks. But generally, if the story is available, there will be a link in the respective area of the site. We keep Special Reports online for extended periods, as many other Web sites link to our work. In general for users, information older than two weeks must be retrieved from our paid archives.

NT: Does the Web site sell many passes to the archives?

GD: A fair number—and the demand is growing. We also sell photographs online.

NT: Some of the free newsletters that are offered are worthwhile. The news update called "News@3" is one of the most valuable. Besides this update, how often is the home page of CTNOW refreshed with new information?

GD: The home page, the nation/world page, the state wire page, and several other pages are updated 24/7. The producers make choices on what will appear at the top of the home page. Late at night, we automate that area.

NT: As a news and Web site professional, do you look to any other particular sites for ideas? Also, what Web sites do you tend to visit regularly on a professional level?

GD: The Tribune sites, the *New York Times*, the *Washington Post*, CNN, and MSNBC.

NT: Does anyone in your business think that newspapers should cease to publish paper copies and just become virtual subscription news sources?

GD: No one has figured out a successful, lasting business model for news Web sites yet. We're all still finding our way.

Broadcast Journalism News Sites

Broadcast journalism sites are created by or run by news organizations that originate at major television or radio entities. Among the first to launch a Web site, CNN Interactive appeared on August 30, 1995. MSNBC followed a year later, and FoxNews.com came on board in October 1996. ABC News began delivering news via the Web in May 1997 and CBS News went online later that year. But the takeoff of broadcast news Web sites goes back to 1997 when Web surfers turned to them for coverage of the automobile accident and, later, the funeral of Diana, Princess of Wales. Within hours of the fatal crash, the main news organizations with Web sites posted breaking news about the incident alongside information regarding the beloved Diana and the final weeks of her life. Although people worldwide watched the funeral of Diana on their televisions in September 1997, others found the coverage on the Web generating a community of international mourners and confirming the Web as a plausible news medium. Major news organizations on the Web at that time, including MSNBC, CNN, and ABC News, noted considerable increases in page views.[19] Although Microsoft's Web-zine *Slate* is not a news site, its founding editor Michael Kinsley said

Diana's sudden death made him realize that a "Web site needed to be on its toes, around the clock."[20]

More recently Nielsen/Net Ratings indicated that 3.9 million site visitors checking in from work and 1.9 million checking in from home went to CNN.com for information on November 8, 2000—the day after the 2000 presidential election—a record audience. Site visitors not only wanted to read the news, they wanted to interact with other readers. They left 13,292 postings on CNN.com's message boards.[21]

The broadcast journalism sites offer depth and timeliness in news coverage. While the most popular is CNN, which the Alexa toolbar shows as ranked 26th out of all Web sites, there are many from which to choose.

CBS News
http://www.cbsnews.com

CBS television viewers can find multimedia clips from their favorite news shows at this Web site. If you missed "60 Minutes" or want to share a segment with a friend, you'll find you can easily locate the stories and send them by e-mail, including the multimedia links. CNN and ABC News have instituted charges for their multimedia clips, but CBS News Videos proudly claim that they are "Always Free." CBS will also e-mail registered users news summaries and breaking news alerts.

CNN
http://www.cnn.com

The first major broadcaster to claim a presence on the Web, CNN attracted one million site visitors in its first two days online. CNN also operates CNN/Money (its financial counterpart at http://money.cnn.com), the "AllPolitics" Web site at http://www.cnn.com/ALLPOLITICS, and CNN/si with *Sports Illustrated* magazine. The top broadcast journalism Web site, CNN's traffic even eclipses traffic to the *New York Times* site. Unfortunately, CNN recently began charging for access to its video stories. The NewsPass is affordable at $4.95 per month or $39.95 per year, and, in August 2002, was the only way to see the exclusive Al Qaeda terrorist training tapes on the Web.

MSNBC
http://www.msnbc.com

This Web site represents a $500 million joint venture between NBC and Microsoft. A strong news site, MSNBC regularly features "Event Chats." Event Chats are online encounters with special guests usually conducted in a virtual auditorium with only chatters' questions and guest answers visible. On some occasions, however, chatter comments are visible during Event Chats. Although Event Chats' guests are often politicians, other guests include sports figures, health professionals, authors, entertainers, and presidential advisors. Another forum, called "News Chats," is always available (where MSNBC viewers can discuss the news online while watching the shows). The chat schedules are posted at http://www.msnbc.com/chat/default.asp.

National Public Radio
http://www.npr.org

Individuals may hear *or* read news at NPR's site. The advantage is that you may continue working on other computer projects while you launch hourly audio news updates or listen to entire shows through NPR Audio Stream, including "All Things Considered," "Fresh Air," or, for laughs, "Wait. Wait. Don't Tell Me!" The emphasis on audio is apropos for the radio shows. (You'll need RealPlayer or Windows Media Player.) Also available: six years of audio archives; if you want to hear everything Daniel Schorr has said in the archive from the past six years, it's a simple keyword search away.

Online Newshour with Jim Lehrer

http://www.pbs.org/newshour

Individuals who enjoy the incisive reporting of Jim Lehrer and others on the erudite staff of the PBS news program will truly appreciate the show's Web site. The site's archives go back to 1996, so site users can search for a segment they remember having seen and revisit the stories they originally found provocative. The Online Newshour also offers video and audio of selected news. Five free daily e-mail newsletters and one special weekly newsletter designed for schoolteachers are available.

BBCi

http://news.bbc.co.uk

The British Broadcasting Corporation's news site ranks at number 39 for popularity on the Web. The site offers e-mail alerts plus something different—a free news ticker that you can download. It is available for Windows and Macs. Once downloaded, the news ticker sits on your desktop and provides automatic updates for news, sports, and weather throughout the day. If you see a story that interests you, just click on the ticker's link and it takes you to the BBCi's news site for details.

C/NET: Tech News First

http://news.com.com

C/NET aims to satisfy a niche—but a big niche. A high-ranking technology site, it is a vortal (vertical portal) specifically tailored to news for techies. Registered C/NET users can choose from up to 28 newsletters (including "Virus & Security Alert," "Handhelds Newsletter," and various shopper oriented alerts). C/NET also provides software downloads, product prices and comparisons, and hardware and software reviews.

Alternate Approaches:
Of Ananova and Weblogs

In the late 1980s, a short-lived television series called "Max Headroom" featured a computer-generated news host whose show brought the viewer "twenty minutes into the future." Long before the World Wide Web, this sci-fi program predicted the integration of video, TV, computers, and on-screen video images with linked databases. Get a glimpse what the show was like by reading "Mad About Max"—the cover story of *Newsweek* on April 20, 1987. If you missed it, there's always the United Kingdom's "Ananova" based in Leeds (http://www.ananova.com). An animated news anchor, age twentysomething with green hair, her first Web cast began, "Hello World! Here's the news and this time it's personal!" Using "your news on your terms" as a motto, the Web site quickly became one of the most avant-garde novelties a news junkie could want.

Ananova has not won a Pulitzer Prize, an EPpy, or a "Digital Edge Award," but *Web User Magazine* has nominated it for "Best News Site." It has over 16,000 links pointing in and a respectable ranking of being in the top 1,100 sites on the Web (compared with CNN at number 25, BBCi is 39, the *New York Times* at 77, *USA Today* at 158, and the *Washington Post* at 165).

Besides having a Web presence, Ananova has moved into the WAP (wireless application protocol) arena and is available on PDAs (personal digital assistants) and a proprietary (subscription) wireless phone network called "Orange" also based in the United Kingdom. Other virtual newscasters have joined the ranks including several available for PDAs and cellphones through 1KTV at http://www.1ktvla.com.

Giving News a Personal Spin: Weblogs

Weblogs have enjoyed attention from the press as well as scholars and anyone interested in the perspectives of others regarding current events. Weblogs are online journals ("Web" + "log" = "Weblog") written by people concerning their own experiences, but many Weblogs go beyond this by interweaving personal experience with what is happening in the news. Daypop, a search engine dedicated to retrieving news and Weblogs, defines Weblogs (also called blogs) as "A new form of personal journalism. Think of them as opinion columns or slices of life. Newspapers give you the international headlines and weblogs give you both a subjective view of current events and a personal view of the author's life." Other characteristics of a Weblog are frequent updates and links between author commentary and articles elsewhere on the Web. Weblogs can be updated frequently because of blogging software. Blog software, such as that offered by Blogger.com, allows anyone with access to a computer on the Web to update and publish entries instantaneously. In fact, Blogger.com not only offers the software but it will host your blog for free, too. (More about creating your own blog in Chapter Eight.)

Blogs emphasize the writer's personality, but there is also a sense of camaraderie between readers and authors and authors and other authors. Dave Winer, a software developer, president of Userland Software, and one of the Web's earliest bloggers (he began a Weblog called "DaveNet" in late 1994), wrote, "A weblog is personal—it's done by a person, not an organization. You see a personality. It's not washed-out and normed-up, the bizarre shows through. That's why weblogs are interesting. ... No weblog stands alone, they are relative to each other and to the world. The Link and Think project, as an example, is part of the weblog community and part of the World AIDS Day community. My weblog, Scripting News (http://www.scriptingnews.com), is part of the weblog community and part of the community of independent developers, particularly those using scripting environments. The same can be said of most weblogs that gain audiences, they connect people together using the Web through common interests."[22]

As a sidebar, Mr. Winer has formally wagered that by 2007, more readers will get news from blogs than from the *New York Times*. Martin Nisenholtz, head of *NYT*'s digital operations, has taken him up on that wager.[23]

Salon's Scott Rosenberg offered this concise definition: "Weblogs, typically, are personal Web sites operated by individuals who compile chronological lists of links to stuff that interests them, interspersed with information, editorializing and personal asides. A good weblog is updated often, in a kind of real-time improvisation, with pointers to interesting events, pages, stories and happenings elsewhere on the Web. New stuff piles on top of the page; older stuff sinks to the bottom." See the Salon site at http://www.salon.com/tech/col/rose/1999/05/28/weblogs.

A few examples will adequately illustrate the connection between the news and Weblogs:

Title: SpinLine
Description: Opinion on politics, technology, and anything newsworthy. Topics in early 2003 included President Bush's tax cut recommendations, the Atkin's diet, leftist movie stars, and the meaning behind your car's "check engine light."
URL: http://spinline.net

Title: Daily Kos
Description: Political analysis and other daily rants on the state of the nation. An extremely well executed blog with plenty of links to other bloggers, opinion journals, and comments from its readers.
URL: http://www.dailykos.com

Title: The Obscure Store
Description: Jim Romenesko mines the Web for offbeat news stories. Extensive links to news sources and other blogs.
URL: http://www.obscurestore.com

Other Weblogs are concerned with the special interests of their authors. The range of interests is universal. If your passion is the arts, you will find Weblogs discussing composers and painters. There are Weblogs discussing librarianship and science. Bloggers who love (or hate) to travel post on the Web. Stephen Levy writes in *Newsweek*, "There are blogs devoted to cats, blogs about knitting, blogs about 802.11 wireless standards, blogs about 'The Golden Girls' TV show, blogs about baseball, blogs about sex (hey, it is the Internet). One blog is written in the voice of Julius Caesar, tracking the Roman's progress as he takes on Gaul. There are blog short stories and a blog novel in progress."[24] Taking Andy Warhol's famous quote to the next logical level, author David Weinberger, considering many of these niche topics, says, "In the future, everyone will be famous to 15 people on the Web."[25] These may provide a sense of the variety of Weblogs you may find:

Library & Information Science News
http://www.lisnews.com

Librarian Blake Carver and his associates compose this collaborative blog for information scientists (see Figure 2.2). News stories relating to technology and libraries are collected from the Web and linked to from this site. Site users contribute stories also. The "see also" section offers links to other library-related blogs.

Other blogs produced by librarians include Jessamyn West's "Librarian.net" and Steven M. Cohen's "Librarystuff.net." Librarians interested in blogs by librarians or at libraries throughout the world may want to visit Peter Scott's directory of weblogs at Libdex (http://www.libdex.com/weblogs.html).

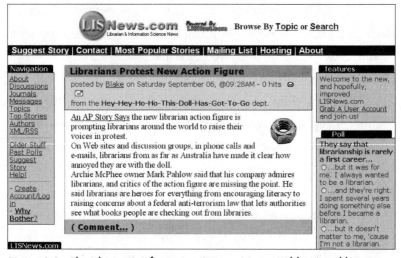

Figure 2.2   The Library & Information Science News Weblog (used by permission LISNews.com and Blake Carver, copyright 2003). Note: The information is library-oriented and the articles link to news stories and other relevant sites.

Oakland Athletics Blog

http://elephantsinoakland.blogspot.com

For baseball fans of the Oakland Athletics and others, this nicely done Weblog discusses broadcasting blackouts, sports books, player's salaries and trades, and last night's game.

Where There's Smoke

http://www.wheretheressmoke.net

Author Kevin Smokler describes his pages as "A weblog of conspicuous cultural consumption." Topics covered include film, books, music, and humor.

Some blogs are very subject specific; they come and go as dictated by events. For example "As the WorldCom Turns: A Blog About WorldCom" was Ben Silverman's running commentary on this fiasco until, on January 6, 2003, he ended the blog writing that he had become "sick of this story." Readers may still view the blog's archive, though, at http://www.dotcomscoop.com/worldcom.html.

Locating the Blogs: Key Resources

Daypop

http://www.daypop.com

You may search for Weblogs by keyword using Daypop (http://www.daypop.com). Daypop searches default to news and Weblogs, but the user can quickly focus on the blogs by using a pull-down menu. Dan Chan, the site's creator, claims Daypop crawls the Web every 24 hours, so the blogs it retrieves should be fresh and updated.

Chan has built some smashing features into the Daypop page. In addition to searching for keywords, one can click on "Word Bursts" to find words that are being frequently mentioned on blogs. The "Top News" link, by contrast, illustrates which Web news articles are currently being linked to. And "News Bursts," like "Word Bursts," tracks increased usage of words, only it tracks them from the front pages of news Web sites. This is a good way to locate the most talked about news items whether you're a news junkie or a blogger watching for hot stories on which to comment.

EatonWeb Portal

http://portal.eatonweb.com

Online since 1997, EatonWeb has grown from 50 active Weblogs to approximately 12,500. Although the portal is searchable, it offers a useful list of categories including "Anime," "Parenting," "Philosophy," "Politics," "Religion," "News/Entertainment," and a hundred others. Clicking "News/Entertainment," I found 776 blogs (in September 2002 the total was 100). Click on a blog's description, and EatonWeb takes you to the site. I visited MyFree Press.com; the author's electronic journal linked to news stories on

Microsoft, genetics, dirty bombs, *The Matrix Reloaded*, SARS, and the United Nations.

Technorati
http://www.technorati.com

Technorati is a service with a "way cool" feature called "Link Cosmos." At Technorati's home page you can enter a URL and see the blogs that are mentioned at the target site. This contrasts with Blogdex, where you can see the blogs that are being most frequently discussed. For example, when I enter the URL for the Library of Congress, Technorati's "Link Cosmos" tells me that the Library of Congress has 302 "inbound links" (as of October 2003). Clicking the links will take you to the inbound blog. You can use this feature to check what bloggers have written about your own pages as well as others! Technorati offers a keyword search of blogs also. At last count, in October 2003, it tracked 360,000 blogs.

Userland
http://www.weblogs.com

Userland does not organize its links by subject or name, but rather by the most recently updated Weblogs. Why? Elementary! The most recently updated blogs have the freshest content and perspectives. Although I'd prefer if it had a search engine or a directory listing, http://www.weblogs.com gets a great deal of traffic and is highly respected among bloggers.

Blogdex MIT Media Lab
http://blogdex.net

The Media Lab at the Massachusetts Institute of Technology created this important and exciting page (see Figure 2.3). Not a list of Weblogs, instead it displays links to the 25 "most linked to" news stories. I initially thought this was satisfactory because it illustrated the topics that bloggers considered top news (and perhaps most interesting). I then discovered that Blogdex also tracks the

Welcome to the newly reconfigured Blogdex. The frontend has changed dramatically, as well as pretty much everything under the hood. Please excuse the bugs while I get things up to speed.

1. **The people who brought you Movable Type announce TypePad**
   typepad.com
   » track this site | 94 links

2. **Guardian Unlimited Online Battle of the blog builders**
   guardian.co.uk/online/news/0,12597,942024,00.html
   » track this site | 51 links

3. **an infusion of investment capital**
   sixapart.com/log/2003/04/six_apart_miles.shtml
   » track this site | 43 links

4. **Sen. Rick Santorum's comments on homosexuality in an AP inter...**
   sfgate.com/cgi-bin/article.cgi?file=/news/archive/2...
   » track this site | 37 links

5. **unprepared to prevent the rise of an anti-American, Islamic f...**
   washingtonpost.com/wp-dyn/articles/A17886-2003Apr22...

INFORMATION

Blogdex News
Search
Add your weblog
XML: RSS 0.91
Contact Blogdex

A YEAR AGO TODAY

1. Yahoo! Sports Golf...
2. comparing the French...
3. Yahoo! News - Photo
4. OBJECTIVE: Creation E...
5. tessellating animatio...
6. Hughes to Leave White...
7. dooce.com | bootylici...
8. Yahoo! News - Photo
9. photojunkie: The Film

Figure 2.3   MIT Media Lab's "Blogdex" lists the most "linked to" news. Users may also click the "sources" link under each listing to view the blogs that have referenced the news stories. Used by permission, Cameron Marlow, MIT Media Lab, copyright 2003.

blogs from which the links come. Librarians call this "citation searching"—learning who cites whom—and find it extremely valuable. You see not only the most discussed news and have the ability to click to the original site to read it, but you can also visit the multiple blogs that generate the links. This arrangement has many implications including comparing individuals' views on specific current events. For instance, on August 16, 2002, 26 blogs were discussing *Salon* magazine's article called "The Media Titans Still Don't Get It." (Big media companies may have lost billions on the Internet because their leaders never actually used it.)

Google

http://directory.google.com/Top/Computers/Internet/On_the_
Web/Weblogs

Google provides another page of Weblog links. The page offers various categories. The "Personal" category has 2,800 listings. Incidentally Google purchased the aforementioned Blogger.com in February 2003—a Weblog search tab from Google can't be far behind.

Other Resources: Yesterday's News

An individual requiring access to older newspaper articles may consider visiting libraries (the "brick-and-mortar" variety) to search their respectable collections of newspapers. Libraries that have invested in microfilm often have a deep backfile of articles from major newspapers. Newspaper Web sites, conversely, have not made digitizing their backfiles a priority. Most only go back a few years and require payment for retrieval of archived news stories. The two sites mentioned here, however, may be useful.

U.S. News Archives of the Web

http://www.ibiblio.org/slanews/internet/archives.html

Maintained by volunteers at the Special Libraries Association, this site serves as a reliable gateway to older newspaper articles from papers in the United States. Daily newspapers from 47 states plus the District of Columbia are represented. Multiple newspapers cover some states. Unfortunately, the backfiles are not very deep, but many of the sites listed do allow free access to older articles.

The Special Libraries Association also maintains links to archives of newspapers outside the United States at http://www.ibiblio.org/slanews/internet/ForArchives.html.

NewspaperArchive

http://www.newspaperarchive.com

The vast majority of Web sites discussed throughout this book have had a relatively high ranking in terms of site visitors and links pointing in; NewspaperArchive does not. First, it's not a free site. You may search the database all you like, but when you have located a relevant document, you'll be prompted to subscribe. Nonetheless, it may prove useful in tracking down older newspaper articles. Coverage is spotty, to say the least, but Chris Gill, president of the site, says he hopes to have at least one major newspaper from each state online by 2003. For example, click Massachusetts, and the site will tell you that *Berkshire County Eagle* is available from 1858 to 1863.

But when you do find something interesting (usually via a keyword search), the results indicate what you will often find all over the Web in the future when a critical mass of newspapers has been digitized. The site presents details of scanned images of the pages of newspapers with the relevant words highlighted. Then the subscribing user may download a copy of the page. The site generates additional revenue by selling reproductions of pages that users have found relevant.

Using News Search Engines

Confirmed news junkies may visit specific newspapers and news sites throughout the day, but they also deploy the services of news search engines and news portals. They access the newspapers and news sites for international and national headline news, and to read the news about specific "beats"—sports, business, books—but they use the engines and portals to track specific topics.

For example, an individual interested in the impact of environmentalists on new housing and home prices in California could access several California newspaper sites and perform multiple searches. Alternatively, he or she could use a news search engine and run the search against multiple sources. Similarly, although the *New York Times* Web site will mention and distill information on a local topic, such as a kidnapping in Modesto, California, by using a news search engine a Web surfer can get links directly to the most updated in-depth articles from the *Modesto Bee*.

AltaVista News
http://www.altavista.com/news

We know AltaVista revolutionalized Web searching, and when it teamed up with Moreover, a major Web news aggregator in its own right, in 2001, it set a benchmark for news searching. Covering 3,000 sources including the *Washington Post, USA Today*, and the *New York Times*, AltaVista news offers a main news page as well as news searching.

The main page offers top stories—this page is refreshed about once an hour. The database goes back a year (with some articles dating back further). The search interface allows the user to specify date ranges or to select from preconfigured intervals. One of the site's main advantages is that the search form allows the user to choose specific world regions or pick from a short list of countries to retrieve news. This could give a reader a nicely rounded view of how various developments are being perceived around the world. For the graphically curious it offers an option to limit searches to articles with images.

Daypop.com
http://www.daypop.com

Emphasizing current events and crawling the "living Web" at least once per day, Daypop searches 7,500 sources including newspapers, news sites, and Weblogs. Daypop defines the "living Web" as "being composed of sites that update on a daily basis: newspapers, online magazines, and weblogs." A search strategy for the keywords "California environmental housing" returned 29 sites (naturally, not all were relevant). Highly recommended for finding up-to-date news, sports, and film reviews.

Google News Search
http://news.google.com

This service culls information from 4,000 of the world's news sources collected over the previous week, a relatively brief time interval. News junkies may want to use this page as their portal to national and international newspapers as well as nonnewspaper sites such as CNN, ABC News, the Associated Press Newswire, and National Public Radio.

The keywords "California environmental housing" (the connector "AND" is not needed in Google searches) found 165 articles. Compare this with the fewer number of hits I located with Ithaki, some of which went back as far as January 2001. Google News also uses auto-generated time of updating.

Ithaki News Metasearch
http://ithaki.net/news

Ithaki searches hundreds of news sources throughout the world. The result is a variety of retrieval. The keyword search for "California environmental housing" retrieves 60 stories. Some come from National Public Radio, some from ABCnews.com, and others originate at the *San Francisco Chronicle* and the *San Jose Mercury News*.

Moreover Showcase News Portal
http://www.moreover.com/cgi-local/page?o=portal

Founded by journalist Nick Denton in 1999, Moreover is a leader in providing news headlines. It keeps site visitors up-to-speed by frequently visiting 2,700 news sources—some as often as every 15 minutes.

World News

http://www.worldnews.com

World News, based in the United Arab Emirates, is a fabulous news site. The home page provides regularly updated news summaries, but its true strength lies in its search engine. Covering 500 international news sites and 20 languages, my quick search on Iraq/fly zone (I omitted the word "no" to avoid confusing the search engine) gathers over 1,000 hits from a wide array of sources including the *Las Vegas Sun*, the *Tehran Times*, *Salon Magazine*, Fox News, the BBC, the *Washington Post*, and dozens of others from Canada, New Zealand, Ireland, and India. I did not browse all the headlines, but I suspect numerous other sources were represented. Each headline links to the story at the original news site. The news search is truly international; you can find news in non-English languages including Swedish, Swahili, Afrikaans, Norwegian, Polish, Italian, Spanish, Slovak, Turkish, Malay, Romanian, Portuguese, Czech, French, Danish, Dutch, German, Hungarian, Indonesian, Hausa, and Finnish.

Setting Up News Updates and Newsletters

Many sites furnish individuals with breaking news, morning and evening news reports, and news on topics that the user defines through e-mail. Employing multiple services allows individuals to get a wide range of news delivered directly to their e-mail. Using services that allow individuals to select the topics they like to read helps people who need specific information.

Updates, usually called "breaking news," consist of a brief headline and a link to the full story. A newsletter is structured and covers a stated topic. Focused e-mailings are a third phenomenon with content based on what you have designated as your search keywords. The frequency of breaking news varies widely. I usually get two a day from CNN, and two a day from the *Hartford Courant*.

Setting up news updates and requesting newsletters at a site is always straightforward. On a newspaper site or a news site, look at the links under "Services" or "E-Mail Services." Sites that provide this advantage will probably offer options such as mailings for entertainment news, technology news, sports news, and political news. If the site offers more generic services, you can still benefit from getting an e-mailed news update once in the morning and once in the afternoon. Even if you love monitoring the news at the sites this chapter has discussed, a single update may be all you need on certain days.

ABC News

http://www.abcnews.com

If you tend to tune into ABC News Tonight or prefer the ABC News Web site, you can register (free) and receive e-mailed newsletters from 18 different points including Peter Jenning's Daily Journal, Nightline, Sam Donaldson's Webcast, Barbara Walters, Weird News, Working Wounded, and This Week with Sam Donaldson and Cokie Roberts. Most of these, however, preview what the next telecast/Webcast will feature, but ABC's Breaking News Alerts provide frequent updates on top news throughout the day.

CNN's E-Mail Services

http://www.cnn.com/EMAIL

CNN's site gives visitors options to receive Breaking News Alerts, headlines in the morning, a weekly political newsletter, and computer and Internet news delivered every Wednesday. It also offers LawWatch, Space Update, U.S. Storm Watch, and Health Week. All are free.

MSNBC

http://www.msnbc.com

At the bottom of the MSNBC home page, click "News Tools" or try this URL: http://www.msnbc.com/tools/newstools. You can get e-mail notifying you of important news as it happens by choosing "News Alert" and choosing from 24 different focused newsletters including daily morning headlines, business headlines, and NBC Nightly News. After clicking "News Tools," go to the "E-Mail Extra" link. Registration is free as are all e-mail services.

Sports Newsletters and Alerts

CNNsi

http://www.cnnsi.com

At the very bottom of the Sports Illustrated home page, a link for "E-mail Newsletters" takes the user to another page where readers can elect to receive three newsletters (daily top stories, golf, and/or football). A breaking sports news alert is a fourth offering. All are free.

About.com

http://about.com/sports/newsletters.htm

Forty-four free newsletters are available under four broad categories including Fitness/Outdoors, Marine, Hunting/Fishing, and, my favorite, Spectator Sports.

Newsletters and Breaking News at National and Local Newspaper Sites

Each of the top five most frequently accessed newspaper sites according to statistics at NewsLink.org (the *Washington Post*, the *Los Angeles Times*, the *New York Times*, the *Miami Herald*, and *USA Today*) can send you e-mail with breaking news and/or other newsletters informing you about specialty topics. Smaller dailies often provide this service also. Check your favorite newspaper's Web site to learn if it offers this feature. Look for phrases such as "E-Mail Services," "News

Alerts," or "Breaking News." These links will walk you through registration and configuring the newsletters you want to receive.

A Free Service Becomes Fee-Based While Two New Free Services Take Its Place

A few years ago I discovered a free feature at the Web version of the *New York Times* called "News Tracker." The service was ahead of its time. It not only e-mailed news alerts to registered site visitors, it allowed them to set up their own customized search strategies for up to three alerts. For example, if you were a big fan of Ozzy Osbourne and his family, you could save a specific alert that would be run against the *New York Times* on a daily basis—any relevant stories would be e-mailed to you. That's quite a bit different than simply getting a generic "rock music" alert. Unfortunately, the Web site sent me several e-mails in June 2003 telling me that this free feature was changing to a fee-based subscription service.

About a month later Google came to the rescue. In midsummer it announced that it was offering "Google News Alerts." Like the New York Times "News Tracker," Google's Alerts allow users to configure keyword searches and search specific news sources (or all of Google's news sources). For example: A person could ask that the word "Osbournes" be searched in the headlines of articles from the *New York Times*! Google runs the searches against the news source and e-mails links to the stories to the user. Google's Alerts are free, and Google allows a user to configure up to 50 searches. (This is a little more cost effective than "News Tracker" from the *New York Times*, which charges $19.95 per year for 10 searches.) You can take advantage of Google's free, customized news alerts at http://www.google.com/newsalerts.

For that matter, if you like CNN's Web site and find it useful to browse its news stories, you can sign up for keyword searches and news delivery at http://www.cnn.com/youralerts. You need to register, but that's free. Then you can set up the alerts focusing on your interests whether they're as mainstream as "stem cell research" or as focused as "Arcane Knights of the Apocalypse." You can also elect to receive the alerts as the news is reported, daily, or batched for weekly delivery to your e-mail address.

Create Your Own News Portal

Having keyword search alerts e-mailed to you, which Google provides, is a solution if you are tracking specific topics. The broad scope of the news pages at AltaVista, CNN, MSNBC, and BBCi, to name a few, are fine if you want a quick glimpse of the top stories. But if you are staying on top of news in various subjects areas, you need a service such as NewsIsFree, located at http://www.newsisfree.com.

At NewsIsFree you can browse the latest headlines; you can search for news, too. But the real attraction, and it's a free feature, is that you can create custom pages of news from the news sources you choose. You can subscribe to its premium services for some worthwhile additions, but the basic service is great when you want to visit a page that has news only on the subjects that interest you. After you register (free), you can create pages from the 6,700 newsfeeds that populate NewsIsFree. When you return to NewsIsFree and login, your pages are available for browsing with updated news about your subjects from the newsfeeds you've chosen. Subjects and newsfeeds are easily organized because each page can have a unique name.

Just for fun let's say we are interested in odd news stories. By browsing the "Offbeat" channel at NewsIsFree we can create a page of weirdness by selecting from over 50 "Offbeat" feeds including Reuter's Oddly Enough, SatireSearch, and Ananova Quirkies. The scholarly types have plenty of choice, too. The "Science" channel includes the Science Web site, Science Friday (NPR), and Eurekalert, to mention a few.

A Journalist Talks About Web News

The vast majority of Web news is quickly accessed, does not require payment, and updates frequently. But getting one's news online still generates questions. Is the content credible? Won't printed newspapers always be preferable? I connected with a media insider to gain more insight on these subjects. Richard Hanley, Ph.D., teaches e-media production at Quinnipiac University in Hamden, Connecticut. Professor Hanley's comments are especially interesting; note that, along with other topics, he discusses Weblogs, the reasons people prefer Web news, and how a news site gains a readers' trust.

INSIDER'S VIEWPOINT FROM YOUR WEB LIBRARY PROFESSIONAL: RICHARD HANLEY, QUINNIPIAC UNIVERSITY

NT: Professor Hanley, let's give readers a perspective on your comments. Would you share some details about your background?

RH: My introduction to the online platform began in 1992 with Prodigy Online Services, the joint venture of IBM and Sears to provide a proprietary computer network for home consumers. The experience—I served as a contributing writer for a module called Timely Topics—showed me the vast potential for delivering content via the online platform and the feedback mechanism it provided. For example, for a story on the "Buy America" fad of the early 1990s, I was able to conduct a poll of Prodigy subscribers and use that information within the story. In addition, I received instant comments on the story from Prodigy subscribers.

After Prodigy, I went to work for CD-ROM encyclopedia publisher Grolier Interactive, which in 1994 had become the world's leading CD-ROM publisher. By then, I was firmly convinced, however, that the Internet as an open network provided the best mechanism for delivering factual information, such as that provided in the encyclopedia. In fact, I saw the Internet as the encyclopedia itself, and one that would eventually compete with Grolier.

In 1995 I was assigned by Grolier to develop the company's encyclopedia products for online distribution. I became the company's first Webmaster, developing free content for its Web site to promote the CD-ROM while helping to prepare the encyclopedia content for online distribution.

Also in 1995, a colleague, Hugh McNally, and I launched the first regularly scheduled, live-video, Internet-delivered sports talk show. Essentially, we modified video conferencing software and applied it to Grolier Interactive servers. The program was netcast every Friday at 4:30 ET from Danbury, Connecticut. Our fans logged on from around the world, including Russia and Finland. For 30 minutes, we poked fun at sports, at ourselves, and at the Internet. The show became so popular that Grolier kicked us off the server because we were causing too much commotion. Actually, Grolier was peeved that we were getting more press than the company's CD-ROM products.

In 1996 I developed "The American Presidency," an Internet presentation that took articles from the three encyclopedia sets owned by Grolier and posted them for free. The presentation included biographies of all American presidents plus detailed articles on politics and the political process. It also included videos, audio speeches, quizzes, and a special feature called Flip Cards, which gave young people the opportunity to click on a presidential portrait or photograph to get baseball-card-like information on the president.

A year later, with the encyclopedia online and available to schools and libraries on a subscription basis, I invented an online magazine for middle school students called Brain Jam. In one of the first instances on the Internet, Brain Jam took long encyclopedia articles and "chunked" them, using the now routine "Back" and "Next" navigation tools for students to follow the article. In addition to a featured article a month, each issue contained a quiz, an events calendar, and other items.

In 1999 I joined *Time* magazine as a senior producer to develop long-form interactive features based on the magazine's articles and materials prepared specifically for the Time Web site. I produced the Web site for the Millennium microsite (a site within the larger site) as well as the microsite for the 1999 Person of the Year.

When AOL merged with Time-Warner in 2000, I decided to help Connecticut Public Broadcasting get a handle on its Internet presence. I developed the Web sites for both CPTV and WNPR.

I joined Quinnipiac University in August 2001.

In addition to my experience on the Internet, I produce, write, and direct historical documentaries for CPTV. I have received numerous Associated Press Broadcasters Association awards and Emmy nominations over the past decade.

NT: That's a great deal of impressive experience. I recently read with great interest your story, which appeared on MSNBC, called "Corporate scandals uncovered. Where was the press while business was cooking its books?" One of your major points was that typical journalists, while able to cover ubiquitous political scandals, are unfortunately unsophisticated in the ways of corporate maneuvering and, therefore, tend to keep their distance when trying to report on business news. Most of what they had said about American companies for several years has been "glad tidings." I realize your article didn't target any one type of journalist as culpable, but I'm wondering about your perception of news reporting on the Web. Nancy Hicks Maynard wrote in the *Neiman Reports* that journalists worry that digitalization of the news may erode its integrity.[26] Nat Hentoff wrote in *Editor & Publisher* that news on the Internet is "dubiously sourced, and as partisan as the U.S. Senate Judiciary Committee ... exposure to ideas and information they [site visitors] might find unpalatable is decidedly limited."[27] As an e-media scholar and historian, what is your take on the trends in Web news?

RH: I would say to Ms. Maynard that the press is more afraid of having its privileges and elite standing undermined by Web sites such as that run by Philip Kaplan (http://www.f----dcompany. com). Kaplan's site prints internal company memos leaked to him by employees. His site was far ahead of the mainstream press in accurately reporting the dot-com bust and the implosion of companies such as WorldCom. Ms. Maynard fails to understand that the Internet allows ordinary folks—not the coddled elite of the mainstream media—to practice journalism, in much the same way the pamphleteers of the 18th century did in Colonial-era America. It is interesting to note that Matt Drudge was the leading journalist in unmasking the Clinton scandals of the late 1990s. The mainstream press was forced to follow his lead on the Internet.

Mr. Hentoff, too, seems more concerned with preserving the status quo. Much of the news in mainstream media is "dubiously sourced." Political agents of both major parties play the press, and this is clear by the propensity of the mainstream media to publish leaks as facts without naming sources.

The trend that Mr. Hentoff and Ms. Maynard fail to recognize is the trend of the Weblog. Individuals that use links to mainstream news stories and postings of observations made by them and their visitors to provide a fresh dimension on the news produce these daily diaries.

The Internet has chipped away at the power and privileges of the mainstream press. And that is good for democracy. Still, the top news sites are administered by mainstream organizations such as CNN, MSNBC, and the *New York Times*.

Ultimately, what the Internet has done is give people the opportunity to get fresh news 24 hours a day, seven days a week. That should dramatically change the way news is delivered via legacy media (television, radio, newspapers). No longer can TV news use teasers to much effect; people who are immersed in the Internet information stream don't tolerate such tactics, for example. The next generation of news consumers will be unlike any that came before simply because they will demand news on their terms on their time.

That, more than any perceived erosion of so-called news values, is the greatest change that the Internet has triggered in the news media/industrial complex.

NT: And how can the reader gauge the credibility of online news, which is produced so rapidly, even when provided by ostensibly authoritative sources such as CNN, MSNBC, the *New York Times* et al.? Are editorial safeguards in place that compare to those used in print journalism? Should the Web surfer simply assume that there is no difference between the printed edition and the Web edition of, say, the *LA Times* and its Web counterpart?

RH: In this context, I would prefer the term Web consumer, as people are more likely to go directly to the site they want instead of surfing mindlessly as they might have in the first generation of Internet activity. Survey data show that people use the Web as an information utility, going directly to sites based on a specific need. For news, people will go to a site that they trust. Web consumers make no conscious distinction between the print and Web editions; in fact, it is likely that many in the future will not even read the print edition, as they will find the Web edition to be better suited to their information consumption wants and needs. Why? Because it is updated constantly even while it is easy to retrieve archived articles.

Let's agree that people will tend to visit news sites that they trust on an informational level, as much as they do now for consuming news via television (note how the networks and cable outlets pound home the trust value in promotions). The difference-maker at the Web level of trust is site functionality. If it's easy to find information, the trust level increases. People won't trust a site that is not updated constantly. In addition, people won't trust a site that doesn't have an archive easily reached via a search mechanism.

So it's important to note that the trust is not only embedded in the information consumed, it's embedded in how it is consumed.

And newspapers, more so than any other medium, have a built-in advantage in that they have a cultural integrity in how they are designed, which is an important distinction above and beyond the mere recitation of perceived facts. The print newspaper has evolved its look and feel into the most efficient interface possible for scanning and retrieving information almost instantly. In the presentation of the information, the hierarchical display of stories, and the inverted pyramid style (most important information in the first paragraph) of writing fit astonishingly well with how Web visitors consume information. They scan and retrieve just what they need at a given moment. The most successful newspapers on the Web such as the *New York Times* are simply duplicating the strengths obtained from decades of experience in designing news pages for print.

By merging the presentation culture of the legacy medium with the attributes of the computer network (instant updating capability with a database that stores articles that can be instantly retrieved), Web consumers will find the best of both worlds. The *New York Times* is by far the best at this.

NT: In 1998 the *San Jose Mercury News* tried to charge for access to its Web edition but dropped the plan not long after. Except for archived news stories, I've found that every online newspaper I access is free. What is the incentive for printed newspapers to promote free Web-based services?

RH: The fee-for-service model is coming into its own now. In the early days, newspapers were forced to open the gates for free to the information they obtained and presented at great cost, because everyone was doing it and no sure business model existed. Now that the Internet has calmed down and is firmly under adult supervision for the first time, it is clear that more and more newspapers can begin to charge for some information on a subscription basis, as long as the subscription is not outrageous. This is already a fact in specialized publications such as *Variety* and *Consumer Reports*.

For daily newspapers, as you pointed out in the question, the subscription fees have been targeted for the archived materials. At some point, however, the fees may surface for high value-added items such as book reviews, dating services, and the like. It is unlikely that ordinary news flows will be subject to subscriptions; in a media-saturated environment, news is a commodity: pile it high and sell it cheap, which in this case means free. Recent survey data confirm this view.

According to an Online Publishers Association report released in August 2002, American Web consumers spent $675 million on online content in 2001, a leap of 92 percent over 2000. The top three categories are Business Content, Entertainment, and Personals/Dating. They accounted for 59 percent of all online content spending.

Thus, it is clear that some sort of hybrid model between the useful (business) and the personal (dating services, investment news) may be the base for a subscription area of daily newspapers.

NT: I've found the "breaking news" options at various news and newspaper sites tremendously interesting and useful. This is something you just won't get from the daily paper you find on your doorstep. Again, from an editorial as well as a financial point of view, why do the news sites offer this feature?

RH: Breaking news features play into the capability of the Internet, where it is cheap to update a site with information that has already been gathered. More than that, though, Internet consumers expect news sites to constantly update their content. Without breaking news modules, news sites are nothing more than a digital version of a legacy product, and that model is destined for failure.

If a newspaper has a site and it is gathering information anyway, it makes sense to post it when the news happens. Otherwise, consumers will go elsewhere and the overall value of the newspaper will fall.

NT: From an insider's experience, have you ever noted an in-house competition between news broadcasters, Web news editors, and newspaper editors?

RH: Indeed, this is a key area of tension within newsrooms. For example, I was interviewed for a job at a major news organization based on my experience on the Web, in television, and in newspapers. The idea was to use the newspaper's vast reportorial army (300 reporters and editors) for the Web and a company-owned television station. When I suggested that the television station should run a crawl at the bottom of the screen with town-by-town news, the state editor of the newspaper almost tossed me out on my ear. "We can't give our content away," she said. The television general manager, meanwhile, didn't want to upstage his news report with such crawls running underneath. I then suggested that at the least the information should hit the Web site when written. Again, the fear, uncertainty, and doubt were palpable.

This illustrates how legacy management in the differing cultures of television and newspaper along with the Web has managed to defeat most attempts at collaboration among the pillars of distribution. There is, however, great hope.

A joint operation of the *Daily Oklahoman* and KWTV News9 in Oklahoma City stands as one of the few successes on this score. The two organizations share stories on a jointly operated Web site—NewsOK.com—and print reporters go on television to report on stories they are covering. It is a seamless convergence. What makes NewsOK.com even more interesting is that the same company does not own them.

Another site, http://tbo.com, has emerged from the convergence of WFLA-TV news and the *Tampa Tribune*. Now, reporters for both the TV and news sides are expanding their capabilities to provide deeper context within stories and the ability to track stories as they evolve more so than they did separately.

Still, these two examples of solid relationships between legacy media organizations on the Web are news simply because they are rare.

NT: Mike Wendland, a journalist and fellow of the Poynter Institute for Media Studies, wrote a piece in the *New York Times* called "Reading the News in the Inkless World of Cyberspace," where he commented on his affinity to newsprint. Apparently he restricted his television news viewing and newspaper reading and for five months he got all his news by reading the electronic editions of his favorite newspapers. In the end he said he missed not only local news, but also the serendipity of finding new stories at leisure while he turned the pages. He also felt that the whole online experience was inconvenient and cumbersome. What about people who love the newspaper? Professor Hanley, how do you perceive the differences between Web newspapers and "the real thing?"

RH: First, I don't believe in that nostalgia-driven attachment to dead trees sprinkled with inky symbols. Mr. Wendland suffers from a desire to find the good in the old, and he has found it, presumably, in that the Web site of his local newspaper is so awful that it doesn't post all the news that it has in its print edition. Second, most Americans work too hard to deal with the magic of serendipity. They want information, they want it fast, and they want it now, because they are too busy raising families and going to work to wait for the moment when a news story will pop out at them as they leisurely stroll through the day's news. That, to me, is the big difference between the digital distribution platform for news and the dead-tree version.

NT: Do you have a preference for any particular newspaper or news site? What makes it stand apart from the innumerable choices you have?

RH: The *New York Times* is without question the top news site, as it takes the strengths from the print version and grafts onto them the strengths of the Internet: detailed articles that are updated if need be, all placed in an intuitive navigation setting, that can be retrieved using a solid search engine at any time.

Conclusion

Newspaper Web sites, news sites, and Weblogs offer a tremendous variety of interestingly presented information to satisfy every taste and need. When assessing the advantages of these resources, we must not only consider that the majority of them can be accessed without charge, but also that they often go far beyond what one can access in physical publications, hear on the radio, or see on television. Apart from the luxury of reading printed news on the subway (or certain rooms in one's home)—and some individuals probably use PDAs (personal digital assistants including handheld devices) and wireless laptops to get around this barrier—their convenience and timeliness is usually superior to their print and broadcast counterparts. In the case of Weblogs, no noncomputerized counterpart exists, unless your affinity to "dead trees sprinkled with inky symbols" (as Professor Richard Hanley stated) is intractable. Also consider the variation you will find in depth of coverage. For example, the *New York Times* will certainly mention an event that occurred in Pittsburgh, but you will get a more complete picture by using a news search engine that brings you to several news Web sites in Pennsylvania. You have to love the value of the Web's coverage of news.

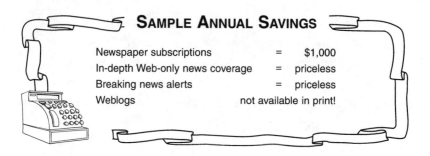

SAMPLE ANNUAL SAVINGS		
Newspaper subscriptions	=	$1,000
In-depth Web-only news coverage	=	priceless
Breaking news alerts	=	priceless
Weblogs		not available in print!

Endnotes

1. "Three more producers announce price hike for newsprint." Paperloop.com. July 8, 2002. San Francisco: The Paperloop. http://www.paperloop.com. July 12, 2002.

2. Lucia Moses. "Newsprint cost should stabilize." *Editor & Publisher.* March 11, 2002. Volume 135. Issue 10. p. 6.

3. "Newsprint price may go up 32%." The Financial Gazette. March 28, 2001. Harare: Zimbabwe. http://www.fingaz.co.zw/fingaz/2001/March/March28/1173.shtml. July 12, 2002.

4. NAA Business and Market Analysis Staff. "Print and Online Components Bring Strength to Newspapers." The Digital Edge. http://www.digitaledge.org/monthly/2000_01/synergize.html. August 13, 2002.

5. Sarah Ryle. "Print Media Loses Out to Internet." The Guardian. July 28, 2002. http://media.guardian.co.uk/presspublishing/story/0,7495,764264,00.html. August 13, 2002.

6. Wayne Robins. "Online Newspaper Consumption is Flat." Editor & Publisher Online. July 1, 2002. http://www.mediainfo.com/editorandpublisher/headlines/index.jsp. August 13, 2002.

7. Marty Beard. "Web's Cool but not the Coolest." Media Life. January 18, 2002. http://www.medialifemagazine.com/news2002/jan02/jan14/5_fri/news5friday.html. August 13, 2002.

8. David Noack. "Poll Says Web News Use Is Mainstream." *Editor & Publisher.* January 16, 1999. Volume 132. Issue 3. p. 26.

9. B. G. Yovovich. "Consumers Trust Web News Providers." *Editor & Publisher.* November 28, 1998. Volume 131. Issue 48. p. 27.

10. Ellen Pearlman. "Web Newspapers Hook Kids Better Than the Paper Kind." *American Editor*. July/August 1996. Issue 777. p. 7.

11. Kathleen O'Toole. "Eye Movement Research Points to Importance of Text Over Graphics on Websites." Stanford Online Report. May 10, 2000. http://www.standford.edu/dept/news/report/news/may10/eyetrack-55.html. August 13, 2002. See also "Online Reading is Different to Newspaper and Magazine Reading." Online Publishing News. May 5, 2000. http://www.onlinepublishingnews.com/htm/n20000505.063238.htm. August 13, 2002.

12. Mike Wendland. "Reading the News in the Inkless World of Cyberspace." *New York Times*. May 25, 2000. Section G. p. 15.

13. Steve Outing. "Charging for Web News." *Editor & Publisher*. February 1, 1997. Volume 130. Issue 5. p. 24.

14. Sharon Machlis. "Web News Site Drops Subscription Fees." *Computerworld*. Volume 32. Issue 22. p. 28. June 1, 1998.

15. "Wall St. Journal" Hikes Online Price. Editor & Publisher Online. July 18, 2002. http://www.editorandpublisher.com/editorandpublisher/index.jsp. August 13, 2002.

16. David Noack. "Kansas Paper Charges for Online Content." *Editor & Publisher*. May 29, 1999. Volume 132. Issue 22. p. 36.

17. "Best Web Sites." *PC World*. July 2002. Volume 20. Issue 7. p. 91.

18. "NAA Hands Out Digital Edge Awards." Editor & Publisher Online. July 15, 2002. http://www.editorandpublisher.com/editorandpublisher/index.jsp. August 14, 2002.

19. Andrew Ross Sorkin. "Diana's Death Expands Web's News Role." *New York Times*. September 8, 1997. Section D. Column 4. p. 3.

20. Stephen Phillips. "Life on a Publishing Rollercoaster: Interview with Michael Kinsley." *The Financial Times*. June 19, 2002. p. 6.

21. Felicity Barringer. "Old Dogs See Opportunities in New Tricks." *New York Times*. September 11, 2000. Section C. p. 4.

22. Dave Winer. "What are Weblogs?" Weblogs.com. November 6, 2001. http://newhome.weblogs.com/personalWebPublishingCommunities. August 20, 2002.

23. Stephen Levy. "Will the Blogs Kill Old Media.?" *Newsweek*. May 20, 2002. Volume 139. Issue 20. p. 52.

24. Stephen Levy. "Living in the Blog-osphere." *Newsweek* on MSNBC.com. August 26, 2002. http://www.msnbc.com/news/ 795156.asp#BODY. September 1, 2002.

25. David Weinberger. *Small Pieces Loosely Joined: A Unified Theory of the Web*. Cambridge, MA: Perseus Books. 2002.

26. Nancy Hicks Maynard. "Digitization and the News." *Neiman Reports*. Winter 2000. Volume 54. Issue 4. p 11.

27. Nat Hentoff. "The Future of News." *Editor & Publisher*. May 6, 2002. Volume 135. Issue 18. p. 26.

Chapter Three

Ready or Not:
Reference on the Web

The days of using the "Very Easy Rodent-Oriented Net-wide Index to Computerized Archives" (Veronica) to help us find documents on Gophers seem prehistoric. Recalling my delight at finding the definition of a word and displaying it on a VT-100 cabled to an old LCD overlay for the fascination of faculty members, I remember the sense of wonder that the Internet was capable of doing such powerful things. In the traditional library, advantages gained by having centralized collections and content accessed by a limited and manageable number of access points are lost in cyberspace. We have replaced that scenario with a digital library, complete with unlimited access points; distributed, varied collections; and content management from all over the Internet.

Admittedly, most computer users find the answers to their own reference questions, but identifying and assessing the strongest reference sites while imposing a semblance of order on them remains a desideratum of many librarians and other information professionals concerned with optimizing the Web's potential. Although individuals may still prefer the printed page over an e-book for bedtime reading, their preference for finding reference information online is demonstrated by the numerous links to free sources such as RefDesk.com, Bartleby.com, Merriam-Webster, and Xrefer.com.

What Is a Reference Question?

In its 1999–2000 statistics questionnaire, the Association of Research Libraries (a not-for-profit membership organization of over 120 leading research libraries in North America) defined a reference question as:

> An information contact that involves the knowledge, use, recommendations, interpretation, or instruction in the use of one or more information sources by a member of the library staff. The term includes information and referral service. Information sources include a) printed and nonprinted material; b) machine-readable databases (including computer-assisted instruction); c) the library's own catalogs and other holdings records; d) other libraries and institutions through communication or referral; and e) persons both inside and outside the library. When a staff member uses information gained from previous use of information sources to answer a question, the transaction is reported as a reference transaction even if the source is not consulted again.[1]

Unlike an open-ended research question, which generates many searches and subsequent queries, a reference question requires a definitive answer. It has a beginning and an end, and librarians answer millions of them every year. Using the Association of Research Libraries's definition, the number of questions posed per year at a college library reference desk ranges from

31,000 at the University of California (Riverside) to almost 600,000 at Wayne State University in Detroit, Michigan. In the middle of the list we find Yale with 156,366 and my alma mater, the University of Connecticut, with 68,405. Librarians at public libraries and special libraries answer their share, too. The Arlington Public Library in Texas answered 675,727 questions in 2001. The Minnesota State Law Library answered 15,000, and the New York Public Library received a total of 6,419,000 reference questions in 2000 (down from 6,588,166 in 1998).[2] Public libraries in Canada field 30 million questions annually.[3] By comparison, this makes the 9,000 total received by the Internet Public Library (IPL) in 1999 seem low— but all the IPL's questions were electronic transactions. The phenomenon isn't limited to the North America—the University of Edinburgh averages about 75,000 queries per annum.

How Much Does It Cost to Answer Questions?

To answer the questions, librarians rely on their knowledge of reference sources. But even the combined knowledge of the best librarians can't help us without referring to the actual reference materials (which aren't cheap to come by).

Typical community colleges, with collections of 50,000 books serving 10,000 users, may have total budgets between $139,000 and $300,000—$20,000 to $30,000 of which purchases their reference books. A medium-sized public university holding 600,000 titles may have a total budget of $1.5 million, and its reference book budget could amount to $100,000. At the Elihu Burritt Library at Central Connecticut State University, the head of the reference department has a reference book budget of $75,000 per year (the budget for electronic databases is $187,000).

Some public libraries also have relatively generous total budgets of over a million dollars. One public library in the midwestern United States allocates $274,000 to its print reference collection.

Another public library reported that out of its $340,000 budget, $50,000 went to print reference. And yet another spends $75,000 on its reference books out of a $730,000 total book/materials budget.

Regardless of the lack of or excess of money, librarians tend to be prudent types. Although in an ideal world every comprehensive, complete reference resource with a catchy/inventive/interesting title or new edition is a temptation, to stretch funds librarians pass on many books. Instead of buying that new edition, they wait a year or two to conserve money.

Besides the limits of budgeting, library reference collections also differ based on library missions, library clienteles, and library types. Many reference collections contain hundreds or thousands of books (the Burritt Library has 15,000). However, there are probably some two dozen or so key ready reference materials that almost any library you visit will have. These items are usually kept at the librarian's desk (and in close proximity to it) to help librarians render rapid assistance to individuals with often-asked questions. It's called the "Ready Reference Collection." This is the collection you want to "house" at your Web library.

INSIDER'S VIEWPOINT FROM YOUR WEB LIBRARY PROFESSIONAL: WILLIAM KATZ, LIBRARIAN, EDUCATOR, AUTHOR

Free, But Are They Really Useful?

William A. Katz, whose *Introduction to Reference Work* (most recent edition is 2002) has been required reading for most graduate library science students for decades, has worked as a journalist and librarian since 1948. Honored by the American Library Association's Reference and User Services Association as the recipient of the Isadore Gilbert Mudge–R.R. Bowker Award, he has been a professor at the School of Library and Information Science, State University of New York (Albany) since 1966. I asked Dr. Katz several questions about the Web and ready reference.

NT: How good a source is the Web for free ready reference information?

WK: Two points: First, the most used aspect of the Net, in terms of information, is ready reference. Second, it is at its best in this information category, as the user need only enter key words for at least some basic, usually current, responses. Whereas, in my opinion, the free Net sites are often less than satisfactory for in-depth information, it is excellent for ready reference. The Net for ready reference vies in number of users only with entertainment (games, etc.), e-mail, shopping, and, yes, pornography.

NT: Will the number of free reference sites diminish?

WK: There will be more, not fewer, ready reference sites for free on the Web because individuals, institutions, etc. find it an excellent way of: a) gaining publicity, b) furthering their interests, and c) keeping in touch with sometimes amazingly narrow fields of knowledge. Although brevity of information, which characterizes most reference information, is not always the key, ready reference is easier to put online than in-depth material.

NT: I've been able to find free, Web-based rough equivalents—not duplications—for a number of classic reference texts. Is this a good sign for individual public Web users, or do you perceive the lack of straight one-to-one equivalents as a failing and a sign of the erosion of authoritative sources?

WK: For both ready reference and in-depth sites, the question is reliability. A major challenge is that a good deal of the instant data is dated, less than objective, and often downright wrong. More important, there is too much of it and little or no way of differentiating the good from the bad. Hence the growing need for experts (for example, librarians) who can make such decisions and, at the same time, save the user valuable hours of searching on the Net.

Concerning reliability and authority, although no one should assume that everything you read, even if it bears the imprimatur of a traditional print source publisher, is true, the credibility of free Web resources becomes less suspect when offered by authorities such as Macmillan, Merriam-Webster, the Mayo Clinic, and others.

Consensus on Ready Reference Sources

Ready reference questions range from people needing information on countries to job descriptions to company data to statistical information. Phone numbers and directory information are often requested. Pithy quotes are needed. Queries about advertising costs in specific publications are common, as are inquiries into definitions of words and examinations of topics.

Many librarians have compiled lists of essential reference resources. At Lehigh University, library help-desk personnel can view a Web page that tells them to become familiar with the *Statistical Abstract of the United States; Encyclopedia of*

Associations; *Ulrich's International Periodicals Directory*; *World Almanac*; *Acronyms, Initialisms, and Abbreviations Dictionary*; *Books in Print*; *Biography Index*; *Merck Index*; *McGraw-Hill Dictionary of Scientific and Technical Terms*; and the *U.S. Government Manual*. At another library site, the *Guinness Book of World Records*, *Who's Who in the World*, and the *Times Atlas of the World* make the top 10. Amazon.com's "Listmania" has contributors who have cited *Merriam Webster's Collegiate Dictionary*, *Roget's Thesaurus*, *National Geographic Atlas of the World*, *Bartlett's Familiar Quotations*, *New York Public Library Desk Reference*, *Emily Post's Etiquette*, *Robert's Rules of Order*, and Strunk's *Elements of Style* as musts. Syllabi in use at various graduate library and information science programs stress knowledge of print resources such as *Current Biography*, *Encyclopedia Americana*, *Encyclopedia of Associations*, *Miss Manners' Guide to Excruciatingly Correct Behavior*, *Directory of Physicians in the United States*, *Occupational Outlook Handbook*, and the *Martindale-Hubbell Law Directory*.

The Top Reference Sources in Print and Online

These eminent authorities notwithstanding, I defer again to Bill Katz, librarian, professor, and author, for his judgment concerning the most accepted and useful recommendations. According to Katz, the top three reference titles are the *Statistical Abstract of the United States*, *World Almanac*, and the *World Book Encyclopedia*.[4] These three titles, along with the *Merck Manual*, were the hottest in large and small libraries according to the results of a year-long survey reported in *Booklist*. Librarians who responded to Mary Ellen Quinn's questionnaire said they based their choices on a preference for what is accessible, authoritative, current, and even enjoyable.[5] If free Web versions of these popular print reference sources could be located on the Web, we'd save money and, most likely, access the information in a more flexible, value-added format.

The Statistical Abstract of the United States

Individuals may add the entire text and tables of *The Statistical Abstract of the United States, 2001* (which retails in print format for about $38) to their desktops for free by downloading Adobe Acrobat documents from the United States Census Bureau at http://www.census.gov/statab/www. But you don't have to download all of it—if specific tables satisfy your needs, you do not need to spend an excessive amount of time storing superfluous information. If, for example, the tables covering "Construction and Housing" interest you, it takes only a couple of minutes to download the approximately 45 tables to your hard drive. Or you can download only the index, which takes two minutes, and then return to the site to download specific tables when needed.

Almanacs

While the *World Almanac and Book of Facts* enjoys wide popularity, some people prefer to use one of many other similar publications. Reputable publishers such as the *New York Times* and *Information Please* make new almanacs available every December, costing $9–$13. Although the *New York Times* does not put any part of its almanac on the Web, *Information Please* does. In fact, if you know where to look, you will find parts of the *Old Farmer's Almanac* (http://www.almanac.com), the *African American Almanac* (http://www.toptags.com/aama), and the *World Almanac for Kids* (http://www.worldalmanacforkids.com).

Péter Jacsó, professor and chairperson at the School of Library and Information Science at the University of Hawaii has reviewed the Infoplease Web site: "[The] Information Please Almanac (http://www.infoplease.com) is part of the new Infoplease free Web site of Information Please LLC that includes other IPA editions for sports and entertainment, plus additional sources such as the Infoplease Dictionary and the Columbia Encyclopedia. The country profiles are excellent, and many of the worldwide statistical tables are the most current you can get. Infoplease was smart enough to use the very good public domain maps of the CIA instead of paying royalties for someone else's high-quality maps. You cannot create customized charts and tables, but the sources are free-text searchable, a feature likely to bring up relevant articles (along with some irrelevant ones). All in all, this source is definitely a pick for its many assets."[6]

The Infoplease home page links to the almanac's index. Because the Web site uses the same section headings that appear in the print almanac, it is easy to locate information in the 180 entries that lead to text, tables, and/or images. Not only does the site offer the general, sports, and entertainment almanacs, a dictionary, and an encyclopedia (as Jacsó stated), it also offers an atlas. Not bad for free.

General Encyclopedias

In 2002 the *World Book Encyclopedia* comprised 22 volumes and retailed for about $950. It is also available on compact disc for about $20. An annual subscription to the value-added World Book Online Web site (http://www.worldbookonline.com) costs $49.95. Article length varies from a paragraph to several pages and most have links to other articles. A number of free Web sites provide encyclopedias including Encyclopedia.com offered by eLibrary (which also provides subscription reference resources), the Columbia Encyclopedia at http://www.bartleby.com/65, and "Free Internet Encyclopedia" at http://www.cam-info.net/enc.html. Most of the free encyclopedias tend to have brief articles, but some of the services have appropriately long articles complete with links similar to those you'd pay for at the World Book site.

Encarta Online Concise Encyclopedia

The Microsoft Network offers free encyclopedia information at http://encarta.msn.com/encnet/refpages/artcenter.aspx.

In terms of factors on which to base a comparison among the free and fee encyclopedias, Encarta Online Concise might not score many points. But when judging resources, a major criterion applied by librarians is authority—who produces the resource and what are the producer's credentials. Although the free Encarta produced no results on a keyword query for "Kandahar," the "Industrial Revolution" search yielded a three-page article with links to related items as well as images and sounds—all free. Moreover, I was very pleasantly surprised to find the article signed by a library director with a doctorate. Encarta scores high on the criterion of authority.

Although the free Encarta Concise site is undoubtedly an appetizer to gain customers for the Encarta Encyclopedia Standard (one compact disc: $19.95) and Encarta Online Deluxe Encyclopedia (three discs: $29.95), it is also a good, free resource, and it should occupy a link in the Web Library.

Britannica Concise

Yahoo! hosts this free resource containing 25,000 alphabetical entries at http://education.yahoo.com/reference/encyclopedia. The articles I looked at, on 10 sample topics, ran between 90 and 600 words. Unfortunately, cross references are not linked to other related articles, and "see also" references to related articles were rare. In another Britannica Concise review, Dr. Jacsó stated: "The longest article is probably the main entry about the United States at 840 words. Remember, however, that the number of articles is not a decisive criterion in comparing encyclopedias. Where *Britannica Concise Encyclopedia* (*BCE*) really shines is with the substantial definitions of many words and names. These are longer than the ones in the comparable encyclopedias and *BCE* has definitions for terms which do not even occur in other concise encyclopedias, let alone as main entries."

The illustration index at http://education.yahoo.com/reference/encyclopedia/illustrations is very handy for locating graphics, though the majority are in black-and-white. It is searchable and browsable by alphabetic range. The illustrations also accompany the appropriate articles, but you should use the index to find a graphic when needed.

Columbia Encyclopedia

The sixth edition of the *Columbia Encyclopedia* became available in 2000. With a list price of $125, it is a comprehensive one-volume work containing 3,156 pages. It also occupies three inches of shelf space. You can access the same information for free at Bartelby.com (http://www.bartleby.com/65). An article on Kandahar ran 316 words and also contained links to other *Columbia Encyclopedia* articles. Similarly the "Industrial Revolution" is handled in a concise manner. The encyclopedia contains a browsable index to its 51,000+ entries. As Dr. Jacsó stated in one of his reviews, "The printed version of the 5th edition has been my primary print reference for many years, although it was not a desk reference as its sheer size made me put it back to the shelf after each use. Indirectly, this was also a workout given the weight of the tome. I will need to find some other exercise now that this excellent source is at my fingertips on the Web."[7]

Encyclopedia.com

Also intended to whet the appetite of searchers for more information, Encyclopedia.com is a free resource offered by the eLibrary.com commercial reference provider (http://www.encyclopedia.com). Encyclopedia.com is based on the *Columbia Encyclopedia*. Upon searching a topic, the user will retrieve brief articles (including links to more specific free information within the article), but the site also entices users by offering magazine, newspaper, radio, television, and journal articles/transcripts and images, which only eLibrary subscribers can view. Not that subscribing to the eLibrary service is such a terrible idea at $79.95 per year.

What can you expect for free at Encyclopedia.com? A search on the keyword "Kandahar" retrieved a 398-word article about the Afghan city. The article included six links to related free information. Premium (subscription) content listings appeared in the sidebar below the basic article.

A search on the Industrial Revolution retrieved a main article, again brief, and five brief subsections including a bibliography. Related Premium content was offered as well. While not a comprehensive source, Encyclopedia.com is worth bookmarking or making a "Favorite."

The *Merck Manual of Diagnosis and Therapy*

The *Merck Manual* is an incomparable compendium of information for physicians, patients, and the general public. It has been in publication for over 100 years and is available in 14 languages. Three hundred experts collaborate on the production of this resource that covers all but the most obscure disorders. "In addition to describing symptoms, common clinical procedures, laboratory tests, and virtually all the disorders that a general internist might encounter, the *Manual* deals with problems of pregnancy and delivery; common and serious disorders of neonates, infants, and children; genetics; drug dependency; psychiatric disorders; and many disorders covered by other specialties. The *Manual* also contains information about special circumstances, such as dental emergencies, reactions and injuries caused by radiation exposure, and problems encountered in deep-sea diving. Current therapy is presented for each disorder and supplemented with a separate section on clinical pharmacology."[8]

A frequently used reference book, the 17th Centennial edition is available at most bookstores for approximately $35 (or on CD-ROM for $90 with illustrations and $35 without). The entire book may be downloaded for $79.95. Or it may be searched/browsed free at Merck's Web site. The Centennial edition appears at http://www. merck.com/pubs/mmanual and includes extensive linking to related text and images.

In 1998 Merck began to reach a broader audience when it published the *Merck Manual of Medical Information, Home Edition*, a freely accessible text version available at http://www.merck.com/ pubs/mmanual_home/contents.htm. An enhanced interactive edition of this book, with animations, photos, sound, tables, videos, sidebars, and illustrations, is freely accessible online at http://www.merckhomeedition.com/home.html.

Frequently Used Reference Materials

Just prior to the onset of the new millennium, Brian E. Coutts, the head of Library Public Services at Western Kentucky University, and John B. Richard, director of the East Baton Rouge Parish Library in Louisiana, published a list of titles that had endured for years and are still considered heavily used ready reference items today.[9] Although the list included several electronic titles, the majority of works were print resources. The choices were made based on the usefulness of the work, longevity, and the practicality of the source for answering questions. The recommendations came from both public and academic electronic discussion lists. The list of 50 works include:

- *Webster's 3rd International Dictionary*
- *World Almanac and Book of Facts*
- *Times Atlas of the World*
- *Statistical Abstract of the United States*
- *Oxford English Dictionary*

- *Bartlett's Familiar Quotations*
- *Encyclopedia Britannica Online
- *Reader's Guide
- *InfoTrac
- *World Book Encyclopedia*
- *Facts on File
- *Encyclopedia of Associations*
- *PDR*
- *Columbia Gazetteer of the World*
- *WorldCat
- *McGraw-Hill Encyclopedia of Science and Technology*
- *New York Times Index
- *Roget's II The New Thesaurus*
- *Statesman's Yearbook*
- *King James Bible*
- *Emily Post's Etiquette*
- *Robert's Rules of Order*
- *CRC Handbook of Chemistry and Physics*
- *Merck Manual*
- *Rand-McNally Commercial Atlas & Marketing Guide*
- *Black's Law Dictionary*
- *Columbia Granger's Index to Poetry*
- *Chicago Manual of Style*
- *Moody's Manuals*
- *Dictionary of American Biography*

- *Occupational Outlook Handbook*

- *Million Dollar Directory*

- *Standard & Poor's Corporation Reports*

- *Guide to Reference Books*

- *American National Biography*

- *Joy of Cooking*

- *Biography and Genealogy Master Index

- *Grove Dictionary of Music and Musicians*

- *Guinness Book of World Records*

- *Science Citation Index

- *Encyclopedia of Religion*

- *Famous First Facts*

- *Routledge Encyclopedia of Philosophy*

- *Peterson's Field Guide Series*

- *Grove Dictionary of Art*

- *American Horticultural Society A-Z Encyclopedia of Garden Plants*

- *New Catholic Encyclopedia*

- *Garland Encyclopedia of World Music*

- *Encyclopedia Judaica*

Top Sources and Free Web Information

The total retail cost for the sources on Coutt's and Richard's list is approximately $35,000. (This figure does not include the asterisked resources that are actually databases, indexes, or subscriptions. We covered these types of resources Chapter One, Free Articles and Indexes.) Few free direct equivalents of the items on this list items exist on the Web; I only found five. Yet the ones on the Web are easy to locate and are preceded by the designation "Located Free on the Web." Also note that expensive business resources, such as *Moody's Manuals*, the *Rand-McNally Commercial Atlas & Marketing Guide, Standard & Poor's Corporation Reports*, and the *Million Dollar Directory* have no free equivalents. The remainder of Coutt's and Richard's hot ready reference titles can be grouped into categories. By grouping the titles it is apparent what types of queries are most often posed and which alternative free resources would render satisfactory answers. While we could not claim that the Web sites listed provide all the information that their counterparts on the above list present, most people will not only find that the free resources contain the basic information they'll need, but, in many cases, will also find value-added components (e.g., sound, animations, discussion groups, links) that complement their research. In cases where several sites are listed under one reference title, I suggest the searcher explore all the sites.

To make the list as an alternate Web resource, the Web site needed to:

1. Be free of charge.

2. Have at least 2,000 links pointing into it as analyzed by Alexa software (indicating its popularity with other Webmasters; see the note at the end of this chapter for information about the Alexa Toolbar).

3. Have been online for a minimum of two years (indicating longevity).

There is one exception to this criteria: The Emily Post Institute does not have the required number of links but remains a good, though abridged, resource.

Category: Words/Language

Listed by Coutts and Richards: *Roget's II The New Thesaurus* $15
Located free on the Web:
- Roget's II: The New Thesaurus, 3rd ed. 1995. http://www.bartleby.com/62

Listed by Coutts and Richards: *Bartlett's Familiar Quotations* $33
Surrogates located free on the Web:
- Bartleby.com (online since 1997)
  http://www.bartleby.com includes
  - Simpson's Contemporary Quotations 1950–1988 http://www. bartleby.com/63
  - Bartlett's Familiar Quotations, 1919, http://www. bartleby.com/100
  - Columbia World of Quotations, http://www.bartleby. com/66

- Quoteland (online since 1997), http://www.quoteland.com

- Yahoo! Graduation Speeches (online since 1995), http://dir. yahoo.com/Education/Graduation/Speeches

Listed by Coutts and Richards: *Black's Law Dictionary* $55
Surrogates located free on the Web:
- Nolo's "Shark Talk" (Everybody's Legal Dictionary) (online since 1994), http://www.nolo.com/lawcenter/ dictionary/wordindex.cfm

- Nolo's Legal Encyclopedia, http://www.nolo.com/lawcenter/ency/index.cfm

Listed by Coutts and Richards: *Chicago Manual of Style* $35
Surrogates located free on the Web:
- University of Wisconsin, Madison: Writer's Handbook (online since 1985), http://www.wisc.edu/writing/Handbook/DocChicago.html

- Chicago Manual of Style FAQ (online since 1991), http://www.press.uchicago.edu/Misc/Chicago/cmosfaq.html

Listed by Coutts and Richards: *Oxford English Dictionary* $950, and *Webster's 3rd International Dictionary* $150
Surrogates located free on the Web:
- American Heritage Dictionary of the English Language (online since 1997), http://www.bartleby.com/61

- Merriam-Webster Online Language Center (online since 1993), http://www.m-w.com

- Dictionary of Difficult Words (online since 2000), http://www.tiscali.co.uk/reference/dictionaries/difficultwords

- Dictionary.com (online since 1995), http://www.dictionary.com

- OneLook Dictionaries—Search 738 online dictionaries at once (online since 1996), http://www.onelook.com

- Your Dictionary (online since 1999) includes foreign language dictionaries, http://www.yourdictionary.com

- Allwords—With Crossword Solver (online since 1998) http://www.allwords.com

- Acronym Finder (online since 1998), http://www.acronymfinder.com

Category: General Subject Overviews
Listed by Coutts and Richards: *World Book Encyclopedia* $950
Surrogates located free on the Web:
- Encarta Online Concise Encyclopedia (online since 1994), http://encarta.msn.com/encnet/refpages/artcenter.aspx

- Britannica Concise (online since 1995), http://education.yahoo.com/reference/encyclopedia

- Columbia Encyclopedia (online since 1997), http://www.bartleby.com/65

- Encyclopedia.com (online since 1998), http://www.encyclopedia.com

Note: A discussion of these free encyclopedias can be found on pages 128–129.

Category: Poetry Information
Listed by Coutts and Richards: *Columbia Granger's Index to Poetry* $283
Surrogates located free on the Web:
- American Verse Project (online since 1985), http://www.hti.umich.edu/a/amverse/

- Bartleby Verse (online since 1997), http://www.bartleby.com/verse

Category: Religion

Listed by Coutts and Richards: *Encyclopedia Judaica* $1,000 (software version: $200)
Surrogate located free on the Web:
- Jewish Virtual Library (online since 1997), http://www.us-israel.org/jsource

Listed by Coutts and Richards: *Encyclopedia of Religion* $35
No surrogate found.

Listed by Coutts and Richards: *King James Bible* $5
Located free on the Web:
- King James Bible at the Electronic Text Center, Univ. of Virginia (online since 1986), http://etext.lib.virginia.edu/kjv.browse.html

Listed by Coutts and Richards: *New Catholic Encyclopedia* $1,500
Surrogate located free on the Web:
- New Advent Catholic Encyclopedia (online since 1998), http://www.newadvent.org/cathen

Category: Medical

Listed by Coutts and Richards: *Merck Manual* $35 (1992)
Located free on the Web:
- Merck Manual (online since 2000), http://www.merck.com/pubs/mmanual

Listed by Coutts and Richards: *Physician's Desk Reference* $90
Surrogates located free on the Web:

- MayoClinic.com—Drug Information (online since 1997), http://www.mayoclinic.com/findinformation/ druginformation/index.cfm

Note: Many drugs include a link to an image; this is a feature for which the *Physician's Desk Reference* is well known.

- WebMD Drugs and Herbs (online since 1998), http://my. webmd.com/drugs

- MEDLINEPlus Drug Information (online since 1998), http:// www.nlm.nih.gov/medlineplus/druginformation. html

Category: Facts

Listed by Coutts and Richards: *Famous First Facts* $130
Surrogate located free on the Web:
- Famous Firsts Trivia Collection (online since 1999), http://www.corsinet.com/trivia/1-triv.html

Listed by Coutts and Richards: *Guinness Book of World Records* $15
Surrogate located free on the Web:
- Guinness World Records (online since 1999), http://www. guinnessworldrecords.com

Listed by Coutts and Richards: *Statistical Abstract of the United States* $38
Located free on the Web:
- Statistical Abstract (online since 1993), http://www. census.gov/prod/www/statistical-abstract-us.html

Listed by Coutts and Richards: *World Almanac and Book of Facts* $10
Surrogate located free on the Web:

- InfoPlease Almanac (online since 1999), http://www. infoplease.com

Category: Geography

Listed by Coutts and Richards: *Columbia Gazetteer of the World* $750

Surrogates located free on the Web:

- Columbia Gazetteer of North America (online since 1997), http://www.bartleby.com/69

- Getty Thesaurus of Geographical Names (online since 1992), http://www.getty.edu/research/tools/vocabulary/ tgn

- United States Census Bureau, U. S. Gazetteer (online since 1993), http://www.census.gov/cgi-bin/gazetteer

- Worldwide Directory of Cities and Towns (online since 1996), http://www.calle.com/world

Listed by Coutts and Richards: *Times Atlas of the World* $175 Surrogates located free on the Web:

- World Sites Atlas (online since 1999), http://www. sitesatlas.com/Maps/index.htm

- National Geographic Map Machine (online since 1995), http://plasma.nationalgeographic.com/mapmachine/ index.html

For street level maps:

- MSN Maps & Directories (online since 1996), http://map point.msn.com

- National Geographic Map Machine (online since 1995), http://plasma.nationalgeographic.com/mapmachine/index.html

- Yahoo! Maps (online since 1995), http://maps.yahoo.com

Category: Directories

Listed by Coutts and Richards: *Encyclopedia of Associations* $150

Surrogates located free on the Web:

- Associations on the Net (online since 1997), http://www.ipl.org/ref/AON

- Associations Central (online since 1998), http://www.associationcentral.com

Category: Special Subject Overviews and Handbooks

Listed by Coutts and Richards: *A-Z Encyclopedia of Garden Plants* $56

Surrogate located free on the Web:

- Botany.com (online since 1996), http://www.botany.com

Listed by Coutts and Richards: *CRC Handbook of Chemistry and Physics* $129

Surrogate located free on the Web:

- Physics and Astronomy Online Education and Reference (online since 1997), http://www.physlink.com/Reference/Index.cfm

Listed by Coutts and Richards: *Dictionary of Art* $4,000

Surrogate located free on the Web:

- Artcyclopedia (online since 1998), http://www.artcyclopedia.com

Listed by Coutts and Richards: *Emily Post's Etiquette* $26
Surrogates located free on the Web:

- Etiquette in Society, in Business, in Politics and at Home, by Emily Post, 1922. (online since 1999), http://www.bartleby.com/95

- Emily Post Institute Etiquette Tips (online since 1996), http://www.emilypost.com/etiquette_index.htm

Listed by Coutts and Richards: *Garland Encyclopedia of World Music* $1,000, and *Grove Dictionary of Music and Musicians* $725
Surrogates located free on the Web:

- University of Michigan Instrument Encyclopedia (online since 1985), http://www.si.umich.edu/chico/instrument

- Internet Public Library Music History 102: A Guide to Western Composers and Their Music from the Middle Ages to the Present (online since 1997), http://www.ipl.org/exhibit/mushist

Listed by Coutts and Richards: *Guide to Reference Books* $200
No surrogate found.

Listed by Coutts and Richards: *Joy of Cooking* $25
Surrogates located free on the Web:

- Boston Cooking School Cook Book (Fannie Farmer) (online since 1997), http://www.bartleby.com/87

- AllRecipes.com (online since 1998), http://www.allrecipes.com

- Recipe Source (online since 1999), http://www.recipe source.com

- GourmetSpot (online since 1997), http://www.gourmet spot.com/recipes.htm

Listed by Coutts and Richards: *McGraw-Hill Encyclopedia of Science and Technology* $100
Surrogates located free on the Web:
- Encyclopedia of the Atmospheric Environment (online since 2000), http://www.doc.mmu.ac.uk/ aric/eae/english.html

- Eric Weisstein's World of Science (online since 1995), http://scienceworld.wolfram.com

- Life Science Dictionary (online since 1985), http:// biotech.icmb.utexas.edu/search/dict-search.html

Listed by Coutts and Richards: *Peterson's Field Guides* $40
Surrogates located free on the Web:
- Peterson Online (online since 1996), http://www.peterson online.com/birds/month/index.shtml

- Virtual Bird Field Guide (online 1999), http://birding. about.com/library/fg/blfg.htm

Listed by Coutts and Richards: *Robert's Rules of Order* $10
Surrogate located free on the Web:
- Constitution Society (online since 1996), http://www. constitution.org/rror/rror--00.htm

(Does not include the modifications of the *Revision*, which is copyright 2000)

Listed by Coutts and Richards: *Routledge Encyclopedia of Philosophy* $3,500

Surrogates located free on the Web:

- Internet Encyclopedia of Philosophy (online since 1993), http://www.utm.edu/research/iep

- Stanford Encyclopedia of Philosophy (online since 1985), http://plato.stanford.edu/contents.html

Listed by Coutts and Richards: *Stateman's Yearbook* $100

Surrogates located free on the Web:

- CIA World Factbook (online since1995), http://www.odci. gov/cia/publications/factbook/index.html

- Library of Congress Country Studies (online since 1990), http://lcweb2.loc.gov/frd/cs/cshome.html

- World Factbook 2002 (online since 1997), http://www. bartleby.com/151

Category: Biography

Listed by Coutts and Richards: *American National Biography* $3,500, and *Dictionary of American Biography* $1,500

Surrogates located free on the Web:

- Academy of Achievement (online since 1995), http://www. achievement.org

- Biography.com (online since 1995), http://www.biography. com

- Biographical Dictionary (online since 1997), http://www.s9. com/biography

- Librarians' Index to the Internet Individual Biography Sites (online since 1998), http://www.lii.org/search?title= People;query=People;subsearch=People;searchtype= subject

Category: Business/Career

Listed by Coutts and Richards: *Occupational Outlook Handbook* $16
Located free on the Web:

- U.S. Department of Labor Occupational Outlook Handbook Online, http://www.bls.gov/oco/home.htm

Listed by Coutts and Richards: *Million Dollar Directory* $500
No surrogate found.

Listed by Coutts and Richards: *Moody's Manuals* $7,000
No surrogate found.

Listed by Coutts and Richards: *Rand-McNally Commercial Atlas & Marketing Guide* $400
No surrogate found.

Listed by Coutts and Richards: *Standard & Poor's Corporation Reports* $3,000
No surrogate found.

Case Study: Sparknotes, Cliff Notes, and *Masterplots*

The *Masterplots* series of reference books enjoys immense popularity with librarians and students. Regardless of a reader's intellectual abilities, some works of literature are less accessible than others. Here *Masterplots* can make a difference, by summarizing the content, providing cursory criticism, and elucidating on characters and themes. *Masterplots* provides an excellent departure point for learning the meaning and action of a piece of literature. With 1,801 plots, stories, and critical evaluations in the main set, it is rare that you cannot find commentary on the work you want. *Masterplots* is comprehensive; *Masterplots* is expensive: $600 for the print and $750 for the compact disc.

Nearly every student has found it necessary, at one time or another, to consult the Cliff Notes analysis of an assigned literary work. Recently a student approached me at the reference desk and requested information on Ayn Rand's *The Fountainhead*. I offered her the *Masterplots Second Revised Edition* summary (about six pages in length), but she said she needed a more detailed treatment—something like the Cliff Notes she'd used for other assignments. I referred her to the Cliff Notes Web site (http://www.cliffnotes.com). With more than 800 titles available, she easily located the perfect download and purchased it for $5.99.

While using the electronic Cliff Notes later, I noticed that a "related site" (according to my Alexa Toolbar) was "Sparknotes." At Sparknotes (http://www.sparknotes.com), I found that the site offered, for free, over 700 study guides covering literature, computer science, psychology, biology, history, and philosophy. A readable and printable 19-page guide for *The Fountainhead* is available. Even though some Sparknotes are also available in hard copy at the Barnes and Noble Web site for $4.99, site visitors can use them free on the Web. And there are more titles available for free than available in print (i.e., *The Fountainhead* study guide was only available at the Web site for free). Sparknotes are written by students at Harvard University. If you can suffer the pop-up ads and you don't mind registering for free access, these study guides will save some time and money.

One-Stops for Ready Reference

First Stop: Bartleby.com

The retail value of the print versions of the ready reference books at this site is $1,200. Get it all at http://www.bartleby.com for free.

Although I mention Bartleby in the chapter on "Books in the Web Library" as a source of full-text books (including fiction and nonfiction), it also laudably succeeds as a reference resource providing Web users with free access to 25 solid sources. Titles include the *Columbia Encyclopedia* (2001), the *American Heritage Dictionary of the English Language* (2000), the *World Factbook 2001*, the *Columbia Gazetteer of North America* (2000), *Roget's II: The New Thesaurus* (1995). You can find quotations from *Bartlett's Familiar Quotations* (1919), the *Columbia World of Quotations* (1996), and *Simpson's Contemporary Quotations* (1988). Several language usage and stylebooks are available, including *The Elements of Style* by William Strunk, and H. L. Mencken's *The American Language: An Inquiry into the Development of English in the United States*. Classic specialty reference titles such as Fannie Farmer's *The Boston Cooking-School Cook Book* and *Emily Post's Etiquette*, though somewhat dated, are searchable as well.

Most World Wide Web users have had the unfortunate experience of discovering that their favorite Web site has disappeared or has changed/reduced its services. For years divine Northern Light (http://www.nlresearch.com) provided excellent coverage of the World Wide Web through its search engine. It even organized results by topic into folders for searchers. Then, just before its sale to divine, the service shifted its focus and became almost exclusively fee-based. And, unfortunately, a notice at divine Northern Light's Web site told users that it had stopped offering a "Special Collection" of pay-per-view documents as of January 2003. Users of free resources are wary of what some might call an Internet "Sword of Damocles." Some resources, on the other hand, can make the claim that they do not plan to alter their commitment to "free." It makes one wonder how they do it. Steven H. van Leeuwen of Bartleby.com quickly responded by e-mail to my questions concerning the durability of his Web resource.

INSIDER'S VIEWPOINT FROM YOUR WEB LIBRARY PROFESSIONAL: STEVEN VAN LEEUWEN, PRESIDENT, BARTLEBY.COM

Nick,

Bartleby.com became a for-profit corporation in September 1999 after being a successful "altruistic" site since January 1993.

Bartleby.com grew quickly in 2000 and 2001 with the influx of private capital investment, which was readily available for Internet companies at the time. In 2002 with the dearth of investment at acceptable terms, Bartleby.com has scaled back our expansion plans; however, our revenue streams are stable and our budget is balanced. For this reason, I can predict a long future for our services as currently structured.

We do have a set of plans for new services; however, we have a long-standing policy of releasing news of services to the press only after they have been rolled out.

Please note one additional revenue stream that was not mentioned in your note, namely, licensing. We have a couple of partnerships that are live, most notably Yahoo! Reference (http://reference.yahoo.com).

On a personal level, I have followed closely the rise and fall of many online "free" services, and look forward to an in-depth analysis of this market.

Sincerely,
Steven van Leeuwen
President, Bartleby.com

Notable Standalone Web Sites for Specific Subjects

Libraries purchase hundreds of excellent reference books that individuals could find useful in their personal collections. Each book has a specific purpose and any amalgamation of Web sites, let alone any single site, will not directly duplicate the vast majority. Nonetheless, we've discovered an ample number of treasures to help answer many of the questions that the most used traditional reference books are continually called on to satisfy.

It is surprising how many reference books written to fill a niche fail, by degrees, to remain current or comprehensive. For example, look at the 12 linear feet of books that cover the subject of movies/films in a library's reference collection, costing an average of $60 per book—none of which can supply a filmography of Alicia Silverstone or Jason Biggs or a summary of *Memento*. But the Internet Movie Database efficiently supplies the answers.

Now that we have discovered Web-based approximations for many of the recommended and heavily used resources, let's complement our Web Library's Reference Department with some additional sites. These resources are noteworthy standalones.

Each resource does one or two things well, but limits its coverage to a specific domain, unlike the one-stop sites exemplified by Bartleby. None of the sites except the Thomas Register, an excellent resource for locating manufacturers, require registration, and all are free.

Art

Artcyclopedia

http://www.artcyclopedia.com

By far one of the preeminent sites for art on the Web because it does so many things so well, Artcyclopedia is a portal to painting, sculpture, installation art, folk art, video/digital/Web-based art, photography, architecture, and the decorative arts on the Internet. Offering several easily navigated indexes, you can look for information by artist name, nationality, subject treated, artistic movement, medium, title of work, or museum name. There is also a separate index for women artists.

Artcyclopedia links to 1,200 art sites. Separate indexes allow you to browse by museum. If planning a trip to Scotland, you can do some reconnaissance by connecting to the Royal Museum's Web pages via Artcyclopedia. The "Art Headlines" link conveys the visitor to third party sites such as the *New York Times, Chicago Tribune,* Atlantic Monthly Online, etc. Apart from the Art Headlines link, you will find that many artist name searches also lead to links for articles that are premium (pay) content; you can ignore or pursue these at your discretion. Whether you desire art news, biographical information on any of 7,500 artists, or to see images of 100,000 works of art, Artcyclopedia is a primary point of departure for research as well as pleasure. For a thorough review please see Péter Jacsó's comments at http://www.galegroup.com/servlet/HTMLFileServlet?imprint=9999&region=7&fileName=reference/archive/200101/artcycl.html.

See also:

Paris Pages' Musee du Louvre
http://www.paris.org/Musees/Louvre

Metropolitan Museum of Art
http://www.metmuseum.org

Web Museum
http://www.ibiblio.org/wm

Smithsonian Museums
http://www.si.edu/museums

Book and Magazine Information

Amazon.com

http://www.amazon.com

Anybody with a credit card knows about Amazon.com and its chief competitor BarnesAndNoble.com. And if you know how to buy books and whatever else from these Web sites, you have probably realized that they can get you anything in print as long as somebody in their network of affiliates has it. That's why it can often be used in lieu of R.R. Bowker's standard *Books in Print* (hundreds of dollars) or its Web equivalent http://www.booksin print.com (thousands of dollars). For comprehensiveness, readers should remember to use the Library of Congress' online catalog at http://catalog.loc.gov; it contains approximately 12 million items. Librarians find it particularly useful for locating MARC records.

Bookfinder.com

http://www.bookfinder.com

Anirvan Chatterjee began a network agent software class in the fall of 1996 at the University of California (Berkeley). His finished project was the forerunner of this metasearch engine for locating books in print or out-of-print, rare or signed. Bookfinder costs nothing to use and your search almost invariably leads to numerous hits collected from the largest book dealers, such as Amazon to the small independents (it searches 40,000 booksellers). A couple of years ago I used several search engines to locate a copy of Mary D. Lake's *Miss Geneva's Lantern*. The copy I found cost $15. I recently used Bookfinder to scour the Web and located a new copy at half.com for $2.99—in seconds. I also want to obtain a first edition of *To Kill a Mockingbird* signed by Harper Lee. Ebay's auctions had a couple of offerings, but Bookfinder retrieved 25 vendors. See Michelle Slatalla's "Online Shopper" column in May 4, 2000's *New York Times* (East Coast edition page G4) for more information.

PubList

http://www.publist.com

Ulrich's Periodicals Directory is a standard ready reference title in most libraries; it retails from $600 to $800 depending on format and proves extremely useful for all types of information involving journals, newspapers, and magazines. Value-conscious people, however, turn to PubList. PubList provides a good deal of the same information without charge (although registration is required). According to its "About Us" page:

> PubList.com is the only Internet-based reference for over 150,000 domestic and international print and electronic publications including magazines, journals, e-journals, newsletters, and monographs. PubList.com provides quick and easy access to detailed publication information, including titles, formats, publisher addresses, editor contacts, circulation data, and ISSN numbers. PubList.com is privately funded and based in Rockland, Massachusetts.[10]

Visitors may search for specific periodicals or browse by subject area. A typical PubList record for a periodical title provides an ISSN, frequency information, address, publisher, and editor. Enhancements include a free table of contents alert service as well as article ordering (for a fee).

Business

Hoover's Online
http://www.hoovers.com

Hoover's public and private company capsules include names, contacts, sales, employment, and ticker symbol information. Hoover's also offers links to external business information including company news and commentary, stock quotes, Securities and Exchange Commission, and individual corporate home pages.
    See also:
Thomas Register (locates manufacturers of specific products in North America)
http://www.thomasregister.com

Securities and Exchange Commission (information on public companies)
http://www.sec.gov/edgar.shtml

North American Industry Classification System/Standard Industrial Classification Codes
http://www.census.gov/epcd/www/naics.html

Dictionary of Occupational Titles (U. S. Department of Labor)
http://www.oalj.dol.gov/libdot.htm

Calculation and Conversion Tools

Universal Currency Converter
http://www.xe.com/ucc

OnlineConversion.com—Convert Just About Anything to
Anything Else
http://www.onlineconversion.com

Robert Fogt, a software developer, provides this page. Supported
by a banner ad, this site offers users free conversion of 28 different
variables including distance/length, area, torque, finance, speed,
time, pressure, density, and energy. With 2,000 links pointing in,
OnlineConversion.com earns a "bookmark" or "favorite" status in
everyone's ready reference folder.

College Information

The Princeton Review: Best 331 College Rankings
http://www.review.com/college/rankings.cfm

According to the "Wooster Survey"* of 532 college freshman, 90
percent of high school students rank the Web as the fourth most
important research tool in choosing a college (behind campus visits and the influence of parents and guidance counselors). The
same students chose the Princeton Review's site as the primary
site search for colleges.

*College of Wooster. http://www.wooster.edu/news/
guiderankings.html

Countries of the World

United States Department of State Background Notes
http://www.state.gov/r/pa/ei/bgn

Many libraries have the $55 annual subscription to the State
Department's excellent *Background Notes* issued in print. The Web
site offers identical information and adds numerous features that
make it infinitely more appealing, and it is free.

When librarians discuss a Web site's credibility, the terms
"authority," "currency," and "objectivity" are always repeated. The
Background Notes site gets high marks on all these criteria. The

notes are frequently revised and contain detailed information on 188 countries. All the standard data such as population, political establishment, economy, geography, trade, defense, and history are clearly laid out; then the site offers links to maps, biographies, and "major reports" (e.g., human rights statements, commercial guides, religious freedom reports).

Although the *Europa Yearbook* is my favorite source for country information, I doubt individuals would pay $700 for the luxury of bookshelf access. The Background Notes site is an outstanding alternative.

Central Intelligence Agency: The World Factbook
http://www.cia.gov/cia/publications/factbook

The World Factbook lists for about $50 at your local bookstore, and it's packed with information, so it's worth the price. But since the information is provided by the C.I.A., United States citizens can download a zipped copy of the most recent data for free at http://www.cia.gov/cia/download.html. The full text can also be consulted on the Web if you choose to use it "on the fly." In addition to country profiles, the *Factbook* is replete with maps, flags, and appendices covering international organizations and international environmental agreements.

See also:
Lonely Planet
http://www.lonelyplanet.com

Directory Information

InfoSpace
http://www.infospace.com

Directory portal for e-mail names, telephone numbers, and "snailmail" addresses of businesses and people. It includes reverse lookup and various links to news, classified ads, shopping, and entertainment sites.

Switchboard.com
http://www.switchboard.com

Find people, businesses, products, and maps. A reverse telephone lookup is available.

WhoWhere
http://www.whowhere.lycos.com

Directory assistance for e-mail addresses, toll-free telephone numbers, and other phone numbers including access to international phone directories.

Zip Code Lookup (United States Postal Service)
http://www.usps.com/zip4/welcome.htm

See also:
AnyWho: Internet Directory Assistance
http://www.anywho.com/index.html

Especially good for reverse lookups.

Facts

Fast Facts: Almanacs/Factbooks/Statistical Reports & Related Reference Tools
http://www.freepint.com/gary/handbook.htm

Gary Price's lists are well known, and this is one of his best. Although very lengthy, it represents a great deal of effort and links to facts from various subject areas. Among the links you will find baseball statistics, presidential pardons, literacy rates, and product recalls as well as crash test information and a computer almanac.

Health Resources

MEDLINEplus
http://www.nlm.nih.gov/medlineplus

Free, reliable, authoritative, up-to-date health information from the world's largest medical library, the National Library of Medicine in Bethesda, Maryland. When asked a reference question about the complications of Carpal Tunnel Syndrome, I used the MEDLINEplus Encyclopedia to provide a considerably detailed answer. The article I excerpted was signed by an orthopedic surgeon and I could even cross-reference the surgeon with the MEDLINEplus directory to further verify my response.

- MEDLINEplus Directory of Dentists and Doctors
  http://www.nlm.nih.gov/medlineplus/directories.html

- MEDLINEplus Drug Information
  http://www.nlm.nih.gov/medlineplus/druginformation.html

- MEDLINEplus Medical Encyclopedia
  http://www.nlm.nih.gov/medlineplus/encyclopedia.html

- MEDLINEplus Medical Dictionaries
  http://www.nlm.nih.gov/medlineplus/dictionaries.html

- MEDLINEplus Health Topics
  http://www.nlm.nih.gov/medlineplus/healthtopics.html

See also:

American Medical Association Online Doctor Finder
http://www.ama-assn.org/aps/amahg.htm

Columbia Home Medical Guide (Columbia University College of Physicians and Surgeons)
http://cpmcnet.columbia.edu/texts/guide

Legal Information

FindLaw
http://www.findlaw.com

Acquired in 2001 by legal publishing giant West Group, FindLaw is still a free metasite providing links to comprehensive state, federal, and international legal information, including cases, codes, law reviews, law firms, United States Supreme Court opinions, and law schools.

Music and Film

IMDB

http://www.imdb.com

The Internet Movie Database (IMDB) has information on 260,000 films and television shows covering 1892 to the present. It catalogs information on stars, producers, directors, film locations, and casts. It also offers 20,000 photos. You can search for information on old films as well as movies not yet released. When you locate a page on a movie that interests you, you'll find links to reviews, news articles, and downloadable trailers. Amazon.com bought IMDB in 1998, so be prepared for merchandising links, also.

A search on 2002's *Panic Room* links to Roger Ebert in the *Chicago-Sun Times*, Salon.com, *Rolling Stone*, the BBCi, the *New York Times*, and 60 additional reviews. Similarly, the page for 1922's *Nosferatu* links to 30 reviews (including Ebert and the BBCi).

I once read a community theater playbill in which the musical director stated he had worked with Roger Daltrey, lead singer with The Who. After a performance, the gentleman explained to me that he had, in fact, acted in a Warner Brothers video called *Pirate Tales*. Unfortunately, the fellow had never seen the final cut. Using the Internet Movie Database I verified that he was listed in the cast and that Daltrey was also in the program. Then using the handy link from IMDB to its owner Amazon.com, I found a copy available for purchase. But, in the event that the better part of this actor's efforts had ended up on the cutting room floor, I went to the database for holdings of the public libraries in state of Connecticut. And—lo and behold—I found that half a dozen libraries owned *Pirate Tales*, including the Hartford Public Library. The following day I offered the maestro all this 411; he was grateful and I got a few kudos.

See also:
All Movie Guide
http://www.allmovie.com

All Music Guide
http://allmusic.com

What the IMDB does for films, the All Music Guide does for music. The dozen or so books in a typical library's reference collection covering jazz, blues, and rock and roll will fall short in terms of currency and comprehensiveness when compared to the All Music Guide. (For classical music see the All Classical Guide.) Besides making it easy to find discographies, reviews, and biographies of composers, performers, and bands in all contemporary musical genres, the All Music Guide provides links to tour information and covers all genres. It also offers a music glossary covering music theory and instruments.

See also:
All Classical Guide
http://allclassical.com

Realty

Domania.com
http://www.domania.com

If you are interested in home prices for a specific ZIP Code, use this free database. Just for registering you can look up the selling prices of specific street addresses. Saves you a drive to the town hall, too.

Realtor.com
http://www.realtor.com

Although highly commercial since it serves as a selling vehicle for the National Association of Realtors, Realtor.com can help consumers compare prices, find homes, look for mortgages, and gain information about moving services, lenders, and more. Other parts of the Web site cover apartments, senior housing, storage facilities, and insurance.

Special Interests

Find a Grave
http://www.findagrave.com

Apparently a lot of people have found "Find a Grave." Google gives it a 7 out of 10 for popularity, and it has over 5,000 other Web sites pointing in to it. According to one reviewer, "A fascinating site for sure. In the famous section, you can find a celeb's burial site (or where the ashes were spread), and very often the cause of death. Great for research or morbid curiosity." According to another, "If you're not listed here, you never really lived." Over 10,000 celebrities' graves are listed and 3.4 million records are searchable. Be prepared for banner ads and pop-up ads.

See also:

Cemetery Transcription Library
http://www.interment.net

Cyndi's List of Genealogy Sites on the Internet
http://www.cyndislist.com

Adflip
http://www.adflip.com

People studying consumerism as represented in the popular media will find this resource interesting. Adflip allows searching and browsing of six decades of print ads. By keyword searching you could get a quick course on the evolution of the camera, or see how Coca-Cola has been marketed, or trace the advertising campaign of Chevrolet's Corvette from 1955 to 2001. You can also browse by year. Why not check out what products were being advertised during the year of your birth? Breck Shampoo was apparently a big seller in 1950s.

See also:

American Advertising Museum

http://www.admuseum.org

AdAccess

http://scriptorium.lib.duke.edu/adaccess

Translation Tools

AltaVista's Babelfish

http://babelfish.altavista.com

Free Translation.com

http://freetranslation.com

Although neither site is comprehensive in terms of languages covered, both are very good for loose translations of words and phrases. FreeTranslation.com can translate up to four or five pages of pasted text, while Babelfish can only translate approximately 150 words at a time. Use these to get an understanding of documents and Web pages in foreign languages

United States Census Data and Demographics

CensusScope

http://www.censusscope.org/index.html

Originating at the Social Science Data Analysis Network at the University of Michigan, CensusScope serves those investigating U.S. demographic trends. Designed for generalists and specialists, CensusScope includes charts, maps, statistics, and rankings for states, counties, metropolitan areas, cities, and towns. Graphic rich; data is exportable.

Great Web Reference Sites— Pick Two and Go with Them

Still looking for more great ready reference Web sites? Searching the Web and using Internet directories (even the important ones such as Yahoo! and the Open Directory Project) can prove frustrating. Although the individual sites already considered range from very good to excellent in terms of usefulness and longevity, a handful of Web guides stand out as worthy of mention. If you have not already visited and bookmarked these sites, prepare to be impressed.

Librarians' Index to the Internet (online since 1997)
http://lii.org

Winning the praise of educators and librarians, the award-winning LII contains links and information on 9,000 Web resources in directory format (i.e., hierarchical by subject) or searchable by "simple" or "advanced" modes. The librarians evaluating Web sites for the LII maintain and apply strict criteria for inclusion; their annotations of each site, added after thorough inspection, will help users target worthwhile pages to explore. You can register for a current awareness service to stay on top of new sites (10 to 20 are added each month). The site charges no fees and requires no registration.

LibrarySpot (online since 1997)
http://www.libraryspot.com

This simple-to-use portal to general and specific library information includes a comparatively lean and useful list of links to ready reference materials. Almanacs, phone directories, dictionaries, encyclopedias, and other quick reference tools are well-stocked here. It is well-organized, but I encountered occasional dead links. Register to get free e-mail updates of newly added sites, but the site is free.

Internet Public Library (IPL) Ready Reference (online since 1995)
http://www.ipl.org/ref

Big and famous, the IPL's reference links are extensive. Clearly, many librarians worked long and hard on these lists, which include dozens of subject categories and ready reference resources. No charge and no registration.

Virtual Reference Shelf: Selected Web Resources Compiled by the Library of Congress (online since 1990)
http://www.loc.gov/rr/askalib/virtualref.html

Plenty of links to authoritative ready reference resources from the world's largest library. Free; no registration required.

RefDesk.com (online since 1995)
http://www.refdesk.com

Bob Drudge, whose credo is "avaritia facit bardus" (greed makes you stupid) is at the core of this resource (son Matthew edits the successful *Drudge Report*). It's a one-person operation where Mr. Drudge performs all the reviewing, indexing, and site maintenance. RefDesk.com has earned accolades from *Yahoo! Internet Life*, *Forbes*, and *U.S. News and World Report*. Back in a 2001 *New York Times* article (January 26, p. 3), secretary of state Colin Powell said RefDesk.com was his favorite Internet site; he'd thrown out his dictionaries and encyclopedias.

RefDesk.com sends a free newsletter to 50,000 subscribers daily. Again no charge and no registration required.

The Observations of a Top Web Reference Librarian

Knowing a librarian who uses the World Wide Web every day to answer reference questions and who would be an instructive authority on the subject, I contacted Patricia Memmott, User

Services and Ask-A-Question service coordinator at the Internet
Public Library (IPL), who graciously answered my questions con-
cerning free reference resources. Among her responsibilities at the
IPL are the coordination of the Frequently Asked Reference
Question (FARQ) pages, the Pathfinder pages, and the Native
American Authors collection. Having earned her master's degree
from the School of Information at the University of Michigan in
December of 1998, Memmott also oversees the many dedicated
librarians-in-training and professional librarians who volunteer
their time to answering reference questions for the service.

INSIDER'S VIEWPOINT FROM YOUR WEB LIBRARY PROFESSIONAL: PATRICIA MEMMOTT, USER SERVICES COORDINATOR, THE INTERNET PUBLIC LIBRARY

NT: The Internet Public Library answers between 8,000 and
9,000 reference questions per year. David Carter and Joseph
Janes indicated that the subject breakdown for reference
queries at the IPL showed that most questions concerned science, history, literature, biography, and the humanities.[11] Is
there a preponderance of questions in any one subject area?

PM: It's basically spread all over the place with no real stand-
outs. Also, the majority are not "ready reference"—we do a
breakdown of our questions into two categorizations—factual
(ready reference) and sources (research type questions where

we get the patron started on a topic), and on average only 27 percent are categorized as factual.

NT: Could you offer some numbers on the breakdown of users of the IPL's reference service?

PM: Essentially, we know that about 52 percent of our questions are homework/school-related. The rest run the gamut from business people (25 percent), teachers (11 percent), librarians (7 percent).

NT: What do you consider the top ready reference Web sites on the Web—the ones the IPL librarians themselves use extensively and consider reliable sources of information? Do any of them excel for certain types of queries and not for others?

PM: A list of ones I teach to new IPL students and use extensively is available at http://www.ipl.org:2000/backroom/class/freeweb.html. [*See list at the end of this chapter for individual addresses.*] There's a few that I might add to those, which are available through links in the IPL reference collection at http://www.ipl.org/ref/RR/static/ref00.00.00.html. They include:

    Bartleby, http://www.bartleby.com

    Infoplease, http://www.infoplease.com

    Internet Movie Database, http://imdb.com

    American FactFinder, http://factfinder.census.gov

    NADA Appraisal Guides, http://www.nadaguides.com

    FindArticles, http://www.findarticles.com

    Babelfish, http://babelfish.altavista.com

I don't know how I would go about indicating what types of queries they might answer better than others. It's mainly an intuitive thing—you look at the question, where they indicated they've already searched, and make your determination that you're either going to go to a search engine or straight to a known resource that you think will answer their question. Most of the time, to be honest, I go straight to a search engine. If it's a case of a younger student or a businessperson whom only needs a little bit of factual info on a topic, then yes, I'll go straight to an online encyclopedia, almanac, or another ready reference site. The older students, though, generally need more extensive information and that's where a search engine is usually more fruitful, to me, now that the more academic ready reference sources like Britannica are no longer free.

NT: To what extent do you believe end-users could have most of their ready reference questions answered by resources such as the reference collection at Bartleby or other reference resources? If they knew of the correct sites, could end-users find most of their own ready reference answers?

PM: I suspect they already are doing just that. We get so few easy ready reference questions that I believe that those people with ready reference questions are getting what they need from search engines. What we do get, instead, are the people who are looking for information on research topics where Web info is scanty or unreliable, or hard to find. I had a student who did some research into our answers to see what sources we were referring patrons to—less than 20 percent of our answers end up using sources already listed in the IPL's reference collection.

NT: Do you think the typical Web surfer is satisfied with what they find?

PM: Will they find an answer that they consider to be "good enough" for most of those questions? I think it depends on their domain-specific subject knowledge. A businessperson may very well know the resources they need to look up share prices, while a high school student may use a search engine and be happy with outdated info from a newspaper article. A parent doing taxes might very well not succeed and then will try to get their search mediated by a library if they want to be sure of reliable information.

NT: What can Web reference sources do that print resources cannot? What can the print resources do that the Web resources can't?

PM: The Web harnesses the power of full-text searching in a way that a print resource (and its table of contents or index) never can, and that's its greatest strength. Have a poetry identification question involving a line that isn't the first or last line? Plug it into a search engine or Bartleby—instant gratification—assuming the patron remembered it correctly and the poem isn't from a greeting card. Unfortunately, the majority of the content lacks any sort of useful authority, which is where print resources get their strength. Editorial review process, subject indexing. Great things, and not easily separated out on the Web.

NT: Is it possible to have a free ready reference collection gleaned from Web sites in lieu of a print reference collection? Is this what the Internet Public Library already has?

PM: I don't think we're there yet, and I don't think that day is coming for a long while. Yes, you can answer a certain percentage of ready reference questions using free Web resources. No, you can't answer all of them. Also, it seems like for every new source that comes up on the Web for free, two more are taken down to go to a fee model. As ad revenues continue to wilt, I don't think most of what I've grown to use daily in answering IPL questions will be around this time next year, since this time last year I was able to use World Book (on DiscoverySchool), Britannica, and Compton's for free and now they're all gone. Bartleby seems like it will hold on, but FindArticles?—I wouldn't get attached to it. Will that hamper my ability to answer questions? Yes, but I also still have the option of doing Web searches and sifting through sites to see if I can find other reliable sources. And when that doesn't work, I can refer people to titles likely to be in their local library's print collection. It's not what they want to hear most of the time, but it's better than the whole-lot-of-drivel they'll get otherwise from the Web.

Conclusion

At the start of this chapter, in my example of happily finding an online dictionary, I mentioned the modest beginnings of the Internet as a conveyer of information to a universal audience. When the Internet was first being explored by the public, the innovators in electronic publishing were computer enthusiasts, information specialists, librarians, and amateurs who had little personal gain at stake, but wanted to make free access to information a reality. Along with the efforts of these individuals came innovations from commercial publishers such as the Merriam-Webster site. These free commercial sites for concise reference information, usually aimed at marketing more lengthy print resources or Web subscriptions, combined with the Web sites of educational institutions and dedicated individuals, has made an array of reference information available that rivals fee-based resources.

In this case, access to the free information is worth several thousands of dollars in terms of what you would spend on subscriptions or one-time purchases. A great deal of physical space is being saved, thankfully, because few individual households could store all these works. We can easily adapt, manipulate, and manage information from the Web sites. They aren't, as Professor Péter Jacsó says, "the poor person's reference sources" but "the smart person's reference sources."

Sample Annual Savings

Bartleby.com	=	$1,000
Country information	=	$1,000
Sparknotes	=	$1,000
"Top Reference Books"/"Surrogates"	=	$1,000s
Authoritative health resources	=	priceless
Updated materials	=	priceless

References

Patricia Memmott's Reference Links (available at:
http://www.ipl.org:2000/backroom/class/freeweb.html):

General

- About.com
  http://www.about.com

- Google's Usenet archive
  http://groups.google.com

- Straight Dope
  http://www.straightdope.com

- Stumpers-L archive
  http://www.cuis.edu/~stumpers

Dictionaries

- Merriam-Webster
  http://www.m-w.com

- Onelook
  http://www.onelook.com

Literary

- Gale Literary Index
  http://www.galenet.com/servlet/LitIndex

Genealogy

- Cyndi's List
  http://www.CyndisList.com

Career

- Occupational Outlook Handbook
  http://www.bls.gov/ocohome.htm

U.S. presidents trivia

- IPL Presidential Info Pathfinder
  http://www.ipl.org/ref/QUE/PF/presidents.html

Science

- Mad Scientist Network's archives
  http://www.madsci.org

Word origins

- IPL Word/Phrase Origins Pathfinder
  http://www.ipl.org/ref/QUE/PF/etymology.html

Law/government

- Findlaw
  http://www.findlaw.com

Geography

- How Far Is It?
  http://www.indo.com/distance

Human experts

- Ask-A Locator
  http://www.vrd.org/locator/subject.html

- AllExperts
  http://www.allexperts.com

For latest news in online reference sources

- Digref-L
  http://www.vrd.org/Dig_Ref/dig_ref.shtml

- ResearchBuzz
  http://www.researchbuzz.com

Supplementary Information

Here are some suggestions to help you maintain your edge on reference sources on the Web:

- Peter's Digital Reference Shelf
  http://www.galegroup.com/reference/peter/peter.htm

- Sign up for the reference site of the day at RefDesk.com
  http://www.refdesk.com

The "Alexa Toolbar"

The free Alexa Toolbar is an excellent addition to your Internet Explorer software. It provides site statistics, contact information, and links to sites related to the one with which you are working. Each time you visit a site, the toolbar will refresh with new information. I use the toolbar to help determine who is responsible for a site, how many other sites link to a site, and which sites may offer similar information. Getting the toolbar is easy and, once downloaded, it will appear on your browser window. The Alexa Toolbar is discussed in detail in Chapter Eight.

Endnotes

1. University of Virginia. Association of Research Libraries Statistics: Interactive Edition. http://fisher.lib.virginia.edu/cgi-local/arlbin/arl.cgi. March 7, 2002. Definition adapted from National Information Standards Organization. Library Statistics. Bethesda, MD: NISO Press. 1997.

2. New York Public Library. 2000 Annual Report. http://www.nypl.org/admin/pro/ar/ar2000.pdf. April 18, 2002.

3. Brantford Public Library and the UNESCO Public Library Manifesto. February 2001. http://www.brantford.library.on.ca/unesco.shtml. March 8, 2002.

4. William A. Katz. *Introduction to Reference Work: Basic Information Services.* Volume 1. New York: McGraw-Hill. 8th Edition. 2002. p. 278.

5. Mary Ellen Quinn. "Field-Tested Reference Titles." *Booklist.* Volume 94. Issue 17. May 1, 1998. p. 1532.

6. Péter Jacsó. "Peter's Picks and Pans." *Database Magazine.* February/March 1999. Volume 22. Issue 1. p. 86.

7. Péter Jacsó. "Free Resources. Columbia Encyclopedia, 6th Edition." Peter's Digital Reference Desk. http://www.galegroup.com/servlet/ HTMLFileServlet?imprint=9999&region=7&fileName=reference/ archive/200006/columbia.html. April 17, 2002.

8. Merck and Co. Merck Frequently Asked Questions. http://www. merck.com/faq/faq.html#mmanual. August 24, 2002.

9. Brian E. Coutts and John B. Richard. "50 Sources for the Millennium." *Library Journal.* November 15, 1999. Volume 124. Issue19. p. 8.

10. Infotrieve Company. "About Publist." http://www.publist. com/about.html. November 21, 2002.

11. David S. Carter and Joseph Janes. "Unobtrusive Data Analysis of Digital Reference Questions and Services at the Internet Public Library: An Exploratory Study." *Library Trends.* Fall 2000. Volume 49. Issue 2. p. 258.

Chapter Four

Reference Part II: Expert, AskA, and Digital Reference Services

We can't always locate the answers we want using books or Web pages; sometimes a person-to-person interaction is not only preferable but necessary. The Web may not seem like the greatest research tool when your search returns 100,000 Web pages. In a DataMonitor report, the "People-to-People" answer market was estimated as a $1 billion annual business. The report issued by this popular market research firm stated: "People searching for answers need other people."[1] This alternative for people who cannot locate an answer themselves can sometimes even be obtained without charge. This is where various "Ask-an-Expert" (also known as AskA) sites on the Web, which feature access to real people, serve a purpose.

At least two types of resources fill the role of human information providers via the Web: library-based sources and nonlibrary sources. Nonlibrary sources may include commercial and noncommercial services, often referred to as "expert services."

The Virtues of Web-Based Assistance

Filling the Gap

Web-based assistance, whether called "experts," "interactive Q&A," "People to People (P2P)," or "Web wizards," fills a gap between online bulletin boards and chatrooms, at one end of the spectrum, and hiring a consultant, at the other extreme. Some "Experts" find motivation in the gratification they get in sharing their interest or knowledge in a subject with others. Even if individual questioners do not receive definitive answers, they may find it helpful to bounce their ideas off other persons.

Someone Must Know the Answer

Because innumerable people access the Web, your chances are high of finding an expert to provide an answer, or at least a kindred spirit. If the question is not of an emergency nature, you may find waiting for an answer acceptable; the wait may only last a couple of hours or a day or three at most. Questioners may also have the opportunity to follow up, provide feedback, and network with other service users and providers. And, usually, it costs little or nothing to participate.

The Problems with Web-Based Assistance

Credibility Issues

While many sources claim to have the answers, results sometimes disappoint searchers. When Andy Warhol said, "In the future, everyone will be famous for 15 minutes," he could not have known that the Internet, with its expansive reach and relentless penetration, would facilitate his prophecy. This democratic vehicle for individuals' ideas also affords a publishing venue for everyone from the most wizened sage to the most shamelessly narcissistic dilettante. Information seekers face this whenever they embark on a knowledge expedition; the information they get may prove worthless.

Charlatans, mountebanks, and con artists have not disappeared from society. The World Wide Web has made it easier to disseminate misinformation. Even the well-meaning online helper may be clueless.

Ascertaining credentials continues to trouble users. We all know Yahoo! is a top Internet portal—my Alexa toolbar tells me it is the number one site, based on traffic, on the World Wide Web. Yahoo! Advice premiered in mid-2001 (http://yahoo.liveadvice.com) and disappeared in May 2003. It wasn't a free service, and advisors signed up to speak with people who had questions and answered them via telephone. The service was quick, but not necessarily inexpensive. Advisors charged anywhere from 75 cents to $10 per minute. And if that failed to shock you, consider that few advisors listed credentials. Out of the 60 advisors listed under "Investing," only three listed credentials. But at least the credentials appeared to have been verified. "LEON4" for instance has an MBA from NYU (as verified by Absolute Backgrounds.com).

Timeliness

While InfoRocket, Keen.com, Kasamba, and LiveAdvice all offer instantaneous feedback from a paid expert, the question of how fast a response is rendered remains an issue with many expert sites. When an expert site is asynchronous (e-mail based) and offered without charge, you must consider several variables in looking for a timely response.

First, though many experts have earned good ratings and post an acceptable average turnaround time, neither their expertise nor their inclination to respond to any given question is assured. Some experts may simply choose to pass on your question. This is particularly exasperating if you have gone through the trouble of looking through dozens of names to identify a suitable expert to receive your question.

Then again, though the designated expert to whom you have written seems qualified, the answer that you wait for may ultimately prove unrewarding—meaning you will have to start all over again, sacrificing more time. I once asked a technology expert at AskMe.com, "How do professionals go about predicting emerging technologies?" The answer, 48 hours later, was: "I tend to just use instinct when picking out market trends." Since no real answer was conveyed, I needed to seek another expert and ask my question again. (The public AskMe.com service has been discontinued; the service is now primarily a business-to-business operation.)

Writers at the Wall Street Journal Online discovered similar problems when they attempted to find answers to their questions. Out of five AskA services, only two provided good answers, and only one was able to do this within the time frame that it promised.[2]

Canards and Just Plain Wrong Answers

Along with the credibility risk is the fact that questions occasionally receive responses characterized by guesswork. Plenty of people are ready to render answers. But if an expert is, as Oscar Wilde said, "An ordinary man away from home giving advice," we do not need a computer to find our share of ultra-crepidarians*— people willing to venture beyond their province of knowledge [*from *Hutchinson's Dictionary of Difficult Words*. Abington, Oxfordshire: Helicon Publishing, Ltd, 2000.]

Two of my favorite questions to ask experts are to "explain the philosophical meaning of the 'Ship of Theseus' phenomenon" and "Why was Lenin transported on a 'sealed train?'" When you receive responses that sound as though they came from the stool across the bar and go something like, "I think Theseus's son had to move a rock to get at his armor" and "Perhaps the train was sealed as a Customs measure," you know it is time to look elsewhere for an expert.

Ask-an-Expert Sites: The Good News

Thomas Pack, an information professional who has worked in digital media for over a decade, reasoned that Ask-an-Expert sites may be the "Next Killer App." As he wrote in *Econtent* magazine, "Logging on to get advice on a personal or professional topic may become part of daily life in the digital age."[3] That's great if individuals can actually connect with others who can provide good information. According to some reports, they can.

The peer-reviewed information science periodical, the *Journal of the American Society for Information Science and Technology*, reported that Ask-an-Expert sites provided responses to 70 percent of the questions posed, and 69 percent of the answers to factual questions contained verifiable information (i.e., as opposed to conjecture, advice, or otherwise unsubstantiated material). Joseph Janes, an expert in technology and information dissemination presently on the faculty of the Information School at the University of Washington, initiated the research with his colleagues. Study associates submitted 240 questions in 10 subject areas to 20 expert sites. The questions were based on actual questions submitted to the Internet Public Library. None of the sites consulted were fee-based.[4]

Librarians consider verifiable answers of the utmost importance; otherwise the answer has no context or credibility. Although some critics may interpret a 69 percent rating in this area as a "D," it indicates that the people behind "Ask-an-Expert" services apparently understand the importance of verifiability as well. Concerning a separate but also important issue, Janes et al. noted that many sites did not bother to post their policies on answering questions; he found that some would respond to every question while others will respond only at their leisure or only to questions they feel they can tackle.

The Nonlibrary Resources

Free Services

When contemplating serious questions that require the counsel of experts, the topics that come to mind may encompass medical, legal, financial, and other areas that fall into the purview of acknowledged professionals. "What are the possible complications of a balloon angioplasty?" "Is the home I plan to buy structurally sound?" "What's the best mutual fund for long-term growth?" These are queries you should submit to doctors, engineers, and investment bankers.

We don't expect a physician to examine us without charge, nor does it shock us when an attorney bills us for half an hour when looking over something as simple as an apartment lease. A veterinarian at Tufts University even charged an anxious cat fancier for telephone advice regarding the best kitty litter. Not only do we pay, but occasionally we must accept that the expert's best advice was wrong. Even specialists can be stumped, but they rarely waive their fees.

Having said this, it is also true that millions of people provide free information every day. They do it for reasons besides money. They are people good at something or with a serious interest in a subject who love talking about what they like doing. They may be volunteering their expertise to promote an idea or Web site or book. Because these services are free, this is probably the option that most individuals will try first. Although many Web-based "expert" sites vied for our attention several years ago, a few have transmogrified into business-to-business solutions (e.g., AskMe.com, Exp.com, AskforFree.com, and Webhelp.com), and others have dropped out of sight altogether (e.g., Knowpost.com). A few endure. These sites get so much traffic that they will likely remain active in the future.

AllExperts

http://www.allexperts.com

Launched in early 1998, AllExperts has the distinction of being the oldest expert service on the Web. It is a commercial service inasmuch as site visitors see sponsored links and banner advertisements. The service has caught the eye (and pen) of writers from the *New York Times, PC Magazine, Yahoo! Internet Life,* and from international publications such as *The Bangkok Post, Japan Times,* and *The Guardian* of London. Its philosophy is admirable: "Volunteers helping people without money exchanging hands!"

AllExperts is easy to use. No registration is required; simply get to the home page, click on a category, and choose a volunteer to answer your question. Volunteer experts await for categories such as "Arts & Humanities," "Homework Help," "Science," "Cultures," "Food & Drink," "Pets," "Religion," and "Money." On the average, six volunteers are listed under each category. You may only find one or two under "British Theatre" (in "Arts & Humanities") or "Horror Books," but numerous experts for "Home Mortgage" and other topics balance out the count. They are called "experts" and "volunteers" interchangeably.

In the disclaimer that appears right after you are informed that by using the service you agree to indemnify and hold it harmless for any liability, AllExpert states "You also acknowledge by using this service that you understand that our volunteers have varying levels of expertise and haven't been certified as 'experts' (or anything else) by us in any professional way. Many of them are professionals in their own right, but AllExperts has not undertaken to verify the credentials or abilities of any of our volunteers" (http://www.allexperts. com/central/disclaimer.shtml).

When you have found the appropriate category, you may read the volunteer's credentials and ratings based on user input. Credentials may include self-reported education attained, publications written, memberships, and personal highlights. Once you've decided whom to ask, you fill out a Web question form. AllExperts asks volunteers to respond within two to three days. Users may rate the volunteers on numerous attributes including clarity, politeness, knowledge, and timeliness. Using this information, an individual with a question can get a pretty detailed idea of what type of service to expect from a specific volunteer.

To become a volunteer at the service, one needs to complete a form describing one's background. Logically, the form emphasizes what types of questions the applicant will and will not be able to answer.

The volunteers at AllExperts have answered 10 questions for me. Although some answers were very good, those that were not bring my average rating for the service down to "fair." Nonetheless, *USA Today* gave it kudos in remarking that it had over 1,800 categories in which answer seekers could find experts. The newspaper gave it its "Hot Site" stamp of approval on February 8, 2000.

Abuzz
http://www.abuzz.com

The history of Abuzz begins in 1996 when it began as Beehive, an Internet tool designed to network people with similar interests. In 1999 it became part of New York Times Digital appearing on several NYTD sites including Boston.com and the New York Times Learning Network. In January 2000 it was launched again with its own URL as a free, shared space to allow questions, answers, and discussion.

In terms of the sheer volume of responses you will receive and, therefore, the number of pieces of information you may be able to compare when attempting to assess a correct answer, Abuzz wins hands down. Eight percent of all questions are answered within one day. It is a good service because the community members seem willing to help, but they do not call themselves experts.

When you ask a question at Abuzz, your query goes to people who have expressed an interest in the subject area into which your question falls, as based on their profiles. To use the service, you need to register. After registering, ask a question, choose a category and subcategory, and submit your query. You are notified by e-mail when someone responds, or you can visit your "My Abuzz" page to see responses. For example, one question I posed was: "What was the popular vote for each candidate in the Nixon–McGovern election?" I chose the category "General" and the subcategory "Reference." Abuzz provided feedback that it had sent my question to 32 people in the Reference category. Within 12 hours I had received five responses. Two were correct, and the answers even included citations to the online Infoplease Almanac (http://www.infoplease.com/ipa/A0781450.html).

During my informal test I asked the Abuzz community six questions and received 20 responses (i.e., an average of 3.3 answers per question). After you receive a response and rate it, you may click on the contributor's screen name to discover more details about the person.

There is one possible, albeit minor, problem. If you want a single definitive answer, be forewarned that Abuzz may give you more than you expected. After all, as the company states, the site is also to foster discussion. If you have asked or answered a question, you are fair game. One exasperated participant wrote: "Look, don't make me sorry I signed up here. I responded to a question and now I am getting everyone's suggestions. I don't want all these responses. How do I get them to STOP?"

Ehow

http://www.ehow.com

Ehow is not an Ask-an-Expert site but rather a community of users posting and seeking "how-to" information. Ehow's revenue comes from its many partners that you may find e-mailing offers to you because you have registered at Ehow (and registration is necessary to gain access to the how-tos).

Ehow is very good at what it does. The home page tells us that it has 15,000 how-to documents available. Just search by keyword for what you would like help with. I took a few projects that I was already familiar with and checked them against the recommendations of the how-tos. For building "pinewood derby cars," Ehow had one document. It provided the classic instructions for building the car, which would be invaluable to anyone who had not tried it before; but it omitted the one or two secrets that really matter if you want the car to win. (I had found them before by performing a generic Web search through Google.) I also found it helpful for finding game rules, specifically darts and pool. When I requested assistance with help for "reseating a toilet" the closest match was "How to repair a running toilet." There was some good advice, including graphics, for instructions of getting started with model rocketry.

My requests reflected my personal interests, but Ehow has a subject directory that includes Computers, Health, Finance, Careers, Automotive, Travel, and several others. You may also submit tips to the site, which Ehow editors will review.

Pitsco's Ask an Expert—The Kid-Friendly Expert Site
http://www.askanexpert.com

Aimed at students, teachers, and parents, Pitsco's Ask an Expert has received such accolades as Popular Science's "Top 50 Web Sites," Library Spot's "Spotlight," and ENC's "Digital Dozen" (ENC is the Eisenhower National Clearninghouse for curriculum resources). Ask an Expert is really a searchable subject directory of the Web pages of cooperating experts. Browsing by category, the student will find links to experts on "Animals," "Science & Technology," "Cultures, Arts & Humanities," "Home Improve-ment," "Law," "Education," "Health," and several others. After the student has found the correct category, a list of experts appears. Clicking on the expert's link takes the searcher to the expert's Web page where an FAQ may answer the question, or you can contact the expert. Under Education, for example, consults are available with the "College Admissions

Guru," "The Braille Expert," "The Conflict Manager," "The K-12 Lesson Plans Expert," and more than a dozen others.

Although Ask an Expert does not have a conspicuously high ranking in terms of traffic, more than 3,000 sites have linked to it.

A Good Free Service Metamorphoses Before My Very Eyes: The Case of AskMe

Launched in March 2000, AskMe (http://www.askme.com) averages almost a million site visitors per month. Boasting 120,000 experts available in numerous categories, the service promised that an individual with a question could receive several answers, comments, Web links, and discussion on virtually any topic. Its free Ask-an-Expert site was alive and well in July 2002.

But AskMe phased out its consumer service and became a business solutions enterprise in November 2002. Using the slogan "Connect employees with problems to employees with solutions," its current mission is helping employees of its client companies interact with co-workers to share expertise.

The free AskMe was a good service; I had queried its experts on several topics and had received sensible answers. Of course, I had also received a few clunkers. But my experience with AskMe is very typical of the reality that resources come and go and transmogrify. Beware, however; you never really know anything about the expert. For a reality check on AskMe and other expert services, read Michael Lewis's article "Faking It" in the *New York Times* from July 15, 2001 (and a related article in August 12, 2001's *Ottawa Citizen*). Lewis describes how a 15-year old became a legal expert with high ratings, even though he had no legal training or experience.

The Fee Services

In a popular new trend, search facilities have begun to offer advice and answer resources. Specifically, Google Answers (http://answers.google.com) initiated its service in early 2002. Tara Calishain, information professional and author of *Google Hacks* (check out her site and subscribe to her free weekly ResearchBuzz newsletter at http://www.researchbuzz.com), reasons, "By charging to answer questions, Google might be able to attract a larger body of searchers to provide answers."[5]

Google Answers

http://answers.google.com

Google has a track record of forward thinking and, appropriately, a solid following of Web users that find it indispensable. Google Answers is a relatively new development for the search engine and a relatively overt nudge toward generating revenue. Otherwise, Web searchers that go to Google to perform a search probably have no idea how the search engine makes money. Google Answers is only part of the company's business model, but probably one that makes most sense to the public.

Google Answers works like this: People with questions register at the site, ask a question, and set the price for an answer. Details include deciding on a window of time in which the question must be answered. Once the question is posted, Google researchers read the question. If a researcher decides they can answer it and that the set price warrants the effort, the researcher "locks" the question and begins working.

After receiving the answer, the individual who posed the question rates the researcher. Theoretically, a better rating will enhance the researcher's prestige and paycheck. Ratings are also used by the Google Answer Team to drop researchers, and researchers have been dropped. Also note that researchers may leave "comments" (as compared with locking a question and declaring the question "answered"), and many of the comments either answer the question or demonstrate to the individual that no satisfactory answer exists.

Google Answers instructs users to "Set a price between $2 and $200 based on your question's difficulty and urgency." Google keeps 25 percent of the take when the question is satisfactorily answered. The researcher gets the rest. Upon looking at some of the subject lines for the questions asked, I rate them as moderately to very difficult. No one seems to want to pay for quick factual answers such as "How tall is the Empire State Building?" which is easily found at an automated answer Web site such as Ask Jeeves (http://www.ask.com). Here are a few examples of Google Answers questions:

- "How do I obtain merchandising licensing for products in the U.K.?"

- "How big is U.S. market for our electronic method of teaching economics?"

- "I saw a candy bar commercial on TV. It had a snow-boarder and a skier, going down a ski hill. The skier ran into a shed. I would like to know where I can get a copy of the commercial, or find out where I can see it." [Note: The Google researcher actually found the archive for the commercials and sent the URL to the requestor.]

Although Google Answers is commercial and fee-based with the bottom line being profit, Google wants the service to shine and tells researchers:

> A satisfactory response answers the question that was asked and provides links to useful sites the customer can visit for additional information. The response is well written and communicates clearly with a helpful tone. Some questions don't have a single answer and in those cases, Researchers should summarize the information found and point the asker to the different sites providing useful information.

Most answers provide links to Web sites that provide edifying content, but some also include references to books, magazine articles, and other printed documents.

FIND/SVP

http://www.findsvp.com

Although not priced for the individual Web surfer, I mention this site because it has proven an effective service for business clients. Charges vary depending on the plan that is chosen. The history of FIND/SVP dates back to 1935 when Maurice de Turckheim founded SVP (S'il Vous Plaît) in Paris. FIND/SVP's experts are employees, not freelancers or volunteers. Andy Garvin, president of FIND/SVP said: "People with business questions simply e-mail their questions via a Web form. That's it. There's no need for the person asking the question to choose from subject categories or lists of experts. Our system delivers the questions to one of the global SVP network's 1,100 professionals most versed in the subject. The response is e-mailed back." Typical answers will run a few paragraphs long and include links to helpful Web sites.

Check these Web pages to locate additional "Q & A" or "Ask-an-Expert" services:

- http://directory.google.com/Top/Reference/Ask_an_Expert
- http://dmoz.org/Reference/Ask_an_Expert

What Happens When Web-Based Assistance Doesn't Work?

Perhaps the people at sites such as AllExperts, Abuzz, and AskMe would disagree, but I believe in the legitimacy of test querying the individuals who answer questions for Web users. Over time, I've asked dozens of questions, and I can count the number of cogent responses on both hands—well, perhaps three hands. I attempt to ask questions that might interest the generally curious information seeker. Following are two answers that sent me back to the site's question form to try again.

Question: "Why are most elections in the United States held on the Tuesday following the first Monday in November?"

[Note that the AllExperts volunteer expert that I chose had a general rating of "7 – Very Good." Stated experience was an interest in American Elections.]

Answer: "I've not a clue to be honest, but it might have something to do with the onset of winter on the east coast of the U.S."

Length of time to answer: 24 hours.

(My mental response: "Wha....?")

Question: Same

[Note that the AllExperts volunteer answering the question was a long-time professor of political science with a doctorate from an Ivy League college.]

Length of time to answer: 4 hours.

Answer: The date of federal elections is specified in the U.S. Constitution; state and local governments have to pay the costs of elections, so mostly they have their elections on the same day as the federal ones.

(My mental response: ".... er, well yes, but....")

Note: For the answer to this question, please refer to Figure 4.5 on p. 207.

What Happens When Web-Based Assistance Works?

The answer to the following question was valuable and worth the time I waited for an e-mailed response. The reply was from an AskMe expert; bear in mind, however, that the service is no longer available for individuals.

Question: I recently rented the comedy film *The Royal Tenenbaums* in which one character wishes to marry his adopted sister. How does the law view siblings who are NOT blood relatives in terms of the legality of their marriage? Thank you very much!

[Note that AskMe.com users could either send a question to all the experts in a category or multiple categories or choose a specific expert. I did not choose a specific expert; my question went to all the experts in the "Civil Law" category. The person who answered my question had the highest rating (five stars) attainable. Listed among the expert's credentials was "J.D., Stanford Law School."]

Answer: The legal term for people who are blood relatives, descended from a (recent) common ancestor, is "consanguinity." Consanguinity is to be distinguished from affinity, which is the relation of a person, through marriage, to the consanguineous relatives of a spouse.

Marriage between siblings (common parents) has generally been forbidden by common law, statutes and church law, as has marriage between those in a lineal relationship such as father and daughter. Many jurisdictions also forbid marriage between first cousins (common grandparents). Marriage between second cousins is permitted in a number of jurisdictions.

Affinity, on the other hand, is generally not a legal bar to marriage, at least in the U.S. In your example, the relation of adoption would probably be treated the same way. Assuming that the adopted daughter is not, in fact, consanguineous with the son (at least to the degree of first cousin), chances are that statutes would not forbid their marriage. Whether church law would disapprove is beyond my knowledge.

Length of time to answer: 3 hours.

(My mental response: "Thank you for the assistance. This is exactly what I needed!")

Finding the Answer: Other Possible Solutions

Specialty Sites

Although I have described a few "Ask-an-Expert" sites, many more exist. As an alternative to posting a question at the broader sites I have discussed, you might try to locate a specialized site. A specialized site may provide a more detailed and appropriate response if your question falls into its purview. The scope of these specialists' sites are as varied as human experience. For educators, teachers, parents, and anyone else with a question about educational research, there is the incomparable AskERIC (http://ericir.syr.edu/About). AskERIC, which has earned awards from *USA Today* and the Internet Public Library, is a question-and-answer service that responds to 35,000 queries per year. E-mail–based, the service has a turnaround time of approximately two days.

Other examples include Culinary.com (http://www.culinary.com), a site that lets you submit questions to an expert chef. At the Smithsonian American Art Museum, you can find "Ask Joan of Art" (http://nmaa-ryder.si.edu/study/nav-joan.html). "Ask Jack" (http://www.naysi.com/ask_jack/ask_jack.htm) is hosted by The North American Youth Sport Institute and covers physical education and fitness. Bird fanciers may like "Ask the Bird Expert" (http://www.upatsix.com/ask-experts), which takes on all-comers; the home page states, "This area is to be used to spread knowledge not only for breeders and professionals, but for the single bird owner or 'newbie' as well."

Bob Drudge of RefDesk.com lists 100 specialty Ask-an-Expert sites at http://www.refdesk.com/expert.html; the Canadian Learning Bank links to a fair number also (http://www.cln.org/int_expert.html). You might also consult the Virtual Reference Desk's AskA+ Locator at http://www.vrd.org/locator/subject.shtml. And for 1,295 links to specialty sites, go to Johnston's Ask the Expert from Johnston Memorial School in Ontario, Canada (http://www.geocities.com/johnstona1/know.html).

Usenet

Usenet's strength lies in its innumerable groups. Usenet groups are divided into various categories usually distinguishable by their names (e.g., alt. or biz. or humanities. or comp.) Because it brings together millions of people with similar interests, it is an excellent complement to Ask-an-Expert services. You should find it fairly easy to identify a group covering your interest, but, if not, just go to Google Groups and enter your keywords. Instead of browsing through each group, Google will pinpoint discussions of your subject.

The Usenet began as a conglomeration of Internet bulletin board postings. As it became more organized, it persisted in being difficult to use. Cantankerous software programs called "news-readers" were required to navigate the Usenet, and they did not always function properly. Google stepped in during February 2001 and made some sense of the Usenet by archiving its 700 million messages back to 1981 and providing a streamlined Web interface that made newsreaders unnecessary.

To access Usenet, go to http://www.google.com and click the "Groups" tab. Once you have performed a search in Google Groups to ascertain which Usenet groups might be most appropriate to monitor or contribute to, you may subsequently access that specific group by typing the group's name in the Google Groups basic search form. When you have accessed your relevant group, you will see numerous messages on which you can comment, or you can post a new message. You must register with Google Groups to post a message, but there is no charge and it takes only a minute. Sometimes your message will create a discussion or "thread," with other users making comments. Sometimes an individual will answer your posting with an e-mail. I have found it useful for several questions, including where to take an especially prized watch for repair (alt.horology) and how much onboard memory I would need to play games on a Palm Pilot m105 handheld device (comp.sys.palmtops.pilot). Figures 4.1 and 4.2 illustrate the utility of Google's Groups.

STUMPERS-L

Many librarians turn to the STUMPERS-L (http://listserv.dom. edu/stumpers-l.html) discussion list when they are, frankly, stumped by a question. Anne Feeney, a former graduate student at

Figure 4.1   Performing a keyword search to determine relevant groups on the Usenet. Courtesy Google, copyright 2003.

Figure 4.2   Viewing the recent messages from a Usenet group discussing PalmPilots. Courtesy Google, copyright 2003.

Rosary College's School of Library and Information Science (now called Dominican University), created STUMPERS-L in 1992.

The site states, "With a worldwide community of over 1,000 librarians and other experts sharing their knowledge and resources, Stumpers-L is the world's largest and most versatile reference desk—and the answers often make for pretty interesting reading."

Only librarians may submit questions to the list, but site visitors may search the archives. Perhaps an individual's question has already been answered.

The Library Answer Continuum: From "A"(synchronous) to Live Reference

No organization or person manages the Web. Anyone can stake a claim to a piece of the Internet frontier that some have compared to the Wild West. The institutions that stood as standards before computers have been given the implicit mandate to "fish or cut bait." Reference services have been challenged more than any other traditional library service. People can often find their own sources of information on the Web, and, when they cannot, there are, as this chapter demonstrates, ample sites hosting experts, volunteers, advisors, counselors, and Web researchers willing to provide assistance.

The Internet Public Library and Its Role as Mentor

The Internet Public Library (http://www.ipl.org) opened its virtual doors to visitors in March 1995. Based at the University of Michigan's School of Information, the IPL is a seminal entity for serving individual information needs on the Web. Many of its projects and features provided a basis for library services that we now perceive as part of the status quo.

When the IPL began its e-mail question-and-answer service (http://www.ipl.org/div/askus), it attracted between 25 and 35 questions per day.[6] Between the inception of the service and September 1998, a total of 12,000 questions were received.[7] The average now, according to Patricia Memmott (the IPL's User Services Coordinator), is between 8,000 and 9,000 per year.[8] This represents a 100 percent increase in the IPL's e-mail reference traffic over the service's first three years.

The service has always apprised users that it cannot accept every query. There are various constraints that make it impossible to handle all the questions that the IPL receives. This fact notwithstanding, IPL's e-mail reference service has served as a working model for librarians who desire to interact "asynchronously" with the public. The staff continues to answer questions via two Web-based forms: one for individuals under the age of 13, and another for older users.

Virtual reference operates in the United Kingdom as well. Co-East, a consortium of 10 public library authorities operating in the East of

England region, offers "Ask a Librarian" at http://www.ask-a-librarian.org.uk. The site offers an e-mail based question-and-answer service that tries to respond within 48 hours. Although based in the U.K., the "About" page at the site states: "The service is designed primarily for U.K. residents. However, we recognize that the Internet is a global medium and we never turn away enquiries from overseas. Questions have come in from everyone from school children to university professors."

Live Reference: Becoming a Standard

When it comes to virtual Q & A, libraries are hardly a "Johnny come lately" (at the risk of another egregious cliché). Many librarians have advocated Web-based reference services through their publications, research, and actions. Libraries all over the world routinely engage in e-mail reference (e.g., question-and-answer interactions). But since that service is perceived as insufficient in many cases, a critical mass of libraries is quickly moving toward live reference—24/7/365.

Good, live reference service, offered by libraries via the Web, is not a new phenomenon, but it is a nascent one—in its chrysalis stage. The Cleveland Public Library, which offers virtual reference through its KnowItNow24x7, receives more than 15,000 questions annually from regional users and logs 22 percent of the inquiries between 9 P.M. and 9 A.M.[9]

Many forward-thinking librarians work to deploy these round-the-clock/round-the-calendar services on a broad scale. These librarians labor behind the scenes to make the experience of connecting with an information professional, "free of charge," part of the standard features of libraries' Web pages. Three administrators of such high-profile programs are Steve Coffman, vice president of product development for LSSI (Library Systems and Services Inc.); Diane Kresh, director of public service collections at the Library of

Congress; and Susan McGlamery, coordinator of reference services for MCLS (Metropolitan Cooperative Library System).

INSIDER'S VIEWPOINT FROM YOUR WEB LIBRARY PROFESSIONAL: SUSAN MCGLAMERY, COORDINATOR OF REFERENCE SERVICES, METROPOLITAN COOPERATIVE LIBRARY SYSTEM, GREATER LOS ANGELES, CALIFORNIA

During a chat session with Susan McGlamery, I learned more about "virtual reference." Ms. McGlamery earned her Master of Library Science degree at St. John's University and followed it up with a J.D. at Emory.

NT: Ms. McGlamery, please give the readers some background on MCLS.

SM: The Metropolitan Cooperative Library System is an association of 32 independent city and special district public libraries located in greater Los Angeles. They have agreed to cooperate in providing library service to the residents of all participating jurisdictions. MCLS provides member libraries a resource-sharing network and a means for enhancing the level and diversity of resources available to library users, while reducing duplication of effort. Our mission at MCLS is to enhance the resources of independent libraries through cooperative services to better serve their local library users.

NT: MCLS uses software called "24/7." Besides offering the software to affiliated libraries, what else can MCLS do for its members?

SM: We sell the software, but we also offer 24-hour reference service to libraries that join our cooperative. Of course a library can simply use our software without using the 24-hour service.

NT: I see; it's a software solution to manage around-the-clock reference, but you've got people standing by to help out when the participating libraries can't cover. From the point of view of a person with a question, the software helps them contact a librarian and interact on several levels, the optimal result being that the patron not only receives an answer, but also receives the benefit of a consultation with a professional librarian, as well as a transcript of the session to facilitate further research. I can certainly see the benefit of live collaboration between the patron and the librarian, but can't individual libraries institute this service on their own? What are the advantages of adopting your cooperative model?

SM: It's true that individual libraries can do this on their own. The advantages of the cooperative model are that libraries can share the cost of the software and, more importantly, share hours of coverage.

NT: Could you comment on the progress of libraries in the United States and internationally that are using various types of "around the clock" reference software?

SM: When we first started this project, there were only about four libraries offering any kind of chat-based reference. Now there are probably well over a thousand, worldwide, that offer live reference. A recent trend is toward doing consortial projects, so that costs and hours of coverage can be shared. Many states (including California, of course) are actively pursuing statewide live reference projects. My estimate is that 1,000 libraries are using some kind of live reference product—probably closer to 1,500.

NT: While we're on this topic, can you estimate the number of actual librarians that are really staffing the 24/7 links from all the participating libraries at any given time? For example, it's 1 o'clock in the afternoon. I click the link to 24/7 at the Los Angeles Public Library; someone responds, but how many people were online waiting to respond? In contrast, it's 3 A.M.; I click the link to the Santa Monica Public Library, a librarian responds, but how many librarians were waiting to respond? Susan, is this how the system really works?

SM: You are absolutely right! At 3 A.M., we only have one librarian answering questions for approximately 50 participating libraries. At certain times of the day, as many as 10 librarians are logged on to answer questions from that group of 50 libraries.

NT: Having done some experimentation with the "Chat with a Librarian" links at various participating libraries, I found the service excellent. The questions have been answered thoroughly and quickly. The librarians have been not only knowledgeable and professional, but also personable. I have noticed that none of the libraries (in my brief trial of half a dozen) required me to offer any proof that I was a resident near the library that I initiated the question from. Do any libraries require "authentication?" In addition, during my session patter I asked a few librarians if the service was overwhelming or demanding. I think that once word gets out about live reference, librarians will be inundated with requests, that the queues will grow longer, as they do at any good library's reference desk. I believe that when libraries come up with a good service, and this is definitely a great service, it's going to get a lot of use, perhaps out of proportion to what can be handled. Do you have any thoughts on this? What's your sense of how participating librarians feel on this subject?

SM: I agree with you—when word gets out we could well become inundated. More and better FAQs and a tiered approach will help us when the floods of people come. Our current software allows one librarian to handle as many as six people at a time. Some librarians enjoy this, and others prefer to only help one at a time. Maybe that first tier of librarians should be culled from the group that enjoys multitasking.

We leave authentication issues up to the individual libraries. Some of our libraries do require that the user type in their library card number before asking a question, but most of them allow anyone to come in—it was their decision. Some ask for ZIP Code, but use this info only for statistical purposes and not to block access.

NT: Do you see any of the participating libraries welcoming all users? Are you aware of any official policies that encourage all users, or any to the contrary? Do any libraries come to mind that are simply stellar in their willingness to "take on all comers?"

SM: All of our participating libraries know that if they do not require authentication, they are potentially taking on the world. This was borne out when a few months ago the *London Financial Times* ran an article on our service and we suddenly had many questions from the U.K. (In these cases, we did remind people about their local public libraries, while still providing an answer to the question.)

NT: Joseph Janes and his colleagues endeavored to analyze the responsiveness of Web AskA services, both commercial and noncommercial. I believe that, on the whole, his findings were positive inasmuch as the services rendered verifiable answers in 69 percent of the cases. You co-authored an *American Libraries* article with Steve Coffman in which you urged librarians to adopt better services than WebHelp and AskJeeves. What's your current perspective on the (nonlibrarian) AskA or Ask-an-Expert services? Do you have any impressions about Google Answers? Does the Usenet have a role in rendering accurate information to posters of queries?

SM: I think there is a place for AskA services and for Usenet groups, but I think the library should make reference services as convenient as possible, hence the idea of a clickable icon with a live librarian at the other end. Librarians should be aware of various referral sources, such as AskA and expert services, so as to send the patron to the most appropriate source. The value of Usenet is like asking the advice of a friend—for example, getting hotel recommendations for Vienna from a group of people who have been (or say they've been!) to Vienna. It's similar to asking your friends and family a question, although these are "friends" that have no clear indicia of reliability.

NT: At the end of many of the live reference sessions I initiated, I was asked to complete a brief survey concerning my satisfaction with the service. Do you ever see the feedback provided by the surveys? How do users perceive the service?

SM: All the librarians see the survey results. The response has been overwhelmingly positive. The users are impressed by the quality of response and the convenience. Many are amazed that the library is providing such an outstanding service, free. Of course it isn't free—their tax dollars support this—but since they have no direct cost it seems free to them.

NT: Is live reference still an experiment or have the participating libraries definitely decided to adopt the services in perpetuity and, for that matter, are more signaling that they wish to join up?

SM: We no longer consider it an experiment but an ongoing program. Almost all of the public libraries in L.A. and Orange County are currently participating, and we receive inquiries all the time from libraries that want to join us.

The World's Largest Library and Its Role in Virtual Q & A

June 10, 2002 was an historic day for "wired" librarians and their clientele. It marked the launch of QuestionPoint, a joint effort of the Library of Congress's (LC) Public Service Collections Directorate and OCLC (the Online Computer Library Center in Dublin, Ohio), the world's leading library vendor. The QuestionPoint service provides subscriber libraries with access to a collaborative network of reference librarians throughout the world. Both LC and OCLC are dominant entities in the information realm; LC's Public Service Collections Directorate maintains a staff of 700 and provides service in 15 of the 21 reading rooms in the world's largest library. OCLC coordinates resource sharing between 41,000 libraries in 82 countries and territories.

For individuals with questions, this means queries may be submitted anytime, day or night, through a participating library's Web site. Librarians or, if appropriate, subject specialists, will begin finding the answers. The interactions may take place by chat, by e-mail, or via a Web-based question submission form. A global knowledge base will hasten response to questions that have already been answered.

For librarians it means the implementation of useful administrative virtual reference tools at a cost lower than services offered by most other 24/7 reference vendors. QuestionPoint automatically routes inquiries to local library staff, to other libraries in a consortia or cooperative, and/or international members of the Global Reference Network. The routing, based on individual library profiles that include staff availability, library resources, and expertise, enables individuals to obtain the best possible answers. Figure 4.3 shows the QuestionPoint screen at the Library of Congress.

While the QuestionPoint concept is brilliant, experts who have worked diligently on other virtual reference projects caution that such services are multidimensional and, unless QuestionPoint is executed flawlessly, problems may hamper its success. But as librarians migrate more quickly than ever to the "just in time" question-and-answer format of the Web, QuestionPoint is perceived as a major advancement, consolidating the power and strengths of its members to offer a high level of professional service.

Chat with a Librarian
an online reference service from the Library of Congress

Welcome to the Library of Congress Humanities and Social Sciences Division chat service. Chat is available from Monday through Friday 2:00-3:00 PM Eastern Time (except Federal Holidays). To contact a librarian during another time, please use our Ask a Librarian web form.

Chat

Monday through Friday 2:00-3:00 PM Eastern Time (except Federal Holidays) - Today is Tuesday January 21 10:26 AM

*Name:

*E-mail Address:

Asterisk (*) denotes required field.   Chat

Humaniti and Soci Science Divisio

Link to Home Pag

If you have any problems with this service, please use our Ask a Librarian Error Report Form.

Figure 4.3   QuestionPoint access at the Library of Congress.

Are You Affiliated with a Leading Edge Library?

Many libraries have already activated virtual reference. Several lists of libraries that offer live reference exist, though none are guaranteed to be comprehensive. Gerry McKiernan, science and technology librarian at the Iowa State University Library in Ames, composed a list called "A Registry of Real-Time Digital Reference Services" (http://www.public.iastate.edu/~CYBERSTACKS/Live Ref.htm). The list breaks the services down by type of library including academic, special, public, and "other." McKiernan's registry also contains links to the software used at these libraries. Bernie Sloan's list of collaborative live reference projects, ones in which several libraries have pooled resources, may be viewed at http://www.lis.uiuc.edu/~b-sloan/collab.htm. The University of Leicester's Library's "ELITE project Electronic Library, IT and staff Education Project" maintains a similar list at http://www.le.ac.uk/li/distance/eliteproject/elib/chat.html.

Live chat with a librarian requires planning and financial support. Until a majority of libraries adopt live reference, individuals would be wise to connect to their affiliated libraries and see if they offer "asynchronous" (i.e., e-mail based) Q & A. Information professional Bernie Sloan provides a list of libraries that deploy e-mail reference at http://alexia.lis.uiuc.edu/~b-sloan/e-mail.html. Sloan's compilation is not necessarily comprehensive, but does provide examples of what individuals may expect. Google's directory offers another list at http://directory.google.com/Top/Reference/Ask_an_Expert/Libraries.

Libraries offering reference assistance via the Web will usually feature that option on their home pages. You may need to look no further than a reference link on your library Web site's home page. Special icons or phrases tell you that you are going to team up with a librarian, but the software or system behind your interaction (e.g., QuestionPoint, 24/7 Reference, LSSI) will be transparent to you. Libraries are free to use any icon to connect you with the service, but a few of the graphics you may come across are included in Figure 4.4.

Figure 4.4   Assorted icons indicating reference assistance.

The Library Difference

Librarians perform research for people, and they facilitate the research of others. Librarians back up their answers with sources. They do not take Web site content at face value, rarely venture an opinion when answering a question, and, though occasionally approached with thinly veiled pleas for personal advice, librarians never render it. When a librarian answers a question, there is no monetary gain at stake; no bias involved. There is no book or Web site to promote. The reward is intrinsic.

If you seek a straightforward answer accompanied by documentation, laced with a smattering of information retrieval instruction, contacting a librarian through the Web will prove satisfactory. Conversely if you wish to discuss a problem, gather consensus on a topic, or have a research question appropriate for a specialist or consultant, you should explore the many AskA options available.

It is also important to note that virtual reference with a live librarian should not be misconstrued as always being the appropriate alternative to discussing a question with a librarian in a physical library. The topic of virtual reference engenders thoughtful dissension within the profession as well as from without. Virtual reference, however, is an additional tool for the client and the librarian, and its usefulness cannot be discounted.

Live Chat with a Librarian: What Happens

When you connect with a librarian via live chat and ask a question, the librarian can "push" your browser to multiple Web sites that contain relevant information while entering comments about the sites you see on your computer (Figure 4.5). If the information isn't clear or relevant, you can immediately tell the librarian. With certain types of reference software, the librarian can also co-navigate with the user. This allows the librarian to show the user how to choose correct databases and how to search the databases. After the session, the user is e-mailed a transcript of the interaction with the addresses of the Web sites that he or she visited along with the librarian.

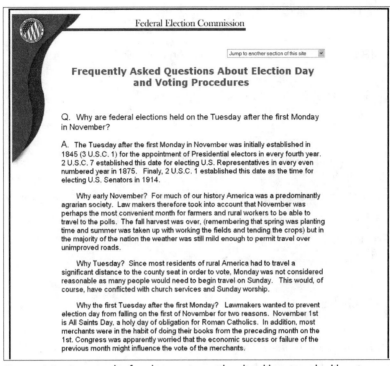

Figure 4.5   As a result of a chat session with a live librarian, the librarian
has "pushed" the client's Web browser to a page from the
Federal Election Commission. The page authoritatively answers
the question concerning the reason elections are held in
November and on the Tuesday following the first Monday.

Here is a transcript I received after a live reference chat:

Thank you for using our Virtual Reference service. We hope that
you found it helpful. Below is a transcript of our session including links
to information.

Nick Tomaiuolo: Can you please help me find an authoritative Web
page that explains the rationale for holding elections in the United
States on the Tuesday FOLLOWING the first Monday in November?
Thanks for your help.

A librarian will be with you momentarily.

[Robb, a library staff member, is coming online...please wait.]

Robb: Welcome to the Virtual Reference Desk at AskYourLibrary. org. My name is Robb.

Robb: Let's see what I can find on this.

Robb: Here's a page from the Federal Election Commission [Item sent—Frequently Asked Questions About Election Day and Voting Procedures]
http://www.fec.gov/pages/faqvdayeprocedures.htm

Robb: Here it is.

Robb: Do you need a site that you can quote that is more authoritative than this one? Although it's tough to find any more authoritative site on elections than the federal election commission.

Nick Tomaiuolo: You've been very helpful, you deserve a raise.

Robb: Thanks, I'll be sure my boss reads this transcript.

[Nick Tomaiuolo—has disconnected]

Robb: Thank you for using the Virtual Reference Desk at Ask YourLibrary.org. Please contact us if you need further assistance.

[Robb—user has closed this session]

Conclusion

How much money is the answer to a question worth? It is difficult to tell, but as we've seen, some fee-based Ask-an-Expert services will help us affix a cost. If you ever have the opportunity to engage a librarian via a 24/7 Web-based chat session, keep the $10 to $12 range per question in mind. That is the approximate cost, with all overhead variables factored in, for a 10-minute interactive Web session with a professional librarian.[10]

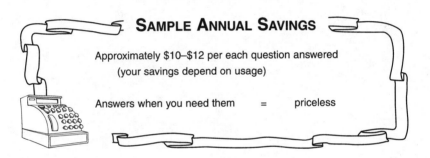

SAMPLE ANNUAL SAVINGS

Approximately $10–$12 per each question answered
(your savings depend on usage)

Answers when you need them   =   priceless

Endnotes

1. DataMonitor. "P2P eCommerce Information Exchanges. Report DMTC0679." April 1, 2000. http://www.datamonitor.com. July 29, 2002.

2. Peter Meyers. "Testing the Online Experts: Which Sites Can You Trust?" Wall Street Journal Online. October 15, 2002. http://online.wjs.com. October 15, 2002.

3. Thomas Pack. "Human Search Engines: The Next Killer App?" *Econtent*. December 2000. Volume 23. Issue 6. pp. 16–22.

4. Joseph Janes, Chrystie Hill, and Alex Rolfe, "Ask-an-Expert Services Analysis." *Journal of the American Society for Information Science and Technology*. November 2001. Volume 52. Issue 13. pp. 1106–1121.

5. Tara Calishain, "Yahoo! Service Offers More Advice Than Expertise." *Information Today*. June 2002. Volume 19. Issue 6. p. 51.

6. Nettie Lagace and Michael McClennen, "Managing an Internet-Based Distributed Reference Service." *Computers in Libraries*. February 1998. Volume 18. Issue 2. p. 24.

7. Kenneth R. Irwin, "Professional Reference Service at the Internet Public Library with Freebie Librarians." *Searcher*. October 1998. Volume 6. Issue 9. p. 21.

8. Personal e-mail from Patricia Memmott, March 2002.

9. Brian Kenney, "Live, Digital Reference." *Library Journal*. October 1, 2002. Volume 127. Issue 16. p. 46.

10. Personal e-mail from Steve Coffman, July 2002.

Chapter Five

Books in the Web Library

How Much Time People Spend Reading

How many books do you read each year? How many books could or would you read if you had no financial or temporal constraints and you could devote as much time as you desired to your avocation? Ten books? Fifty? Five hundred?

In October 1999 the Gallup News Service released the results of a poll that tallied the responses of 1,698 Americans over age 18. It showed that at least 84 percent of Americans had read all or part of one book during the previous year (and that number has stayed approximately the same for the past 20 years). Thirty percent of the public reads between one and five books and 16 percent between six and 10 books; about 40 percent reported they had read more than 10 books in a year; and 7 percent read over 50 books (http://www.gallup.com/poll/releases/pr991004b.asp).[1]

Although individuals engage in many diversions, some of which they spend more time on than ever (television, Internet access, listening to music), according to the U.S. Census Bureau, Americans' reading habits have remained steady. People have been reading about 100 hours a year for the last decade. The professional journalism magazine *Quill* distilled this information and stated that Americans spent 1,595 hours watching television in 1997 (or about 4.4 hours per day), but read a book for only 17 minutes per day.[2] Figure 5.1 is derived from the *Statistical Abstract of the United States, 2001,* and illustrates book reading compared with other types of leisure time use.[3]

For readers concerned that they are not reading enough, consider that with all the great literature in the world, it would be difficult to tackle even the tip of the iceberg. A few years ago, when the Modern Library (http://www.randomhouse.com/modernlibrary/100best novels.html) issued its Board's decision on the Top 100 Novels

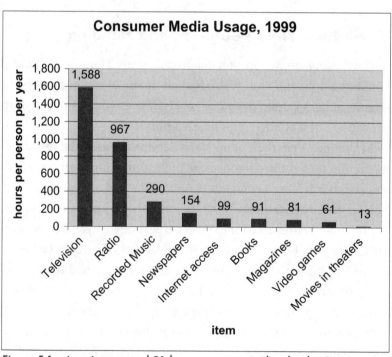

Figure 5.1 Americans spend 91 hours per year reading books. Source: *Statistical Abstract of the United States,* 2001.

since 1900, led by James Joyce's *Ulysses*, many readers took exception with the list. One way to put the argument into perspective is to consider not the "Top 100" books but the top 10,000. That's the scope of the vastness that readers are really dealing with.

Let's suppose you have unlimited time to read. Let's suppose your goal is not only to divert yourself, but also to elevate your thoughts and expand your intellectual reach. Think about the great masterpieces of literature you may have already read. If you are like many people, you've probably had a taste of Shakespeare, Dickens, Twain, and perhaps Kafka, Poe, and Zola. What about the other classicists and classics you've yet to become familiar with? Plato, Homer, the *Bhagavad-Gita*, and *Gulliver's Travels*? Again, with all the time in the world available to you, you may want to begin with best literature available. How much would it cost to stock your personal library with the world's most enduring works?

How Much Money People Spend on Reading

The fact that people buy plenty of books is demonstrated by the financial figures from companies like Amazon.com, Barnes and Noble, and Borders. Having done more than $2.5 billion in sales in 2000, Amazon.com is one of the biggest players in electronic commerce. Most people who use computers know that Amazon sells more than books these days. But back in its infancy in 1996 and 1997, Amazon was still doing a very brisk business, based chiefly on online book sales. In 1996 its sales hovered around $12 million, which shot up to $118 million in '97. Borders Books, a retail bookstore chain based in Michigan, reported net income of $111 million for its fiscal year ending Jan. 26, 2003, according to *Publishers Weekly* (March 17, 2003). In February 2001, Barnes and Noble, Inc. reported over a billion dollars in sales. Its online counterpart (http://barnesandnoble.com) reported sales of $320 million. The *U.S. Statistical Abstract 2001* reported that individuals spend about

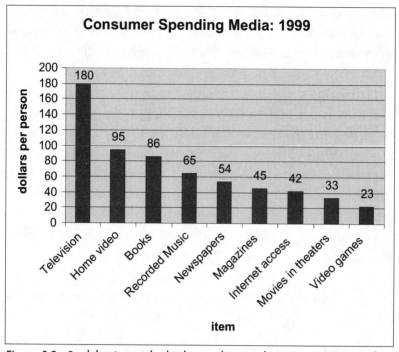

Figure 5.2   Book buying ranks third in media spending. Source: *Statistical Abstract of the United States*, 2001.

$86 each per year on books, and those dollars add up to big sales for book retailers and book publishers. Figure 5.2 shows that book buying ranks third in individual recreational spending with only television and home video outpacing it.

In the United States, wise consumers often visit their libraries to borrow the books they might otherwise purchase. In interpreting the government's figures for consumer book spending, we may wish to bear in mind that public, academic, school, and special libraries spend about $2 billion a year on books. Libraries serving populations of over 500,000 (e.g., cities about the size of Atlanta, Georgia or Cleveland, Ohio) spend an average of about $1.3 million on their adult book budget; of that amount $168,000 goes to popular fiction and another $78,000 for mysteries. Incidentally, libraries spend most of their money on current titles—less than 10 percent on replacement copies.[4] While hardly surprising, it may affect whether a copy of something less "in vogue" will be available at the library.

If Amazon.com, Barnes and Noble, Alibris, and dozens of other companies run Web sites that *sell* books, why do enterprises that distribute free e-texts such as Project Gutenberg, the text collection at the Internet Public Library, and Bartleby "Great Books Online" continue to expand and attract users? What are the philosophies, mechanics, and rules that prevail in these electronic text Web sites? How do the creators of these sites assess the value of what they offer?

Traditional Books, Electronic Texts, and Electronic Books

Let me define the terms I will use relating to books accessible through the World Wide Web. The important items under discussion are electronic texts (e-texts or etexts) and electronic books (e-books or ebooks). For most purposes, electronic texts can be equated to words written on a page of indeterminate length. They usually lack any conspicuous formatting and, therefore, could be presented in plain ASCII—simple text that any computer can understand—or formatted in hypertext markup language (HTML) to appear more Web-friendly. In other words, electronic books prepared in ASCII will look as though the simplest word processing program created them, while those prepared in HTML will immediately exhibit visual embellishments.

Electronic books are virtual representations of printed books. Although many titles can be read at the computer as "Web versions," individuals may need special software (e.g., Adobe Reader, Microsoft Reader) and sometimes special hardware (e.g., portable, book-sized or smaller devices) to use e-books. The University of Virginia's E-Book Library (http://etext.lib.virginia.edu/ebooks/ ebooklist.html) is a prime example of an electronic book archive; 1,800 titles out of its total collection are e-books readable using Microsoft Reader software for PCs, or AportisDoc software for Palm handhelds. See Chapter Eight, Software Keys to the Web Library, for information and Web sites to download free book reader software.

Portable Document Files (PDFs) are also used to present e-texts. PDF texts are flexible because they can be used independently of the hardware, software, or operating systems used to create them. For individuals using online books, PDF files are great because they can be searched easily. You can download a free version of Adobe Reader (the software needed to read PDFs) at http://www. adobe.com.

Yet another format for e-texts is called "embedded image." When you view an e-text in the embedded image format, you usually look at the representation of the text offered as an image file (i.e., a graphic file). An e-text in the embedded image format may look more like the printed page of a book to which people are accustomed. When e-book distributors scan an entire book and you experience it encountering all the original fonts and illustrations, you are enjoying an embedded image.

The providers of many electronic books and electronic texts might argue that in terms of the actual text of any given book, there is no difference between the physical book or an e-book/e-text. Others would argue that there is a tactile, palpable, and even sensual dimension to a physical book that electronic books and electronic texts can never duplicate.

Purists, bibliophiles, and scholars may contend that only definitive editions of books are worth reading. But what is the definitive edition of a book? An author starts with an idea and begins to create a text. The author revises, alters, deletes, and expands the text.

Handed over to the editor and publisher, the text may undergo more changes. Furthermore, the author may continue mentally (and physically) to rework the text. The text goes to the printer where it may again be altered. Somewhere in this process the author has lost some control over the text. So where is the definitive edition?

In *The Future of the Book*, Luca Toschi writes a fascinating account of the definitive edition of a classic of Italian literature. Alessandro Manzoni first published *The Betrothed* in 1827, but he put a great deal more effort into an edition published 13 years later.

For the 1840 edition Manzoni managed a group of designers, block cutters, a printer, and illustrator Francesco Gonin. His objective was to present a new edition of *The Betrothed* that would include hundreds of illustrations. His collaboration with Gonin was intense. Manzoni had Gonin and the printer place the illustrations at the precise points in the text that he conceived as perfect. In *The Betrothed*, writes Toschi, illustrations are not simply ornamental, but part of an "indivisible text" in which "the relationship of the alphabetic text and the illustrated elements is so close that removing the pictures means modifying a very complex structure."[5] Through Toschi's discussion we become convinced that the illustrations were conceived and mandated by the author. Any reading of *The Betrothed* without these very special graphics is invalid.

I can find one copy of *The Betrothed* on the Web. Using the Internet Public Library's Online Text catalog, I discovered that it resides at Bartleby.com, specifically at http://www.bartleby.com/21. The electronic text has no illustrations. Incidentally, that copy is an HTML text from the respected Harvard Classics.

Unfortunately none of the six different editions of *The Betrothed* (or *I Promessi Sposi*) at the library where I work are illustrated. The oldest edition was from 1907 and the newest was a 1984 Penguin Classics edition. Therefore, none of the editions conveniently available to the reader, including the free electronic version or the Penguin Classics edition available at a friendly online bookstore for $12.80, includes the important illustrations. What's a modern reader to do?

George Paul Landow, Professor of English and History at Brown University, in the same collection of essays, essentially rejects the deification of some printed editions because very few people have access to them. He writes an account of a conference presenter who offered up Ben Jonson's own copy of *Euclid*—a well-designed, well-printed, Moroccan bound work of art—and proceeded to juxtapose the craftsmanship of his antiquarian's specimen with electronic texts that seem poorly rendered by computer monitors. Professor Landow points out that the majority of readers do not have access to such a rare treasure, and that even the textbooks students use (ill-designed, fragile, and short-lived) may pale in comparison to many electronic texts.[6] In an e-mail response to me, Professor Landow added, "Most online texts are no worse than paperback editions. My argument was emphasizing the point that critics take an ideal print text to compare to an existing electronic one—hardly a fair comparison."

Online E-Text Collections: Cornerstone of Your Own Web Library

While it is true that a skilled searcher has a good chance of finding the electronic text of a book, short story, poem, or play by skillfully using relatively comprehensive finding tools such as Google (http://www.google.com), a more organized plan for developing the literary and nonfiction portion of your own Web Library should involve getting acquainted with the online text resources available on the Web. Once familiar with the history, scope, and usability of about a dozen online text libraries, you can adopt them; then you'll have the resources of some of the Web's heaviest hitters right at your fingertips (and at the desktop of your computer).

What's Available Online

Given: We want access to free, first rate books electronically. We have to consider what types of texts Web sites will probably give away. The answer is uncopyrighted texts and, in those cases where authors have given permission, a few copyrighted works. Commercial Web sites may give away some copyrighted texts as promotional incentives to readers. Some self-publishing writers might give away their electronic books to whet your appetite. Many Web sites provide free electronic texts. One of the first things the reader may notice, however, is that the vast majority of the items at these sites are older titles. This, however, does not make the electronic texts any less valuable. To understand why you won't see any John Grisham novels or Stephen King works on these sites is merely a matter of comprehending some basic copyright law and the phrase "public domain."

Another factor to consider in building your own electronic text collection is whether the site offers documents readable online (and therefore theoretically printable) or documents not only readable but also downloadable. For example, when an electronic text distributor such as the University of Virginia Electronic Text Library states, "6.4 million free ebooks were shipped since August 2000" from its Web site, it actually counts the number of books downloaded to the computers of readers who have visited its site. To date, the University of Virginia has given away $26 million in electronic books! Many sites permit downloading of electronic books and electronic texts—perfect for offline viewing. Others provide online texts and books for browsing while connected to the World Wide Web.

A Note on Copyright and the "Public Domain"

Although this is not meant to be a legal interpretation of the copyright laws of the United States, the following information summarizes the publicly accessible circulars concerning the present state of copyright from the Library of Congress's pages ("Extension of Copyright Term" explained at http://www.loc.gov/copyright/circs/circ15t.pdf, and "New Terms for Copyright Protection" is explained at http://www.loc.gov/copyright/slcirc1 5.pdf). The net effect of the laws currently in force is that any work copyrighted by an author living now, for practical purposes, will not enter the public domain in our lifetimes.

Works Published Before 1923

United States Copyright Law states that if a work was written before 1923, it is in the "public domain." Public domain means that it belongs to the people, and is not protected by copyright.

Works Published 1923 to 1963

A work published between 1923 and 1963 was copyrighted initially for 28 years and, if copyright was renewed, for an additional 47 years. This was extended an additional 20 years by the "Sonny Bono Copyright Term Extension Act" of 1998.

Works Published 1964 to 1977

The "Sonny Bono Copyright Term Extension Act" of 1998 also affected the materials published from 1965 to 1977 that are now copyrighted for an initial term of 28 years with an automatic extension of 67 years.

Works Created Since 1978

For materials created and fixed in a "tangible medium" since 1978, copyright is the life of the author plus seventy years.

Thankfully, the law did not restore copyright protection to works already in the public domain. But readers can easily see the reason their favorite contemporary authors are not represented in the electronic text archives. Many creators and volunteers at the archives are extremely concerned that copyright extension will go out of control, adversely affecting human knowledge. Despite the case made by Eric Eldred, founder of a well-known nonprofit Web site providing free online access to public domain books (Eldritch Press at http://www.eldritchpress.org), the United States Supreme Court decided on January 15, 2003, by a vote of seven to two, to uphold the right of the United States Congress to pass legislation extending the length of copyright. In an Information Today NewsBreak (http://info today.com/newsbreaks/nb030120-1.htm), law professor and library director George H. Pike of the University of Pittsburgh School of Law wrote that the court's decision was seen as a "major victory for large-scale commercial copyright holders, such as Disney and Time Warner, whose creations, like Mickey Mouse and the great movies and compositions of the 1920s and early '30s, are now protected until the year 2020 and beyond." Copyright law varies from country to country.

INSIDER'S VIEWPOINT FROM YOUR WEB LIBRARY PROFESSIONAL: GREGORY NEWBY, PROJECT GUTENBERG

Professor Gregory B. Newby of the School of Information and Library Science at the University of North Carolina at Chapel Hill is not only active in copyright research and paperless publishing, but he is also the technical guru for Project Gutenberg, the original and still largest e-text service. We discussed copyright and the public domain.

NT: As a Gutenberg researcher, could you comment on the outlook of the future of copyright restrictions relative to when books will enter the public domain? For example, are new laws being made to augment copyright in the U.S., or are they in the offing? What type of lobbying motivates changing the laws?

GN: There's not an easy answer. The future outlook is that before 2019 there will be further extension of United States copyright laws. [*This is when works published from 1923 to 1977 will first enter the public domain.*] Disney/ABC supposedly spent $20 million lobbying for the current laws, and they do not want the Mouse to enter the public domain, ever. Lobbying by U.S. citizens, librarians, and civil libertarians (as well as content providers) essentially fell on deaf ears during the debate for the 1998 copyright extension (the Sonny Bono Act, also the Digital Millennium Copyright Act).

NT: Michael Hart, founder of Project Gutenberg, said that some copyrighted works are available at Project Gutenberg. How did Gutenberg manage to include copyrighted texts?

GN: We got permission from the copyright owner. In GUTIN-DEX.ALL [*a link on the Project Gutenberg home page*], copyrighted e-texts have a "C" on the end of the line. Our e-text #3001 is a great example of this: the copyright owner gave us permission for the lyrics, and recorded the song for us. Of course, we mostly have texts, not music, but #3001 is particularly neat, being a Grammy winner and all.

NT: Can you briefly explain why information published by the United States government is automatically considered to be in the public domain?

GN: Because the United States citizenry paid for its creation. So, they should not have to pay again for rights to use it.

Free E-Text Collections and Catalogs on the World Wide Web

The World Wide Web is often perceived as a democratic and egalitarian vehicle for spreading information. The prevailing philosophy behind electronic text archives is an altruistic motivation to distribute books, not only fiction but also nonfiction, to a widespread audience. I could not list all the sites that offer e-texts, but I will discuss several prime sites and list more in an accompanying sidebar. My Web site at http://library.ccsu.edu/library/tomaiuolon/theweblibrary.htm contains links to these and many others.

Project Gutenberg

The "granddaddy of them all," as far as electronic texts is concerned, is the venerable Project Gutenberg (http://www.promo.net/pg). At least 20,000 Web sites link to the various Project Gutenberg sites/mirrors, making it a preeminent entity on the Web. Founded in 1971 by Michael Stern Hart, it is the longest enduring e-text undertaking on the Internet. Hart graduated from the College of Liberal Arts and Sciences at the University of Illinois at Urbana-Champaign in February 1973 with all available University honors, having already started Project Gutenberg while earning a degree in Human–Machine Interfacing. Beginning with one brief document—the *Declaration of Independence*—Hart envisioned the output of his online collection reaching every "connected" person in the universe.

In a December 2001 *Project Gutenberg Newsletter,* Hart wrote, "People ask me how I managed to keep working on Project Gutenberg during a long initial period of 17 years before anyone ever had any response other than that it was crazy to put Shakespeare in a computer ... the answer is that I could see every word I typed being read by 100,000,000 people." Hart began to build this collection of chiefly public domain works (works for which copyright has expired) with a goal of serving the average reader with unlimited distribution. Project Gutenberg's objective is to provide authoritative electronic text editions. Because of copyright law, you won't be able to read Al Franken's latest book in cyberspace via Project Gutenberg. Ninety-nine percent of Project Gutenberg works are in the public domain; just a few are copyrighted.

Project Gutenberg is an excellent starting point for individuals seeking to not only read electronic texts, but to understand what texts they can acquire for free and even to become involved with helping to provide them. Although funding is always a concern, Hart is equally interested in finding people who want to see their favorite books contributed to the Internet. He asks would-be volunteers to imagine what they've added by being read by 100,000,000 people. If you doubt whether people use this site, consider anecdotal evidence such as this excerpt from an early 2002 *Project Gutenberg Newsletter*:

> I'm an Italian teenager of 17 and I visited your Web site more and more times to search some books, but I can't read whole books in English!! Can you tell me where I can find Italian translations of your "telematic" books? In particular, I'd want to read *Flatland* by Edwin A. Abbott. My compliments and greetings to you all. I hope you'll write me soon.
> —T. Landi.

Besides its Web addresses at http://www.gutenberg.net and http://promo.net/pg, Project Gutenberg has many "mirror sites" (copies of the original site) throughout the world. At the sites you will find over 5,500 documents, mostly literature, but also medicine, science, nonfiction, and even music files. Aside from the recent/copyrighted titles posted with authors' permissions (e.g., Janis Ian's lyrics to and performance of the Grammy winning "Society's Child," Ed Krol's *Hitchhiker's Guide to the Internet* [1992], etc.), the collection contains the text of items in the public domain. And there's quite a selection. From Shakespeare to Somerset Maugham, D. H. Lawrence to Joseph Conrad, Emily Brontë and Virginia Woolf to Jane Austen,

United States Government publications to interviews, the list is extensive. Project Gutenberg also contains reference works such as almanacs, encyclopedias, and dictionaries.

E-texts created by Project Gutenberg use the "Plain Vanilla ASCII" format, which is the simplest, easiest-to-use format available to the majority of computer users. Although this format lacks the adornment of Web pages with graphics and multimedia familiar to many Internet users, people with even the simplest computers can take advantage of the thousands of books Hart and his volunteers offer through Gutenberg.

Finding an electronic text at Project Gutenberg is easy. The home page has search options familiar to any library catalog user: author, title words, an advanced search, help, and a browse by author or title function. The advanced search page permits searching by Library of Congress Classification (i.e., subject area). The Project Gutenberg home page is shown in Figure 5.3.

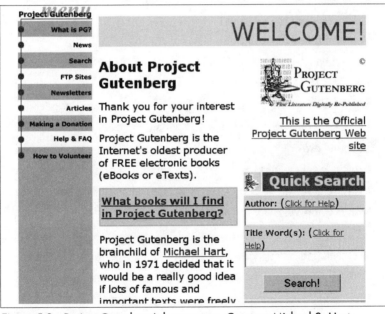

Figure 5.3   Project Gutenberg's home page. Courtesy Michael S. Hart, copyright 2003.

INSIDER'S VIEWPOINT FROM YOUR WEB LIBRARY PROFESSIONAL: MICHAEL S. HART, FOUNDER, PROJECT GUTENBERG

Michael Hart envisions the distribution of information on the World Wide Web as the Neo-Industrial Revolution. He named his project after Johannes Gutenberg, the 15th-century developer of movable type. Hart considers Johannes Gutenberg the forerunner of the Industrial Revolution because the concept of movable type presaged the concept of interchangeable parts that spawned mass production at Eli Whitney's (the inventor of the cotton gin) New Haven, Connecticut, musket factory in 1798. Dean Roland Holmes, the director of Hart's degree program at the University of Illinois, said that Hart "is not walled in by a blind acceptance of the 'normal ways' of doing things." Project Gutenberg, the oldest e-text distributor on the Internet, demonstrates this attribute.

Hart is the son of a Shakespearean scholar and a mathematician. In 1971, Hart's associates, operators of the Xerox Sigma V Mainframe at the Materials Research Lab at the University of Illinois, granted him access and opened a computer account providing $100 million in computer time. I talked with Professor Hart, and these were his remarks concerning the philosophy of offering books free to users of the Internet and the World Wide Web.

NT: Michael, your creation and sustained efforts in running Project Gutenberg over the past three decades have made thousands of texts available to anyone connected to the Internet. What motivates your altruism?

MH: It's not really altruism. I want the world this way. There are a few volunteers at Gutenberg that think like me, and there are many who are simply altruistic. But when I was a kid, I couldn't find information. A kid walks into a library and the librarian looks right over them—doesn't even see them. I'm doing this as much for my younger self and other kids as for anyone else.

NT: You've been involved with distributing texts on the Internet since 1971. How did you feel when you made your first posting of the *Declaration of Independence* on the networks, and why did you choose that document?

MH: Well it was just one of those serendipitous things. It was a hot Fourth of July night. I stopped at the grocery store to pick up some snacks before heading over to the lab. In the grocery bag there was a copy of the *Declaration of Independence* on faux parchment. My friend Fred made me an account on the mainframe. I had a vision of the entire Internet—the way it was going to be for the next 25 years. I realized it was never going to disappear. I had seen radios go from the size of small refrigerators to transistors. So when I started to tell my friend Fred that I imagined computers could be as small as laptops, he thought I was crazy.

It was a classic moment. Right place. Right time. Right friends. Right background. I wanted to do something that would be around for a hundred years. Something that would be around forever. So I typed up the *Declaration of Independence*. Once I put the *Declaration* on the computer, it became a virus. Nobody can stomp it out. Once you digitize something important or something of interest and put it on the Net, you can't calculate the number of copies that will be made. Anything that can be put into a computer can be reproduced an unlimited number of times.

NT: Is that what you meant when you coined the term "Replicator Technology"?

MH: Right. For the next 17 years I was just waiting for the world to realize I'd knocked it over. You've heard of "cow-tipping"? The cow had been tipped over but it took 17 years for it to wake up and say "moo."

NT: In 1999 Project Gutenberg averaged putting 36 e-texts on the Web per year. How many e-texts are now available at Gutenberg, and given the increase in the texts you've made available over the years, can readers expect the collection to grow more rapidly in the future, or do you see contributions leveling off?

MH: Ten years ago there were 18 e-texts on the Internet, and I put them there. The Internet Public Library now has 20,000. Without any changes in the current rate that texts are being added, there will be 18 or 19 million in 10 more years. Drives keep driving, the Net keeps netting. Right now Gutenberg has 6,300 e-texts, and it only took us 11 months to add the last 1,000. We're hoping to do 100 a month until the end of 2003. Then I'm hoping to change the schedule to 200 a month in 2004. We hope to do everything in the public domain: pictures, sculptures, and music.

NT: What makes putting books online for free so revolutionary?

MH: It's a paradigm shift. It's the power of one person, alone in their basement, being able to type in their favorite books and give it to millions or billions of people. It just wasn't even remotely possible before; not even the Gideons can say they have given away a billion Bibles in the past year. We have always lived in civilizations based on the fact that there is never enough for everyone, but now everyone can have as many copies of tens of thousands of books as they could want.

If everyone has diamonds, nobody wants diamonds. Some people become upset when I make their favorite books available on Gutenberg. I used to get lots of nastygrams from professors who thought their favorite books should *not* be "for the masses." They say that I'm casting their pearls before swine. The prevailing philosophy is "limited distribution." The whole thing I've been doing for years is unlimited distribution. The main problem is that the developed world is still so totally into limited distribution that most of the people there can't see the potential of our new ability to make unlimited copies of any book available at virtually no cost, at virtually instantaneous download speed, to anyone around the world or in range of our satellite transmissions—and they never go out of print. Those at the top of the food chain would just as soon flood the marketplace with so much "information overload" that no one can search for what they might want—even if it were there.

Under "ye olde" system, versus under the new system, if you've got a library of 1,000 books, you're pretty cool. A personal library of 1,000 books in a room is impressive. Now you can fit 10,000 books on a DVD, and nobody knows how cool you are because your collection looks small. Harvard has 14 million books. Put them on DVDs and the collection is a foot high. Under the "olde" system you can look cool just by *displaying* the books. Under the new system you actually have to *read* them to look cool. It's a big difference. In "ye olde" way you are defining yourself by what you own as property; in the new way you are investing in yourself by reading, not simply in possessing the physical books.

Without the electronic text of the Human Genome Project, Project Gutenberg occupies 2.5 gigabytes of space. The default storage on a computer these days is 40 gigabytes. So Project Gutenberg wouldn't even take one-sixteenth of your hard drive. One sixteenth of your hard drive could hold 100,000 copies of *Alice in Wonderland.* Considering the cost of disk space, that comes to about a quarter of a cent per copy. That's what I was thinking back in 1971.

NT: What powers Project Gutenberg? Help readers imagine what goes into making e-texts available for them to read or download at their computers.

MH: It's too much for me. I'll change my job description and focus on public relations and fund-raising soon. Project Gutenberg has lots of volunteers, but I haven't met many of them. A couple of them have teased me. They say, "It takes five of us to do what you do alone." Half the volunteers type their contributions, and half of them scan them in. The scanners do more, but they have less fun. Say it takes 200 days to type in a book, and then everyone in the world can have a copy. That's Replicator Technology.

NT: In an article in the *Chronicle of Higher Education* 10 years ago, scholars claimed that your efforts weren't really reaching the 99 percent of the population you intended to reach—the average person—because most computers and the Internet were only in use in academia. Given the state of home and business computer usage, would you agree that those comments need to be revisited?

MH: They just have to eat their words. Nobody thought about the future; they thought the way it was would be the way it would always be. One volunteer working one hour a night can type three pages. As soon as it goes online, everyone has a copy! That's a big paradigm shift, and it angers some people. The status quo can't stand that this is coming from nowhere. We're working on a shoestring, but we have leverage.

NT: Could people browsing the Web just as easily use search engines to locate e-texts instead of going directly to Project Gutenberg?

MH: Most of the search engines have been corrupted by people who pay big money to be at the top of the results. You have to be good with searches to get past that stuff much of the time. I took a graduate school course in searching and it *still* frustrates me a lot of the time. I know it frustrates readers, too. I get a note nearly every week that says someone has been looking for e-texts for years and finally found our work. Makes you wonder—before the pay-for-placement corruption Project Gutenberg was at the top of all the search engines. You can still find our books but you need to do advanced searches.

NT: If you compare the monetary value of the Gutenberg collection with the cost of buying the same titles at a bookstore—assuming that they were all actually available—how much is the collection worth?

> **MH:** Well, I put the cost at $1.00 per title. But you could esti-
> mate more, up to $3.00 or $4.00 a title. If I gave you a diskette
> with 100 Gutenberg books on it, and then you went out and
> bought the same books, it's going to come to several hundred
> dollars. That's serious money. You wouldn't throw that money
> away. About a half trillion copies of books in the Project
> Gutenberg collection have been downloaded. At $1.00 each,
> the collection is very valuable.

Hart often uses the number 100,000,000 readers in assessing the value of Project Gutenberg, observing that 100,000,000 is just one to two percent of the world's population. In late 2001 a Project Gutenberg newsletter stated: "With 4,161 eTexts online as of December 4th, it now takes an average of 100,000,000 readers gaining a nominal value of $2.40 from each book, for Project Gutenberg to have given away $1,000,000,000,000 [*one trillion dollars*] in books."

Other Extraordinary E-Text/E-Book Resources

The Internet Public Library Book Collection
http://www.ipl.org/reading/books

Linked to by more than 32,000 other Web sites, the popular Internet Public Library (IPL) is another bookmark for readers desiring access to free electronic texts and books. What began as a collection of links to the works of William Shakespeare, the IPL now serves as a clearinghouse and organizer for 20,000 electronic texts on the World Wide Web. Whereas Project Gutenberg creates and distributes e-texts, the IPL Online Text Collection scoops up all the electronic texts from other distributors, catalogs it for searching by various means, including Dewey Decimal subject classification, and provides links to electronic documents throughout the Internet.

None of the online texts found through the IPL actually originate there. The texts emanate from different sites and exist in different formats. For example, you may click on the IPL's entry for Mary Shelley's *Frankenstein* and go to the University of Virginia's Electronic Text Library, but clicking on an entry for H. G. Wells's *Invisible Man* will transport you to Bartleby.com. For some Sherlock Holmes, you may find your browser has pointed to the Adelaide University in Australia at http://www.library.adelaide. edu.au/etext, where you can download the book to your own machine for offline reading. (Actually, there are at least three copies of *Frankenstein* offered by the IPL. One resides at Bibliomania, where it can be read online. Another is readable or downloadable from Project Gutenberg. A third comes from the "Litrix Reading Rook" at http://www.litrix.com.)

David S. Carter, founding director of the Internet Public Library and a faculty member at the University of Michigan School of Information and Library Studies, located and cataloged many of the 20,000 online texts (representing six years of work). Carter has stated that, for inclusion in the IPL Online Texts collection, the electronic document must not appear as a traditional nononline text. An intermittent criticism of electronic texts and, to a lesser extent, electronic books is that they lack the quality control of printed editions. Detractors mention that omissions, typographical errors, and proofreading mistakes are problems inherent in materials available, especially for free, over the World Wide Web. In *The Internet Public Library Handbook* Carter offered a comment that addressed these criticisms, "As an example, when I add a text from Project Gutenberg (PG) into the IPL's Online Text collection, I assume that the text I'm adding is a complete version, without any deliberate or accidental errors or omissions. I can assume this, because I know something about the process that texts go through to be accepted into PG (which includes copyediting, proofreading, and revision), and because PG has gained a reputation over the years for providing texts at a certain level of quality."[7]

There are many sites to explore for electronic texts, but the Internet Public Library should be one of your first stops.

The Online Books Page, University of Pennsylvania
http://onlinebooks.library.upenn.edu

John Mark Ockerbloom, a digital library planner and researcher at the University of Pennsylvania, is the founder and editor of this prominent collection. The Online Books Page offers 15,000 freely accessible electronic texts. This site represents Ockerbloom's extraordinary effort to locate and link to free material from all over the Web. Works included may be in e-book reader formats, PDF, page images embedded into Web pages, HTML, and ASCII. Ockerbloom prefers the last two formats because they are most readable on any computer connected to the Web. Many of the texts are illustrated.

Ockerbloom also includes links to dozens of other e-text collections and special archives at http://onlinebooks.library.upenn.edu/archives.html. Other highlights include pages featuring Banned Books and Award Winners.

Individuals may search for authors or titles. Browsing by author or by title is also available. Ockerbloom has listed most of the collection by Library of Congress Subject Classification headings and provides a list of subject category links to books within subject areas.

Only a subset of the Online Books Page's collection actually originates at Ockerbloom's institution, specifically, a digitized rare book collection at http://www.library.upenn.edu/etext called the "Schoenberg Center for Electronic Text and Image" and "A Celebration of Women Writers" at http://digital.library.upenn.edu/women edited by John's wife Mary Mark Ockerbloom. To discover the others, he uses a combination of strategies including rechecking active online book sites (though many e-mail him notices of recent acquisitions), performing his own Web searches on "in demand" subjects, and old-fashioned human interaction.

INSIDER'S VIEWPOINT FROM YOUR WEB LIBRARY PROFESSIONAL: JOHN MARK OCKERBLOOM, FOUNDER, THE ONLINE BOOKS PAGE

I wondered how Mr. Ockerbloom perceived the future of electronic access to free books. Among other things, he observed that electronic texts are practical because they are usually searchable and good to have on hand when you don't have a physical copy of the book around. Here are his comments.

JMO: Right now, I have no shortage of books to list. They're going online, and I'm hearing about them, faster than I can list them. So right now I have to set priorities to a certain extent, based in part on what sorts of materials seem to be in demand or are on topics that seem to merit fuller coverage.

I hope that before long you'll be able to find nearly any public-domain book, and a fair number of (legitimately online) copyrighted books, online for free reading. While I still prefer reading book-length texts in print form (as most people seem to, judging from the low sales of most commercial e-books), the online form is extremely useful for consultation, searching, quick browsing, and certain kinds of interesting enhancements. It's also an easy way to look at a book when print copies are inconvenient or impossible to obtain. (Some copyright holders have also found that having their books online has increased the sales of the print version; while I don't expect that this will always hold for all

> books, there do appear to be some interesting cases where it does.)
>
> The collection of online books listed on my page represents the efforts of a growing community of interested readers, authors, publishers, and educational projects over a number of years. It's a bit like the "Stone Soup" story—we might not have started with much, but we have managed to help build the beginnings of an increasingly useful free library over time, through the help of lots of people who care about sharing knowledge and literature with the world.

Bartleby.com

http://www.bartleby.com

Like all substantive Web sites Bartleby.com (named for the intractable copyist in Herman Melville's classic short story *Bartleby the Scrivener*) attracts a large number of users (15 million unique visitors in 2000) and can boast over 18,000 links pointing into it. Headquartered in New York City, Bartleby.com began as a personal research experiment by Steven H. van Leeuwen in January 1993. Van Leeuwen had worked as a science editor for publishing giant Elsevier. This resource calls itself "an innovative Internet publisher providing students, educators and the intellectually curious with unlimited access to books and information on the Web, free of charge." Bartleby runs banner advertisements, has an Amazon.com link on its home page, and maintains its own Bartleby Bookstore (which amounts ultimately to a search of Amazon.com). But its eclectic collection offers the full text of the Harvard Classics (a 70-volume set of fiction and nonfiction); Henry Gray's authoritative *Anatomy of the Human Body*, which includes 1,247 excellent illustrations; as well as a couple of hundred other books, including some copyrighted titles—all without charge. Unlike the books at some other sites, the documents at Bartleby cannot be downloaded and stored offline for later consultation.

As with Project Gutenberg, the Internet Public Library, and the Online Books Page at the University of Pennsylvania, the Bartleby Web site does not require registration and does not require the user to submit personal information in order to use its collection. Although the actual number of electronic texts is not as extensive as the resources previously discussed, the special attention to the format of the text and the value-added features that accompany many works are noteworthy. If the individual chooses to see works by a specific author, the site brings up a biographical sketch with links to further information about the author or author's works within Bartleby's own collection (e.g., the *Columbia Encyclopedia* or the *American Heritage Dictionary of the English Language*). Most works in the collection include a bibliographic record with more hyperlinks for exploration. As Figure 5.4 shows, Bartleby seeks to not only offer the texts, but adds value to each entry.

Bartleby also provides multiple access points to the collection. Begin with a simple search of the entire Bartleby site or focus the search by selecting a specific collection or author. Besides searching, the site is navigable by author, subject, or title index. While the collection is perhaps not so impressive when juxtaposed to even smaller public libraries, you can use it 24 hours a day.

University of Virginia Electronic Texts
http://etext.lib.virginia.edu

Here's the scenario: The "Quick Facts" page states that the site has 30,000 daily visitor sessions. Those visitors access 130,000 documents per day (compare this with the statistic that 5,930 people visit the University of Virginia's physical libraries on any given day). Five thousand of the electronic texts and electronic books are

Figure 5.4 Bartleby.com: From internal links to pronunciation to biographies, this free Web site strives to add value. Courtesy Steven van Leeuwen, copyright 2003.

publicly accessible without charge; many others are accessible only to the VIVA—the Virtual Library of Virginia. These 5,000 electronic texts include about 1,800 electronic books for the Microsoft Reader and Palm handheld devices; according to the site, 3,181,129 free e-books "shipped" from this resource to over 100 countries during its first year in operation. Sixteen thousand sites on the Web link into the University of Virginia's Electronic Texts.

If you want to read or collect e-books, go directly to the "E-Book Library" page at http://etext.lib.virginia.edu/ebooks/ebooklist. html and browse authors or subjects. You may also search the full text of the e-book collection.

Several e-book collections at the site deserve closer inspection including "Illustrated Classics," "Civil War," "Women Writers," and

"Young Readers." Within these collections, you can download e-book versions, including illustrations, for the Microsoft Reader or Palm devices of such titles as *The Red Badge of Courage*, *Little Women*, *Leaves of Grass*, and a colorful *Alice's Adventure's in Wonderland* for free. This is a great site if you want to download books and set up your own library on your computer or handheld device.

University of California Press eScholarship Editions
http://escholarship.cdlib.org/ucpress

Four hundred titles, most of them out of print, but not necessarily in the public domain, are available free of charge to the public.

Blackmask Online
http://www.blackmask.com

In contrast to some electronic book collections, Blackmask Online is not underwritten by donations or grants, nor does it receive free hosting on a university's server. Its creator, David Moynihan, is solely responsible for the collection and its maintenance. I include the site here as an example of an independent e-text/e-book site that one person manages and offers to Internet users. It exemplifies the eclectic sites for free e-text readers that one can find on the Web. It presently offers nearly 10,000 e-books.

INSIDER'S VIEWPOINT FROM YOUR WEB LIBRARY PROFESSIONAL: DAVID MOYNIHAN, CREATOR, BLACKMASK ONLINE

Although originally built to distribute pulp fiction, horror stories, and mysteries, David Moynihan began to see that his e-texts of classic literature by Sir Arthur Conan Doyle, the

Brontë sisters, and Joseph Conrad were among the most popular e-texts being read on his site. In an e-mail, David explained how he gauges what readers are looking for, and what spurs interest in a specific writer's work.

DM: The number one book on my site is *The Importance of Being Earnest* by Oscar Wilde—I think. My site's way of tracking books is a little strange, where I only have a clean way of recording the "main" simple HTML link (which is generally the least popular format). I get something like 500,000 visits a month; it's a bit hard to tell how many of those are unique.

I know from some "not-very-reliable" site-tracking software that roughly 15 percent of my traffic comes from Google. I also have noticed that certain events—like, say, *New York Times* Op-Ed page editor Gail Collins discussing Bellamy's *Looking Backward From 2000 to 1887* in one of her pieces will move interest in that book [*Bellamy's book is available free at the Blackmask site.*]— similar effects for Nostradamus in the wake of 9/11, etc. [*Blackmask also offers* The Writings of Nostradamus *free.*]

I wanted David to cover two other issues. First, I had read that the Blackmask site sometimes took public domain material from other sites and then added value such as converting it into e-book reader formats. Since many items in his collection are not only immediately readable, but also downloadable for e-book readers such as the Microsoft Reader, how did he manage to convert the free e-texts he had access to? And how does a free e-text provider like the Blackmask Online site sustain itself? Some of his responses become somewhat technical, but they demonstrate what individuals are doing to make electronic texts accessible. For individuals looking for free electronic books, the point is that David Moynihan and other entrepreneurs are thinking of ways to offer more, and putting their expertise to work for themselves and other readers.

DM: The first thing is to convert the texts into HTML—I've done this a lot, so I have macros that do most of the work for me. I also use a freeware program called "HTMLDOC" that, in addition to creating PDFs, generates a table of contents for the books.

After I have the HTML, I write a little batch file that'll do the Rocket eBook, Acrobat, iSilo (Palm thing), and zipped versions. Then—I'm not done (I've only recently started this)—I do some searches and replaces (with BK Replace'em and something called XCHANGECL) that convert a copy of the HTML version into an XML OEBPS document (table of contents, package file, source file, cover page). (Sigh.) That document is then converted into MS-Reader and MobiPocket (for Franklin eBookman). I'm still getting the hang of the XML thing (after 6,000 MobiPocket conversions), so I haven't been able to add quite as many books a day as I would normally.

I used to carry banner ads, etc., but every time I hit a milestone they'd raise the bar (awhile ago, if you had 250,000 page views a month, you could sign up for engage.com and be guaranteed $1,250 each month; Engage stopped doing that right when I hit that number last year; then when I hit doubleclick.com turf—1 million page views—it killed its "run of network advertising," and near as I could tell weren't letting publishers sign up), so instead I sell CD-ROMs. You know, I already have the content, move a couple dozen disks a month off my site (more if it's around Christmas), eight or 10 each week on eBay, adds up, and the margins on CD-ROMs rival Microsoft's. Longer term, I do plan on selling original e-books.

Sites for Electronic Books

In addition to the numerous Web sites that provide electronic texts, some sites also offer free electronic books for one or more of the many free book readers that individuals may download and use on their computers or handheld devices. Locating free electronic books for these readers isn't as easy as finding electronic texts, but these Web sites helped me build a cozy and attractive electronic book library with my Web connection and a browser:

Adobe E-Book Store
http://bookstore.glassbook.com/store/default.asp

Amazon.com eBooks Free Downloads
http://www.amazon.com/exec/obidos/tg/browse/-/556968/104-7464443-1538330

Blackmask Online
http://www.blackmask.com

EBookMall Free eBooks
http://www.ebookmall.com/free-downloads.htm

University of Virginia's E-Book Library [1,800 titles]
http://etext.lib.virginia.edu/ebooks/ebooklist.html

Note: See Chapter Eight, Software Keys to the Web Library, for information and Web sites where you may obtain the free software you need to read these electronic books.

In Practice

Free e-texts exist on the Web not purely for academic reasons; creators do not produce sites simply "because it's there." My son Ben was reading a respectable edition of Daniel Defoe's *Robinson*

Crusoe (illustrated by N. C. Wyeth). I had read the book years ago, but I wanted to reread it so we could discuss it. Using the sites I have already described, it did not take long to find an e-book version of the classic. (Several HTML versions and ASCII versions were also available, but I wanted a version I could download to my computer's Microsoft Reader.) I found the electronic book at the "University of Virginia's E-Book Library for the Microsoft Reader and Palm." Every day I read a couple of chapters and was ready to talk about the adventures the next time I saw Ben.

Similarly, Eric Lease Morgan's Alex Catalogue at http://www.infomotions.com/alex provided several free short stories that I downloaded to my PalmPilot, and could enjoy them on my small handheld in all sorts of situations that might have precluded carrying a book. Contrary to a popular comic strip's humorous depiction of a handheld's text display (i.e., first page displayed "Call me Ish" and the second page displayed "mael"), my PDA is easy to read, not at all the nuisance one might imagine.

Other Web Resources with Links to E-Text/E-Book Sites

These resources will provide more options, so if you want to explore and experiment, here are several worthwhile starting points.

Google's Directory of Electronic Text Archives
http://directory.google.com/alpha/Top/Arts/Literature/Electronic_Text_Archives

This list presents many noteworthy sites not covered in my annotated list (e.g., "Online Literature Library," "Daoist Scriptures," and "Bookvalley"). Not all the sites on this list are free, though many are.

Refdesk.com: Electronic Texts on the Internet
http://www.refdesk.com/factelec.html

Over 80 links; many sites are free but some, unfortunately, are subscription services. Includes links to Jane Austen's letters, Walt Whitman, and many other e-text sites.

SearcheBooks
http://www.searchebooks.com

A no-frills search engine for locating electronic texts and books on the World Wide Web. Just enter your keyword(s) and click "Search." My search on the author Boethius retrieved 80 hits with links to online text (not all writings by Boethius). A search on the string of words "rime of the ancient mariner coleridge" resulted in 12 links. Finally, just for fun, I tried a search for "Buffalo Bill" and located some free online dime novels including *Adventures of Buffalo Bill from Boyhood to Manhood* by the turn-of-the-twentieth-century writer Colonel Prentiss Ingraham.

A Cost-Benefit Analysis of Online Electronic Texts and Books

Earlier in this article, we discovered that a considerable amount of money changes hands when individuals leave a bookstore with their purchase or click "Add to Cart" at their favorite online book retailer. (Of course, people could wait until their local libraries buy, process, and make a book available.) But a person interested in transforming their home computer into a worldclass book collection will find no dearth of free titles waiting to be read or saved on disk. The old adage "You get what you pay for," especially in regard to classic books, may not apply in the connected world. Let's compare the cost and availability of some titles in the traditional print format with their availability in the virtual format.

Great Books of the Western World: Case Study

Offered by Encyclopedia Britannica, *Great Books of the Western World* is a collection of the world's exemplary literature. First published in 1952 and now in its second edition (1990), the anthology is a handy yardstick for determining what works our civilization might find indispensable. According to the "Britannica Store" at Britannica.com (the publishers of the *Encyclopedia Britannica*): "From the ancient classics to the masterpieces of the 20th century, the *Great Books* are all the introduction you'll ever need to the ideas, stories and discoveries that have shaped modern civilization."[8] There we have it. Britannica, an authoritative publisher, has packaged an outstanding selection of novels, short stories, plays, poetry, and other documents on history, politics, economics, ethics, mathematics, the natural sciences, philosophy, and religion. The long list of authors covered includes Homer, Virgil, Shakespeare, Molière, Jonathan Swift, Rene Descartes, Francis Bacon, Voltaire, Herman Melville, Mark Twain, Jane Austen, Francis Bacon, Benedictus Espinoza, Sir Issac Newton, Willa Cather, James Joyce, George Eliot, Michael Faraday, Niels Bohr, and Albert Einstein.

Didn't I see writings by some of these authors in my visits to free electronic text collections? Absolutely. In fact, when I checked the contents of the *Great Books* with my favorite electronic books sites, I found 61 percent of the titles available for reading and 47 percent available for reading and downloading. Bear in mind that the "Syntopican: An Index to the Great Ideas" (an alphabetical list of ideas with accompanying essays) is a proprietary work from the *Great Books*. But writers with works in the public domain have authored the majority of the collection. Some of the works contained in the *Great Books* show up several times on the Web for free.

The estimated retail cost of the *Great Books* is $995 and it occupies six feet of shelf space. If a reader browses and/or downloads the portion of the works also contained in the *Great Books* available free on the Web, storage only involves a few megabytes of a computer's hard drive.

Some of the literary highlights available on the Web that appear in the *Great Books* include a readable/downloadable version of Cervantes's *Don Quixote* (found at three different sites). Dante's *Divine Comedy* seems very popular; located in readable/downloadable formats at 12 different sites. Ten sites offer a readable/downloadable *Paradise Lost* by John Milton. *Moby Dick* is readable/downloadable at multiple sites, as is *Gulliver's Travels* and Voltaire's wonderfully cheeky *Candide*. You can read or download Henrik Ibsen's *Master Builder* (or his *A Doll's House* or *Hedda Gabler*, if you prefer). Jane Austen's *Emma* appears on two different sites.

Similarly, 75 percent of the titles Martin Seymour-Smith chose to comment on in his *100 Most Influential Books Ever Written* (Secaucus: Citadel Press, 1998) are readily available. I quickly located entries for them at the Internet Public Library's Online Texts link. At the back of an old Penguin Classics edition of a George Eliot novel appears a list of similar titles that Penguin offers for around $6 each; every one of them appears online for free.

No Brainer: Download a Book for $2.69 or Get It for Free

Consider the costs of downloading electronic books for the free e-book readers I previously mentioned. There are plenty of electronic books available at online booksellers. Quick searches at Amazon.com will find numerous "classic" electronic book titles. And they are inexpensive. If you purchase one for immediate download, you can keep it on your computer's hard drive, Zip drive, or CD-R/W drive, and read it or consult it whenever you wish. You can often download the books to other platforms and read them on handheld devices as well.

Once the book is downloaded, the display on your computer's e-book reader (e.g., Microsoft Reader, Adobe Reader) or portable device will look attractive. You can search the book and make notes in the text. Your collection of handsome e-book classics could begin with Thomas Hardy's *Tess of the d'Urbervilles* for $2.69 at Amazon.com; add Mark Twain's *Innocents Abroad* for another $4.45 or E. M. Forster's *A Room with a View* at $4.45, also from Amazon. Flaubert's *Madame Bovary* costs $5.35 for downloading to the Microsoft Reader or $2.99 for the Adobe Reader. Shopping at the electronic book retailers has the added advantage that you can purchase, download, collect, and read contemporary titles as well. I couldn't find the Harry Potter novels for download, but I did buy Stephen King's *Black House* (for $19.95).

As to classics, if you look for Dickens at the Amazon ebook store, you will find 57 electronic editions. Thomas Hardy's e-book catalog numbers 27. But there are only three e-book titles listed for Dostoyevsky and only one by Tom Wolfe. Over at the Barnes and Noble Web site, you can buy Anne Rice's *Blood and Gold* for $21.50 or an older title such as Robin Moore's *French Connection* for $5.95. Older books generally cost less. Edith Wharton's *House of Mirth* downloads for $3.95. So you still spend some coin for the electronic books (and some significant coin at that for the newer titles).

Compare the cost of these books with the titles available from free e-book distributors such as the University of Virginia's Electronic Text Library, Web-Books, and Blackmask Online. There you will also find, at no charge, attractively formatted editions for e-book readers of Hardy, Wharton, Dickens, and Dostoyevsky et al. Of course, unless more contemporary authors grant permission to provide copyrighted works, you still won't find their works for free. But then again, you don't find too many contemporary authors' works for download, even when you are willing to pay and, when you do, the books are not really a bargain.

Add to Cart or Save to Disk?

On a shopping spree at the corner bookstore, mall, or favorite retail book Web site, you may gravitate to attractively packaged editions of the newest books and many classic titles as well. Perhaps you will discover a real antiquarian treasure in an out-of-the-way used bookstore or have your book autographed at a bookshop-sponsored author signing. These are components of the sensual dimension of books. You may spend a few dollars or a few hundred, but you will add some nice volumes to your personal library.

Trouble in paradise: A book you want is out of print; the library never replaced its copy. Perhaps you have special ordered it from a bookstore. Weeks have gone by, but no one has called you. Or maybe you love books but no longer have the space to house more. Or what if you want to take some reading material with you on a trip, but have exceeded your luggage quota? The University of Virginia's Electronic Text Center states that it shipped 6.8 books per minute for 21 months.

As a quick experiment, I arbitrarily searched for various titles at online bookstores and then compared their availability and cost with where you can find them free on the Web. Note that some titles you locate in bookstores cannot be readily found for free on the Web, but conversely, a few you can find for free on the Web are not readily available from online bookstores. Of the 15 titles I sought, 13 were available as free electronic books, whereas the same 13 titles in print would have cost up to $159.79. Two books were still in copyright and may never be available for free electronic distribution. Note that Winston Churchill's *A Far Country* was completely unavailable at the retail Web sites but was available free on the Web. Table 5.1 shows the availability options for the books I was looking for—most were available as free e-books on the Web.

Table 5.1   Availability options for an eclectic selection of books—most of them can be found free on the Web

Title	Author	Commercial Availability	Price	On Web Free?	Where is it on the Web?
A Far Country	Winston Churchill	unavailable	n/a	Yes	Project Gutenberg: http://digital.library.upenn.edu/webbin/gutbook/lookup?num=3739
I Know Why the Caged Bird Sings	Maya Angelou	ships in 24 hours	16.00	No (in copyright)	
Leaves of Grass	Walt Whitman	ships in 2–3 days	6.98	Yes	http://jefferson.village.Virginia.EDU/whitman/works/leaves/1855/sgml/1855.sgm
Nostromo	Joseph Conrad	ships in 2–3 days	8.00	Yes	http://digital.library.upenn.edu/webbin/gutbook/lookup?num=2021
Oblomov	Ivan Goncharov	ships in 24 hours	11.65	Yes	Eldritch Press: http://www.eldritchpress.org:8080/iag/ob1-1.htm
Our National Parks	John Muir	download	8.95	Yes	http://etext.lib.virginia.edu/ebooks/Mist.html
Rabbit Run	John Updike	ships in 2–3 days	11.20	No (in copyright)	
Scarlet Letter	Nathaniel Hawthorne	ships in 24 hours	5.95	Yes	Litrix Reading Room: http://www.litrix.com/scarletr/scarl001.htm
Sense and Sensibility	Jane Austen	ships in 24 hours	6.95	Yes	http://www.blackmask.com/cgi-bin/links55/cgi/search.cgi?query=sense+and+sensibility&catid=
Simpson's Contemporary Quotations	James B. Simpson	ships in 2 days	24.50	Yes	Bartleby.com: http://bartleby.com/63/
Tenant of Wildfell Hall	Anne Brontë	ships in 24 hours	9.95	Yes	Bibliomania: http://www.bibliomania.com/0/0/9/15/frameset.html
The Time Machine	H. G. Wells	ships in 2–3 days	15.36	Yes	http://www.bygosh.com/timemachine/TOC.htm
Ulysses	James Joyce	ships in 24 hours	13.60	Yes	http://www.bibliomania.com/0/0/29/61/frameset.html
Who's Not Working and Why (1999)	Frederic L. Pryor	ships in 2–3 days	37.95	Yes	Electric Press Reading Room: http://readingroom.elpress.com/readittoc.jsp?Book=0521651522
A Young Girl's Diary	Sigmund Freud	download	9.95	Yes	University of Virginia Ebooks: http://etext.lib.virginia.edu/ebooks/Flist.html

Interesting Developments in Electronic Books

"Not all those that wander are lost."[9] Hypertext and the World Wide Web have created fascinating opportunities for augmenting, embellishing, and otherwise adding value to electronic texts. With respect to most of the public domain e-text providers covered in this chapter, many of these possibilities have yet to be implemented. Though the fine sites discussed offer a broad choice of electronic texts and offer them in ways that will accommodate many uses, circumstances, and situations (e.g., downloadable, readable on alternative devices via different platforms, and, in the vast majority of cases, without any fee whatsoever), several features of other electronic text Web sites bear note. Everyone knows that clicking a link on one Web page will transport the Web surfer to related Web pages or Web sites. Researchers, scholars, and other enterprising individuals are interested in discovering ways to extend the experience of reading through hypertext. The hypertext Web sites that these people have created differ from electronic texts available in hypertext markup language (HTML), such as those that reside at Bartleby.com. The Web sites in this section have some interesting, special properties.

One benefit to linking to other documents on the Web is that you can quickly view material related to the page you are reading. This advantage affords writers and researchers numerous possibilities. For example, an author can experiment in creating several plots to a work of fiction and, depending on the link the reader chooses, reveal different outcomes. Take it a step further by imagining how the fabric of a work of fiction may become woven, rewoven, embroidered, and rewoven again as a function of the links embedded in the story and the links embedded within the text of the links' targets. Reading such literature requires a certain degree of energy because these works transcend the usual expectations of fiction. Authors Vladimir Nabokov and Julio Cortázar experimented with this idea in *Pale Fire* (in which the reader is challenged to connect a poem with a narrative) and *Rayuela* (literally "hopscotch" in English), respectively. Flann O'Brien's *At Swim-Two-Birds*, published in 1939, is also diversely arranged. O'Brien wrote in the book's first paragraph: "One beginning and one ending for a book was a thing I did not agree with." Consequently, the *Dictionary of Literary Biography* states, "So the novel has three beginnings and three endings, and the different strands run alongside each other for much of the book. But there is also a curious involution, or confusion of realms."[10] Other authors writing before the advent of the World Wide Web undoubtedly could be mentioned. But how much more simply could hypertext accomplish such author objectives?

One organization, called The Electronic Literature Organization (ELO) at http://www.eliterature.org, aims to facilitate and promote the writing, publishing, and reading of literature in electronic media. Also, publishers dedicated entirely to hypertext works, such as Eastgate Systems "Serious Hypertext" at http://www.eastgate.com, have developed a presence acknowledged by publications such as *Salon*, the *New York Times*, *Los Angeles Times*, and *London Guardian*. Perhaps in the future the variety of hypertext embellishment presented at the Web sites described here will become *de rigueur*. This will certainly be the case if the proponents and creators of these initiatives have their way. Here is the short list of hypertext entities that may serve as examples:

The Victorian Web
http://www.victorianweb.org

Funded by the University Scholars Program at the National University of Singapore, this hypertext project is the Web translation of Brown University's Context 61, a resource for courses in Victorian literature, according to Professor George P. Landow of Brown University. These materials ultimately derive from Context 32, the Intermedia Web that provided contextual information for

English 32, "Survey of English literature from 1700 to the Present" at Brown University.

The operative word in Landow's description is "context." Explore the Victorian Web and you will discover that the links appended to various sections of text help the reader place the information in context. One example occurs right on the home page called "Victorian Web Books." From here the reader may choose from various links such as Barbara P. Gates's (Alumni Distinguished Professor of English and Women's Studies, University of Delaware) *Victorian Suicide: Mad Crimes and Sad Histories*, a Web version of the full text of her book of the same title published in 1988 by Princeton University Press. Clicking the link *Victorian Suicide: Mad Crimes and Sad Histories* displays the contents (including illustrations); the links take the reader to chapters with more links including explanatory, augmented material not included in the original print version. In checking out Gates's chapter called "Oscar Wilde's Picture of Dorian Gray," I clicked a link about the magazine *Punch* and was transported to a list, with additional comprehensive links to material about *Punch* written by several other Victorian scholars. The Victorian Web is an excellent example of not only electronic books, but also how hypertext can add value to them.

The Republic Pemberly
http://www.pemberley.com/janeinfo/janeinfo.html

A haven for fans of Jane Austen's novels and the films adapted from them, the Republic Pemberly offers electronic texts of Austen's works annotated and illustrated through hypertext links. The hypertext for *Pride and Prejudice*, for example, is complete with links to Victorian C. E. Brock's illustrations of the novel, as well as other images of representative clothing from the early 1800s. Links to the genealogical tables of the characters are provided, as well as links to brief illustrations of the uses of the themes of "pride" and "prejudice."

Edward Picot's Independent Fiction
http://www.edwardpicot.com/index.html

This site is a solid example of nonlinear fiction capitalizing on the potential of hypertext. Picot, a graduate of Cambridge University with a major in English Literature, also holds a doctorate from the University of Kent in the same subject. He allows visitors to his site to access excerpts of two novels, several short stories, and samples from his compact disc hypertext collection of poetry and short stories titled *Heronsbrook*.

Regarding his work Picot says, "To make the stories truly non-linear, I have randomized the order in which the sections are displayed. Each time you visit one of the stories, its contents list will appear in a different sequence. One of the interesting consequences of this is that there are so many possible sequences in which the stories could be read that I haven't tried them all myself." Concerning the material on *Heronsbrook*, Dr. Picot states, "There are four other nonlinear stories on the CD, which have all been written according to the same basic principles: the narrative has been split into sections, and the sections have been randomized. This simple structural device seems to open up a very large range of new possibilities, and I like to think that each story explores some slightly different ground. There are also some poems on the compact disc, and one linear short story, written before any of the others, which seems (to me) to belong to the same cycle, and to anticipate my ventures into nonlinear fiction."

Conclusion

A considerable body of literature exists for free on the World Wide Web. The original electronic text sites such as Project Gutenberg even serve as databanks for newer undertakings such as Blackmask Online, the site that can convert ASCII into PDF files and formats for electronic book readers. The individuals responsible for these sites, adept as they are in the technical issues of loading and reformatting the texts for computer users, see no end to the number of books they can offer, barring the one nagging issue of copyright extension in the United States. By visiting the sites mentioned in this article, you can download or read online as many books as you want.

Are people really interested in reading books at their computers? Depending on the circumstances, it may be preferable to have a nice copy of a classic book on one's nightstand. The trouble with that is some people don't read very much before being lulled to sleep. The strengths of your own digital library, stocked by electronic text archives and electronic book distributors, are that you can quickly get the all the books you want without having to consider physical storage questions. Remember that you saved six feet of shelving in the *Great Books* example, and, if you had used Bartleby.com to read the contents of the Harvard Classics, you saved five additional feet. You can search the texts easily, in many cases "mark them up," and all for free. If any of these features appeal to you, perhaps you should take advantage of the resources discussed here.

The early proponents of electronic books may have been mistaken. Many publishers and authors attending "Epub University" at BookExpoAmerica 2002 in New York City agreed that general acceptance of e-books is just a matter of time—and they also agreed that many things must be done to make e-books more acceptable. Yet many compelling reasons for using them already exist. Bob Tedeschi made a case for e-books in a May 5, 2002 *New York Times* article "Lighter loads for traveling readers" when he favorably discussed e-book reader hardware. For example, he asked, would a traveler prefer to lug a suitcase containing a book weighing three pounds and occupying 64 cubic inches or an entire library on one small handheld device?

As you visit these sites, you may find some newer copyrighted works available, also. Though this will not occur frequently, free electronic texts exist in most subject areas and genres.

As every Web user has found, sites come and go. The Internet Public Library has been up and running for over seven years. Project Gutenberg has been around since 1971. Bartleby.com went online nine years ago. I maintain a Web site at http://library.ccsu.edu/library/tomaiuolon/theweblibrary.htm that links to all the resources I have discussed. Nevertheless, if a Web site you've "bookmarked" becomes unavailable, remember you can always find others. Go to a reputable, robust, and durable Web search engine, Google (http://www.google. com) for example, and perform a quick search using keywords such as "electronic text archives" or "free online books."

But the Web is not simply textual. A great deal of what we want to use from the Web appeals to our senses of sight, and one of the things the Web is sometimes best at is presenting images. Chapter Six, which follows, provides information on finding images, saving them, and using them.

SAMPLE ANNUAL SAVINGS

Bartleby.com	=	$1,000
Blackmask Online	=	$10,000
Britannica's *Great Books*	=	$500
Project Gutenburg	=	$10,000
University of Virginia electronic text library	=	$14,350
UPenn's online books	=	$15,000

Supplementary Information: E-Book/E-Text Web Site Annotated List

Adelaide University Library E-Books
http://www.library.adelaide.edu.au/etext

From "down under" come 147 electronic texts for reading online or downloading for offline reading. Many titles from the Britannica's Great Books collection appear here.

Alex Catalogue of Electronic Texts
http://www.infomotions.com/alex

Created by North Carolina State University librarian Eric Lease Morgan, Alex is an ongoing project providing free access to selected American literature, English literature, and Western philosophy. Alex even lets you download the entire library of 700 titles by visiting http://www.infomotions.com/alex/downloads. Books may be downloaded in several formats including PDF, PalmPilot, Rocket eBook, or Newton Paperback. Morgan is responsible for many digital library innovations, so it's no surprise that he has a streamlined search mechanism, but has also added (for most titles) the ability to analyze the occurrence of words with an online concordance. For example, you can search the text of George Eliot's *Silas Marner* for the word "daughter," and analyze the context and meanings of its use throughout the book.

Bibliomania
http://www.bibliomania.com

With approximately 9,000 links pointing to it, Bibliomania is a prolific resource. Besides its free texts, it offers reference works and study guides. Although texts may not be reproduced, the fiction, nonfiction, and study guides are worth the trip for an online read. Some options require registration (free), but they're worth it.

BookRags

http://www.bookrags.com

Has 1,500 electronic books, but a small, growing collection of book notes for students offered for free.

CARRIE

http://www.ukans.edu/carrie

CARRIE, named in honor of Carrie Watson, the first professional librarian at the University of Kansas and the true founder of its library system and collections, by creator Lynn H. Nelson, professor emeritus at that institution, is not an e-text collection in itself (like Project Gutenberg, the University of Virginia project, or Blackmask Online). Instead it points to other collections where electronic texts reside. The upside of this is that it lists texts from some sites that would be difficult to identify; the downside is that some of the links are dead or have moved.

Pointing mostly to history, literature, and philosophical writings, CARRIE lists not only works in English, but a respectable body of texts in Latin, Italian, Japanese, Spanish, Greek, Portuguese, Dutch, Scandinavian, French, and Esperanto. Texts ultimately emanate from Virginia Commonwealth University, Rutgers University, Georgetown University, the University of Colorado, and many others.

The EServer (formerly "The English Server")

http://eserver.org

Begun in 1990 on a Macintosh Plus by the English Department at Carnegie Mellon University, the EServer has grown into a research project with 42 major collections covering the arts and humanities. Although the EServer's primary objective is to facilitate collaborative research, it welcomes use by the general public and attracts a million visits each week. Readers interested in fiction, poetry, and drama will discover extensive collections of classic and contemporary works.

Humanities Text Initiative
http://www.hti.umich.edu

The University of Michigan's Digital Library Production Service oversees this Web site, which has provided online access to full-text resources since 1994. Some of the site is restricted to use by affiliated faculty, staff, and students. The numerous works you can search include the *Koran*, the *King James Bible*, and E. M. Forster's *A Room with a View*.

Making of America Books
http://www.hti.umich.edu/m/moagrp

If you've got an American history school assignment or want to view primary source documents in American history, click to the priceless collection of 8,500 volumes at the University of Michigan's Making of America Web site. Comprising scanned images from primary source materials (books and journals), the collection has been read by optical character recognition (OCR) software to facilitate searching. The search mechanism includes searches within pages or within entire works and supports Boolean or proximity searching.

Renascence Editions
http://darkwing.uoregon.edu/~rbear/ren.htm

Fourteen hundred sites, including scholarly and peer-reviewed literary journals, point toward Richard Bear's effort to provide readable Web editions of early modern English works and translations. The 154 works residing at Renascence Editions were originally written between 1477 and 1799.

Web-Books.Com

http://www.web-books.com

Another site with a bare minimum of explanatory remarks, Web-Books carries 1,000 fiction and nonfiction classics. Many of the books require the user to download the "Web-book reader" (a simple step, but requiring free registration). The result is nicely formatted e-texts on your computer's screen (and on your hard drive).

Zeroland's Live Text Databases, Online Literature,

E-Libraries (New Zealand)

http://www.zeroland.co.nz/literature-etexts.html

Includes links to the standards Gutenberg and the University of Virginia, but adds some interesting sites such as "Logos" (a multilingual electronic text library).

Endnotes

1. Darren K. Carlson. "Poll Shows Continuing Strong American Reading Habits." October 4, 1999. Princeton, NJ: Gallup News Service. http://www.gallup.com/poll/releases/pr991004b.asp/December 3, 2001.

2. "1,595 T.V. Hours." *Quill.* January/February 1998. Volume 4. Issue 1. p. 7.

3. United States Census Bureau. "Media Usage and Consumer Spending: 1995 to 2004. Table No. 1125." *Statistical Abstract of the United States: 2001.* p. 704.

4. Barbara Hoffert. "Book Report: What Public Libraries Buy and How Much They Spend." *Library Journal.* February 15, 1998. Volume 123. Issue 3. p. 106.

5. Luca Toschi. "Hypertext and Authorship" in *The Future of the Book.* Geoffrey Nunberg, ed., Berkeley: University of California Press, 1996.

6. George P. Landow. "Twenty Minutes into the Future" in *The Future of the Book.* Geoffrey Nunberg, ed., Berkeley: University of California Press, 1996.

7. Joseph Janes, David Carter, Annette Lagace, David McLennen, Sara Ryan, and Schelle Simcox. *The Internet Public Library Handbook.* New York: Neal-Schuman. 1999. p. 63.

8. Britannica Store. Great Books of the Western World. http://store. britannica.com/escalate/store/DetailPage?pls=britannica&bc= britannica&clist=04c41400140c45&pc=GBWW&cc=columnpromo_ topseller/January 2, 2002.

9. J. R. R. Tolkien. *The Fellowship of the Rings.* Boston: Houghton Mifflin, 1965, p. 182.

10. *Dictionary of Literary Biography, Volume 231: British Novelists Since 1960*, Fourth Series. Edited by Merritt Moseley. University of North Carolina at Asheville. The Gale Group. 2000. pp. 207–220.

Chapter Six

When Image Is Everything

The Web's major attraction, apart from the information shared by authors, scientists, government agencies, businesses et al., lies in its rich offerings in terms of sounds and graphics. At one time, looking at the original (or even a copy) of the Mona Lisa or a Matthew Brady daguerreotype necessitated a trip to a museum, bookstore, or library. The Web has made it possible to conveniently start with almost any search engine, type in a few keywords, and pull a facsimile out of the haystack of more than a billion Web pages.

Uses of Images from the Web

The most basic graphics you can find on the Web include icons, buttons, wallpapers, and backgrounds. Surfers and Webmasters find these items and download them to enhance Web pages, reports, desktops, and presentations. As we move along the continuum, we discover a broad range of spectacular and ubiquitous drawings and photographs; for example, a strikingly crisp image of the "four-toed litter skink" can be captured by grade school students for a paper on rainforests, while an image of Bill Clinton from his grand jury testimony might make its way into a professor's law and ethics presentation in a freshman philosophy seminar. The range of Web images encompasses everything from animations of spinning compact discs to the infamous crowd-control-gone-bad scene captured in John Filo's Pulitzer Prize winning photo taken at Kent State University on May 4, 1971. It can include an .avi (audio/visual interleaved format) of the frequently discussed Zapruder film of J.F.K. in Dallas or one of Monet's Rouen Cathedrals. It's all there for study, research, or enjoyment. Many images may be used for personal as well as commercial purposes; many are free, but many are not. Depending on what the individual needs, finding images on the Web can save considerable time and, in some cases, a significant amount of money.

Search Engines

Searchers once found image files by combining a keyword with a file type. For example, a search using the general search engine Overture (http://www.overture.com) for "polar bear and .jpg" would probably yield links to sites where an image of a bear resides in the Joint Photographic Experts Group (JPG) format. A keyword search for "deer and .jpg" using Microsoft Network's MSN Search (http://search.msn.com) leads to similar results. But image search engines make it unnecessary for the searcher to perform these operations. They offer their own image searching options. These options merely require the user to type in a keyword and the matching of the keyword to sites with images occurs transparently.

How do image search engines work? To summarize Paula Berinstein's work from 1998:[1]

- The engines sometimes look for graphics files. By "detecting the presence of the "IMG SRC" (image source) tag or the GIF or JPG file extension, the engine verifies the presence of an image.

- By matching a keyword search with the file name, the engine can roughly determine the content of the file. This might happen by simply reading the filename, for example dragon.gif, or by looking in the path for the file name, for example /public/dragons/flying.gif.

- The engine may look for Web sites whose titles indicate the presence of pictures on a certain subject. This strategy works occasionally, but relies on the existence of titles that describe content well, which is next to impossible. For example, "New Mexico Photo Gallery" tells you that you'll find images of New Mexico at the site, but it doesn't indicate whether you'll find pictures of pueblos, geologic formations native to the state, or the Santa Fe opera house.

- The engines might employ human intervention to seek out and catalog images. This method results in the most accurate system, but its labor-intensiveness limits the number of images processed.

- Berinstein also wrote that an ideal image search engine would display results by showing a thumbnail, the URL of the image, the URL of the site where it resides, and some information about the image. Most image search utilities now do this.

Searchers focusing on Web images should also consider Daniel Amor's proposition, which expands on Berinstein: "Image search engines are using the information that accompanies a picture, such as the file name (e.g., "href='cat.jpg'"), the alternative text (e.g., "alt='this is a picture of a cat'"), or the text next to the image ("the following image displays a cat"). As long as your search is very generic, the existing image search engines work very well. The problem arises as soon as you search for more specific images. 'A red cat with a little ball' could be a very common request. Although it is highly unlikely that the filename will contain all this information, the alt-text may contain it and the accompanying text as well, but don't be too sure."[2]

Numerous image search tools exist. Some tools comb the Web for images, archiving thumbnails of what they find. Others partner with commercial providers and offer pictures at various pricing levels. Some services maintain their own collections that searchers may employ in various ways depending on the terms and conditions of use. If you're interested in finding an image, you should have no trouble if you first bookmark some of the following sites.

AltaVista Image Search

http://www.altavista.com/image/default

AltaVista does not share statistics on the number of images it archives, but the retrieval from some eclectic searches (e.g., Baron von Richtofen, reclining Buddha, Sydney Harbor Bridge) indicated extensive coverage. Besides a thumbnail, AltaVista image listings state the image size and format and link to the hosting URL. AltaVista allows users to search by color/black and white, photos, graphics, and buttons and banners. Retrieval may come from personal or commercial Web sites or AltaVista partners such as Corbis or *Rolling Stone Magazine.*

Ditto

http://www.ditto.com

Ditto.com delivers relevant thumbnail images and links to the relevant sites that host the original images. If the user chooses to see a "detail view," Ditto shows filename, file size, a link to the original URL, and keywords indexing the image. The user can click on keywords for related images. Ditto says, "… we have compiled the largest searchable index of visual content on the internet via proprietary processes."

Excite

http://www.excite.com

Select the "Photos" radio button. Excite has two image indexes. "Member Photos" are user-posted images. "News Photos" originate at Reuters and the Associated Press. Results of image searches may come from professional collections (free to download as wallpaper or send as an e-card, and usually accompanied by an offer to buy the photo as a poster), free from a member of the "Webshots" community, or a news photo that usually links to a news story but cannot be freely downloaded.

FAST Multimedia Search

http://multimedia.alltheweb.com

FAST offers an easy image search; clicking on thumbnails provides larger image and details including file size, file format, image size, and a link to the hosting URL. Most thumbnails carry the statement: "This image is copyrighted to its rightful owner(s)." Use the Fast Advanced Multimedia search (http://multimedia.alltheweb.com/cgi-bin/advsearch) to narrow to file type, color/black and white, etc.

Google Image Search

http://www.google.com/advanced_image_search

Google boasts 250 million images. After you retrieve some material, just click the thumbnail to see a larger version of the image, as well as the Web page on which the image is located. From the advanced image search page (the address recommended above), you can narrow results down by image size (icon-sized, small, medium, large, very large, wallpaper-sized, filetype (.jpg or .gif), and color (black and white, grayscale, or full color).

Like most search utilities, Google admonishes users of the copyright protection attached to many images. Google further states, "Although you can locate and access the images through our service, we cannot grant you any rights to use them for any purpose other than viewing them on the Web."

HotBot
http://www.hotbot.com

Click "Advanced Search," type your keywords, and then scroll down the screen until you reach "Page Content." Besides image searching, you'll notice many other helpful content searches.

Ithaki Image and Photo Metasearch
http://www.ithaki.net/images

Ithaki is a metasearch tool that covers some of the Internet's well-known engines (e.g., Fast, Google, Hotbot, Altavista) and directories (e.g., Yahoo!, Dmoz, Looksmart). Advanced search options support Boolean, phrase, or natural language searching.

IXQUICK
http://www.ixquick.com

By selecting the "pictures" radio button, the searcher uses IXQUICK to metasearch AltaVista, Art.com, FAST, and Yahoo!.

Lycos Multimedia Search
http://multimedia.lycos.com

To limit to still images, select the "pictures" radio button. Search by keyword. A copyright notice appears with most photos, as does a "license professionally" link.

Picsearch
http://www.picsearch.com

This search engine for pictures and images has many features that make it unique. It has a relevancy unrivaled on the Web due to its patent-pending indexing algorithms. Picsearch states that it has a "family friendliness" that "allows children to surf in safety as all offensive material is filtered out by our advanced filtering systems." Use the Advanced Search to limit to animations, specify size of the images retrieved, and limit to color or black and white.

Yahoo! Picture Gallery

http://gallery.yahoo.com

The Yahoo! Picture Gallery is searchable or browsable by category. According to Yahoo!: "From the Dalai Lama to baby llamas, we have an incredible variety of pictures that you can use in a number of ways." Having a primary partnership with Corbis, most of what you retrieve from Yahoo! will come from Corbis and, therefore, be usable in limited ways according to the terms and conditions.

Big Search Engine Index to Images

http://www.search-engine-index.co.uk/Images_Search

If you want to save some time, you may wish to bookmark the Big Search Engine Index's link to 19 engines. Besides most of the aforementioned services, Big's links include Photo Disc (http://www.photodisc.com) and the Animation Factory (http://www.animationfactory.com).

What's Wrong with This Picture?

Copyright is the biggest problem when using images from the Web. If more than a billion Web pages exist, we conservatively estimate that 20 percent of them contain an image. Therefore, over 200 million pictures exist out there on the Web for people to study, learn from, enjoy, and, if they fancy the notion, download. Most of the richest sites I have visited stridently declare that the images residing on their pages are not to be copied. For example, the Smithsonian Institution Office of Imaging, Printing, and Photographic Services (http://photos.si.edu) boasts 15,000 images ranging from the "Star Spangled Banner" to pandas Tian Tian's and Mei Xiang's arrival at the National Zoo. None of them, however, can be reproduced without written permission from the Smithsonian.

The devil's advocates will postulate that the Web is a public and democratic forum, that if people post their documents, sounds, files, and graphics, those people should accept the inevitability of user sharing. While such a position may seem logical and practical, it isn't necessarily legal. At one end of the spectrum you have people who want to drive others to their sites, and at the other end you may actually have people who feel extremely proprietary about their site content. Furthermore, you may find that some people who want site traffic (such as professional artists and photographers) are particularly possessive about what you may do with their material. You might counter this by claiming "It's possible to password protect your site, write code into your pages that will avert crawlers from indexing it, place watermarks on your work, or otherwise protect it." But some authors and Webmasters retort, "That shouldn't be necessary and we shouldn't have to do it." This seems more like obstinacy than reluctance.

Retailers (e.g., the physical ones we visit at the mall) have their wares in full view, yet you usually exit through portals that sense anti-theft tags. Libraries try to hang onto their collections by buying millions of strips of "Tattletape" each year. While taking copyright seriously, some creators/owners of copyrighted material believe that the vastness of the Web makes it difficult to apprehend perpetrators. Bob Kern, content/acquisitions manager for "IN Jersey—New Jersey's Home on the Internet" (http://www.injersey.com) conceded that there has been unauthorized use of IN Jersey's content but added, "We obviously cannot go around checking all the Internet sites in the world to see what is being used and what isn't, so there is little you can do to keep people from pulling stuff off."[3]

Perhaps image purveyors would be wise to more zealously protect their property. And some do. In 1997, Playboy Enterprises won a case of copyright infringement when defendant Webbworld was found to have "willfully infringed" by posting 62 Playboy copyrighted photos on its site. (Webbworld was penalized $5,000 per infringement for a total of $310,000.)[4] Playboy signed an agreement in the same year with Digimarc to place digital watermarks on images that could potentially be downloaded from Playboy's Web site. The technology is available to individual photographers for approximately $100 and runs between $800 and $5,000 for corporate users. Digimarc not only sells its ImageBridge and ImageBridge Pro watermarking tools to safeguard images, but also offers the MarcSpider Image Tracker—software that can find watermarked images on the Web. Blue Spike is another company that offers digital watermarking. See http://www.digimarc.com/products.htm or http://www.bluespike.com/art.html to read more about the technology that protects images from indiscriminate hijackers.

People copy many of the images they like and send them to friends, use them on their own sites, post them on Usenet, add them to their presentations, and illustrate reports. But a strict interpretation of United States copyright law would probably make most of this illegal. Without the permission of the originator of the work, proper payment, or licensing, this cornucopia of eye candy turns into a monumental tease. People who download and reuse copyrighted images from the Web without permission do so at their own risk. Although the ease with which this can be done is alluring, the mere novelty of the technology doesn't always make it right.

In 1998 the *Boston Herald* paid Bill Swersey, a freelance photographer, $3,500 in an out-of-court settlement that revolved around its use of a photograph that Swersey took that originally appeared at http://www.discovery.com.[5] A more notable case, *Kelly v. Arriba Soft*, involves photographer Les Kelly and Ditto.com (formerly the Arriba Soft Corporation). Ditto (which searches the Web and indexes its images) successfully defended itself in December 1999 when plaintiff Kelly sued claiming that, without permission, the firm takes thumbnails of images and places them in a searchable database. Kelly claimed the firm supports itself by making money on the work of others by creating the database of copyrighted work (in many cases). Mr. Kelly brought the search engine to United

States District Court where Judge Gary Taylor decided that Ditto's operations constituted "fair use."[6] The plaintiff further claimed that the firm breached the Digital Millennium Copyright Act (DMCA) by initially taking his images out of context and then eliminating the original copyright information on Ditto's thumbnail.[7] On appeal in February 2002, the United States Federal Court of Appeals for the Ninth District decided to affirm the display of "thumbnail" low resolution images by search engines but also found, in favor of Kelly, that the display of framed, full-sized images was not "fair use."[8] That decision meant that search engines could not display full-sized images out of the context of the originating Web site.

The case does not end there. The debate has resulted in the articulation of several compelling and opposing viewpoints. On one hand, we have Les Kelly and similarly minded entities (e.g., The American Society of Media Photographers, The Author's Guild, The North American Nature Photographers Association, et al.). On the other hand, the voices of Sorceron (Ditto.com's owner) along with the Electronic Frontier Foundation and others declare that decisions limiting the ability to freely link or display images threatens to jeopardize the backbone of the World Wide Web—namely "linking." The latest news is that the Ninth Circuit Court of Appeals revised its February 2002 opinion on July 7, 2003. While it still holds that Ditto's display of low resolution thumbnails is "fair use," it deleted the part of the decision that addressed full-sized images, again floating the question that framing images without acknowledgment may be fair use (see "Current Developments: Copyright" in *Computer and Internet Lawyer*, September 2003, Volume 20, issue 9, page 25).

There are two Web sites that offer differing viewpoints on the linking to and displaying of images and fair use: Netcopyright.law (http://www.netcopyrightlaw.com) clearly states Les Kelly's perspective, while the opposing side can be viewed in the Electronic Frontier Foundation's Amicus Brief at http://www.eff.org/IP/Linking/Kelly_v_Arriba_Soft/20020227_eff_amicus_brief.html.

Copyright Refresher for Image Acquisition

Creators of images have cause to be concerned if someone:

1. Copies/reproduces the image without permission.
2. Creates a new image derived from the original work (for example, by distorting it).
3. Sells or gives away the image.
4. Displays the image in public.

The standard defense in a case of copyright infringement invokes the "doctrine of fair use." Fair use allows the reproduction of an image, notwithstanding the creator's rights, for purposes such as criticism, satire, news reporting, teaching, and research. In determining fair use, the purpose of the copying (e.g., was it for profit?) and the effect the copying may have on the market for the original image would be considered (e.g., copying might be more permissible if it is unlikely to cause economic harm to the creator of the image).

In the United States, copyright was augmented when the Digital Millennium Copyright Act (DMCA) was signed into law by President Clinton on October 28, 1998. The DMCA addresses a number of important copyright issues, and Titles I and II are the most salient concerning would-be image acquirers of copyrighted material. Title I covers circumventing technological measures used by copyright owners to protect their work; it also addresses tampering with copyright management information (such as a copyright notice). Title II creates limitations on the liability of online service providers for copyright infringement when engaging in certain types of activities such as system caching. (Remember Les Kelly, previously noted in *Kelly v. Arriba Soft*, claims that in taking his image out of context and eliminating his copyright management information, Ditto.com is guilty of copyright infringement.) A summary of the DMCA appears at http://www.loc.gov/copyright/legislation/dmca.pdf.

I have noticed that most search engines that specialize in finding images, including Ditto, AltaVista, and Google, post either an overall disclaimer or a notice with each image warning searchers that images may be copyrighted and advising them to obtain permission before using a retrieved image. For example, at http://www.picsearch.com/menu.cgi?item=Copyright%20Info, Picsearch posts a rather inclusive statement that covers itself while helping searchers and copyright holders:

> Many of the images on the World Wide Web are protected by copyright. Although Picsearch locates and displays links to these images, Picsearch does not hold, grant or imply permissions or licenses to use these images for any purpose. If you would like to use any images linked to from Picsearch you must contact the Webmaster or copyright holder in order to obtain the appropriate permissions to do so. Picsearch downloads the original pictures only to create thumbnail images. Afterwards the original pictures are removed. Thus, users can only access the thumbnails when searching for a specific picture. The thumbnails are accompanied by references to the original page it was indexed from. This enables the users to visit the original page and obtain the appropriate permissions to use the picture. The crawling technology employed by Picsearch follows the robots exclusion standard and the robots meta tag. If you do not wish Picsearch to index your pictures please add 'psbot' to your robots.txt file in accordance with the Robot Exclusion Standard. If you do not have

access to the robots.txt file, Picsearch also obeys the robots meta tag.

Here is some other language regarding "image grabbing" that I have encountered on Web sites. Notice that while some pages are strict and warn users to refrain from taking images, others permit copying.

From "Rigby's World of Egypt"
http://www.powerup.com.au/~ancient

"I receive requests every week from around the world for permission to use photographs and/or text on personal, educational and commercial Web sites. This defeats my original purpose in having devoted considerable personal resources to create an appealing, educational site containing original content with images not found elsewhere on the Internet. Therefore, I do not grant permission for use of the Web site material on Web sites, CD-ROMs or any other form of reproduction. However, I have no objections to links being made to Rigby's World Of Egypt—preferably to the homepage."

From "Sunda Images," a travel photography Web site
http://www.geocities.com/TheTropics/Harbor/5983/
homeimages.html

"Use of images: Permission for use of images will generally be given upon notification of publication or webpage where used. All images are subject to copyright unless permission has been granted."

From "Images of American Political History"
http://teachpol.tcnj.edu/amer_pol_hist/_use.htm

"The intent of this collection is to support the teaching of American political history by providing quick access to uncopyrighted images for inclusion in teaching materials. All images are strongly believed to be in the public domain. They were obtained from non-copyrighted U.S. government holdings and publications and from published works with clearly expired copyrights. Thus there are absolutely no restrictions on their use."

(An image from this uncopyrighted collection appears in Figure 6.1.)

From "University of Pennsylvania Professor Ali Ali-Dinar's K-12 Electronic Guide for African Resources on the Internet"
http://www.sas.upenn.edu/African_Studies/K-12/AFR_GIDE.html

"These materials are available for use by students, teachers, librarians, the business community, and the general public." (See Figure 6.2.)

From "Les Kelly's California's Gold Rush Country"
http://www.goldrush1849.com/about.html

"All images and text copyrighted 1997 by Leslie A. Kelly/Les Kelly Publications. Terms of use: All content on this website, including all the text, graphics, photographs, data, and images are the property of Leslie A. Kelly. Any use of such content without the express written permission of the owner, including but not limited to, reproduction, modification, distribution, transmission, republication, storage or display is strictly prohibited under federal law."

From "Paris Pages' Musee de Louvre"
http://www.paris.org/Musees/Louvre

"Up to 5 documents or images from the Paris Pages may be used in whole, or in part, provided the use is strictly personal, not for commercial or financial gain, attribution and a link is made to the Paris Pages, together with the words 'used with permission' nearby

Figure 6.1   President Herbert Hoover, Henry Ford, Thomas Edison, and
Harvey Firestone at Edison's 82nd birthday. Ft. Myers, Florida,
February 11, 1929. A public domain image, according to the
Web site that posted it.

Figure 6.2   King Tut's "Golden Mask" from an educational site where the
author stated anyone could use his images.

... you send The Paris Pages a message indicating your usage of material, and your URL."

INSIDER'S VIEWPOINT FROM YOUR WEB LIBRARY PROFESSIONAL: SIMON KIRWAN, PROFESSIONAL TRAVEL PHOTOGRAPHER, THE-LIGHTBOX.COM

The Artist's Perspective

Simon Kirwan is a professional photographer. His Web site, called The Lightbox (http://www.the-lightbox.com), specializes in displaying travel photographs from hundreds of exotic destinations. Kirwan consented to answering several questions that may edify the viewpoint of the site author for the image seeker. Incidentally, Kirwan's photograph of the "Himal Chuli, Manaslu & Peak 29, Nepal Himalaya" appears in Figure 6.3. The fact that Mr. Kirwan allowed me to reproduce his copyrighted work here is a testimony to what may be accomplished when the consumer can interact with a generous image professional.

NT: Could you explain what motivates you, as an artist and photographer, to mount a Web site and what you would hope site visitors might use it for?

SK: Originally, the Web site was a personal project, although it has always offered images for commercial usage. As the profile of the site has risen, traffic has increased, enquiries have become more frequent, and more of my time and energy has been spent marketing myself and the site as a picture library, I have come to take it more seriously as a commercial entity. I now hope that although many visitors are simply casual surfers interested in travel, and travel photography, there will be enquiries from professional agencies looking to purchase stock travel images, or commission original photography.

NT: Do you allow site visitors to make copies of the images?

SK: I allow personal, noncommercial use of images, but otherwise request payment, although this is not strictly enforceable as I do not watermark the images or otherwise prevent their use. The low resolution of the images is deliberately intended to stop commercial piracy.

NT: To provide readers with a sense of the value of the images at your site, how much do you charge for commercial use?

SK: Prices are variable, depending on usage—for print reproduction I normally charge £100 UK Sterling, £50 for Web usage. I have files available for immediate dispatch of most images; higher resolution images are available if necessary—higher scanning charge then applies.

NT: Could you provide a perspective regarding the work an artist/photographer needs to do and your stance concerning copying when using a Web browser?

SK: I do try to protect the copyright of my images; I have allowed various Web sites free usage provided they always attach a credit and link back to The Lightbox, and I also provide some free wallpaper images, but otherwise I expect to be paid for commercial usage of my work. The Web is a great democratic medium for allowing anybody to become a publisher; this also allows for the potential for original material to be pirated. What steps the artist takes to protect him or herself depends on their attitude toward the usage of the work in question. I have been fairly relaxed up to now, as the free usage of some content has definitely raised the profile of the site, and led to sometimes dramatic increases in traffic, and while this is not an end in itself, traffic equals exposure, equals business—in theory. So I accept that there may be low levels of image theft in return for the possibility of increased exposure to a wider market.

Figure 6.3   Himal Chuli, Manaslu & Peak 29, Nepal Himalaya. Courtesy of Simon Kirwan, http://www.the-lightbox.com, copyright 2003. Permission to publish requested by the author and generously granted by the photographer.

Permit Me, S'il Vous Plaît

Although gaining permission to use images at sites where they are apparently copyrighted yields varying degrees of success, the potential graphic user is obligated to do so. The key to using the image you want legitimately lies in either your diligence in obtaining permission or your good fortune in locating images at sites granting permission in advance. The caveat in the latter case, however, is you must be confident the site creator is really the copyright holder and hasn't pirated the images himself. While preparing this chapter I attempted to secure permission from several Web sites.

Newseum (http://www.newseum.org/cybernewseum) offers an exhibit ironically entitled "Capture the Moment: Pulitzer Prize Winning Photographs." I was skeptical, but I contacted Newseum's marketing and communications department and asked for permission to capture one image and include it in this chapter. Indira Williams, an associate in the graphic resources, research, and news history department, responded that if I was writing an article about the exhibit, I could use the images. If I were going to take the image out of context, I would need to get permission from the copyright holders. Because this chapter is not specifically about the exhibit, using the image would have been inappropriate.

While searching I located an image of the Leaning Tower in Pisa, Italy. The image (shown in Figure 6.4) is copyrighted by Professor Michael D. Calia, a professional photographer and the Associate Director of the Ed McMahon Mass Communications Center at Quinnipiac University. Although I was delighted when Prof. Calia e-mailed the following positive response after I requested to use the image, I noted that his consent possibly did not cover using his image in this book. (Note the text that I have italicized.)

Dear Mr. Tomaiuolo:

Thank you for your inquiry. I would be happy to grant you permission to use one of my photographs, provided you adhere to the following restrictions:

You agree that I am licensing to you one photograph, "Leaning Tower of Pisa/Italy-Sept. 2000," for a one-time use only and for illustrative purposes; that you will provide the following credit: "Photo by Michael Calia" on the page immediately below the image; *that you will not sell the photograph, nor transfer the license to any other person or entity; and that you will not edit or alter the photograph in any way.*

Best wishes for a successful project.

Michael D. Calia
Associate Director, Ed McMahon Mass Communications Center and Assistant Professor of Communications (adjunct)
Quinnipiac University Hamden Connecticut 06518

Figure 6.4   The Leaning Tower, Pisa, Italy. Photo by Michael Calia, copyright 2003. Permission to publish requested by the author and granted by the photographer.

While this type of image could be employed by a student, researcher, or general computer-user in a research paper, presentation, or online gallery, I found that, for my proposed use, I needed to follow up with Professor Calia. I was more specific in my second request, and the photographer graciously extended his consent to cover publication in this book. His original photo of the Leaning Tower appears in Figure 6.4. You must, however, take considerable care before reusing another person's images. I was glad I clarified my point with the photographer.

Types of Image Files

To effectively use the images you find, you need to become familiar with some of the file types that images come in. There are a number of image file formats used today for various purposes. Some are designed to reproduce ultra-high-quality, 24-bit color images suitable for printing. Others are designed to result in the smallest file size possible for transmission over the Internet. Some are used for video applications, such as animation and video editing, while others depend on particular platforms (such as Microsoft Windows or Apple Macintosh) or devices (Truevision's Targa video capture and display cards). Most images on Web sites are saved in one of two of the most popular formats: JPEG and GIF.

BMP

BMP, which stands for bitmap, is a standard file format primarily used by the Microsoft Windows operating system. The format can handle millions of colors, and so has very large file sizes; this explains why you won't encounter too many on the Web where less is more. Webmasters also prefer platform-independent formats such as JPEG rather than BMP files, which usually run on Windows.

GIF

GIF is an acronym for Graphics Interchange Format. The old CompuServe online service developed the format to allow the quick electronic transfer of highly compressed raster graphic files. Well-matched to the capabilities of most computers, two versions exist: GIF87 and GIF89. The differences are minor, however, and any program that can read a GIF file can read either variety. GIF reduces file size partly by limiting the palette of colors it can reproduce, and so, though adequate for viewing on computer monitors, is not suited to other uses that may require full 24-bit, high-resolution files.

JPEG

The Joint Photographic Experts Group lent its name to the standard it developed for handling digitized photographs. Its objective was to find a method of data encoding and compression to significantly reduce the size of image files while maintaining an acceptable level of quality. JPEG compression technology can reduce the size of image files saved in other file formats such as TIFF, so it is both a file format and a technology used to enhance the features of other formats. JPEG supports 24 bits of color data, which allows it to reproduce millions of colors.

The platform independence of JPEG images, combined with their small size and acceptable quality, make them common on the Internet. JPEGs are most often used to preserve image quality in photographs and images that have subtle variations in color. Because it has a "lossy" compression method, resaving and recompressing JPEG files will eventually degrade the image. (Lossy applies to compression methods that actually discard some image data.)

PCX

The PCX format first used by the PC program Paintbrush is now used by many paint programs; it is the PC equivalent to the Macintosh PICT format and also handles low-resolution photographs.

PICT

Originally used by Apple's MacDraw program, PICT is a "loss-less" format. Unlike JPEG, PICT does not discard image data. Files therefore tend to be fairly large. PICT is often used for video editing, video frame capture, animation, and other video-related applications.

PNG

The Portable Network Graphics format (PNG) provides a patent-free replacement for Compuserve's GIF format. Some graphics users postulate that eventually PNG will completely replace GIF. It supports indexed-color, grayscale, and true-color images. For more info, see Greg Roelof's page at http://www. libpng.org/pub/png/pngintro.html.

SVG

The Scalable Vector Graphics format is based on XML (eXtensible Markup Language—a license-free, platform-independent, and well-supported method of structuring data) and, as such, it is an "open platform" that flexibly incorporates vector graphics, bitmap graphics, text, and style sheets. Consult Bill Trippe's *Transform Magazine* story "The Next Wave for Graphics" at http://www.transformmag.com/db_area/archs/2002/04/tfm0204 xm.shtml for more information on the SVG format. Once you have downloaded the free SVG Viewer from Adobe (http://www.adobe. com/svg/viewer/install/main.html), go on to http://www.adobe. com/svg/demos/main.html to see how it works.

TIFF

Developed by the Aldus Corporation (creators of the original *Pagemaker* desktop publishing software) in the mid-1980s, the Tag Image File Format (TIFF) image file format was designed to serve as a standard file format for saving and transmitting high-quality images from sources such as scanners, paint and photo-editing applications, frame capture devices, etc. TIFF images work on different platforms such as Microsoft Windows, Apple's Macintosh, and UNIX. TIFF images can be compressed or uncompressed.

The number of "flavors" in TIFF format versions can cause problems. You might have difficulty opening a TIFF in a given application. Nonetheless, the ability to save high-quality images in color, grayscale, black and white, and palette-color make TIFF an industry-standard file format that you may encounter.

Key Words

You'll need to acquaint yourself with several terms that surround the use of some images, especially concerning images that you find from commercial image vendors and, at times, through the image search engines. Depending on the intended use of what you retrieve, you may need to understand this jargon.

- Comping—Short for "comprehensive rendering." Comping images are medium-to-low resolution images that you can use to "try out" in your layouts to see how they will look. Corbis allows individuals to use downloaded images for comping purposes.

- Royalty-free—These are images that are purchased outright for use in any way you want. Royalty-free images are often priced based on file size; the smaller the file you purchase, the less you can do with that image (artistically), so the fee drops. Apparently no effort is made to monitor where the images will be used.

- Rights-protected—These images are "rented" for specific purposes at a specific price. Once you negotiate a fee with the photographer or rights-holder for the specific use you have in mind, any other use is subject to an additional fee. Theoretically, records are kept of each publication to eliminate conflicts.

Examples of Image-Rich Sites

Whether you only wish to view images or want to download and use them, explore some of the sites on this list, which offer a good snapshot of the many excellent sites that provide images. To find these sites I performed a variety of "keyword" and "similar to" searches on Google. I also zipped over to ProFusion.com (http://www.profusion.com) and searched there by keywords "images," "stock photos." Searchers who wish to explore more sites that offer a variety of graphics should do likewise. And, always read the FAQs or copyright statements.

American Memory at the Library of Congress
http://memory.loc.gov/ammem/amhome.html

The American Memory home page declares it "is a gateway to rich primary source materials relating to the history and culture of the United States. The site offers more than 7 million digital items from more than 100 historical collections." LC says that some materials in the collections *may be protected by the U.S. Copyright Law* (Title 17, U.S.C.) and/or by the copyright or neighboring-rights laws of other nations.

Artcyclopedia
http://www.artcyclopedia.com

By searching Artcyclopedia you not only retrieve images, but you are also provided with a list of links to collections on the Web where related images are located. For example, a search of "John Singer Sargent" provided one image and a list of other Sargent exhibitions that contain more of his works.

FreeFoto.com
http://www.freefoto.com

The comprehensive, yet easy-to-navigate site features 50 main sections with over 1600 subheadings. Photographs are free to private noncommercial users and for sale to commercial users.

FreeFoto.com contains more than 40,000 images with new pictures added every week.

Free Images.com
http://www.freeimages.com

A moderate collection of images that you may use, according to the site's FAQ, for some personal and commercial purposes (such as Web sites), but may not redistribute.

Free Images and Free Stock Photos
http://www.freeimages.co.uk

These images are free provided the user doesn't redistribute them to others. The site says, "Spread the URL not the files!"

FreeStockPhotos.com
http://freestockphotos.com

A minor gold mine. Here you can download stock photographs absolutely free, not just royalty-free. Use in any Web site or publication you wish—personal or commercial. Use without any royalty, use fee, or cost of any kind. Users must credit the source by domain name, FreeStockPhotos.com, and may not crop out a credit if it appears on a photograph.

Thinker Image Database
http://www.thinker.org

Launched in 1996, the Thinker Image Database represents more than 82,000 images from the collections of the Fine Arts Museums of San Francisco. Personal use is not mentioned under "Use of Images," which says "Any commercial use of images or requests for publishable-quality copies of images must be arranged through our Photo Services office." Recommended: go to "Advanced Search" and use the fielded search options.

Public Domain Images
http://www.pdimages.com

While exploring Web sites where I could find unfettered free images to reuse, I discovered "Public Domain Images," a resource offered by Scott Tambert. At one of the pages on the site, Tambert generously offers well over 50 images for free (http://www.pdim ages.com/web6.htm). As a dutiful librarian, I followed up by reading Tambert's *How to Find Free and Low Cost Images on Almost Any Subject* (Washington, D.C.: S. Tambert). Mr. Tambert lists (on page 30) 38 sites from which computer users can legally copy images. Although the list relies heavily on links to U.S. government resources such as the Library of Congress and the United States National Archives and Records Administration Web sites, valuable free material is available for the clicking. The reasoning here is that taxpayer money goes into information created by the United States government and therefore belongs to everyone. Using Tambert's book I found several interesting photos of President Richard Nixon with Elvis Presley at http://www.ibiblio.org/lia/president/NixonLibrary/audiovisual/photos/BasicNixon-photos.html (see Figure 6.5).

Being cautious, however, I did write to "Project Nixon" at the Nixon Library and received this response:

> The photograph in question is the work product of a government employee, and as such, is probably in the public domain. The National Archives exercises no intellectual property restrictions with respect to these photographs. This is not to say that other entities (the participants' estates?) might not have such claims.

As you can see from the tentative permission that the letter rendered, receiving approval to use even a so-called uncopyrighted photograph may be complicated.

Figure 6.5   President Richard Nixon and Elvis Presley. December 1970: the single most requested image from the National Archives. According to the Archives, it is "probably" in the public domain.

Image Services Requiring Payment

Art Today

http://www.arttoday.com

This site provides unlimited access to more than 2,600,000 clip-art images, animations, photos, fonts, and sounds. Subscriptions are available for periods of one week, three months, six months, and annual. Example rates: $7.95 per week, $153.40 per year. The database is easy to search. A FAQ states: "Feel free to use ArtToday content in commercial or noncommercial projects to create Web pages, T-shirts, posters, book covers, art, advertising, newsletters, presentations, logos ... you name it. There are no per-image costs, royalties, or extra payments for ArtToday's content when you follow the Usage Guidelines below. We make it easy for you to use our files for virtually any purpose—except to compete with us."

Corbis

http://www.corbis.com

Bill Gates owns this company that has acquired the rights to more than 70 million images and photographs. The gallery is open to professionals and other end-users for free searching and e-cards, but you can only download images without the Corbis watermark for a fee. Corbis's terms allow users to download one copy on a single computer for personal, noncommercial use (such a copy would bear the Corbis watermark).

Getty Images

http://www.gettyimages.com

Pricey and for professionals, this is a hub of access to over 200,000 images, some royalty-free and some rights-protected.

GoGraph

http://www.graphsearch.com

GoGraph includes directory categories for Animated GIFs, Clip Art, Icons, Wallpapers, and Photos. This is a commercial site; by searching it you will retrieve thumbnails and have an opportunity to buy the image, visit the creator's site, or find copyright information about the image. The GoGraph FAQ states: "For personal purposes, you may use the images found on GOgraph's website and include a limited number of those image(s) on a personal, noncommercial website."

Imagestate

http://www.imagestate.com

Imagestate provides rights-protected and royalty-free imagery serving graphic designers, ad agencies, corporations, and small businesses. Customers can search and preview the entire image collection, and purchase and download royalty-free images 24/7. Good quality royalty-free images begin at $49. Rights-protected images are also available. Comping images (what most people do when they right-click their mouse and save a file) is free at Imagestate, though you must register first.

TimePix
http://www.timepix.com

You must register, but once you have established yourself as a site visitor you'll have access to news photos of current events, famous images from the pages of *Time* and *Life* magazines, celebrities attending last night's parties, as well as beautiful nature and wildlife images. TimePix is an excellent source for stock photography, but it is a professional site created to facilitate both print and Web publishing. As such, all images are protected by watermarks and high-resolution images must be purchased.

How to "Grab" an Image from the Web

Once you have obtained permission, paid for, or found an uncopyrighted/public domain image you want, here are two slick ways to copy that image from the World Wide Web:

On a conventional PC:

1. Using your mouse, click the right mouse button.
2. In Netscape 7.1 select and click new "Save Image As." (For internet Explorer 6.0 select and click "Save Picture As.")

3. You will be prompted with a default filename (which you may change) and a default location in which to save the image (which you may change). Under the filename a default file type will usually appear with the appropriate file extension.

4. Select the destination you desire to save the image to, and click SAVE.

On a Macintosh:

1. Point your cursor over the image.

2. Click down and hold the mouse button, wait for options.

3. Select "Save this image as."

4. Release the mouse button (dialogue box will open).

5. Select desired location.

6. Rename the file if desired.

7. Click SAVE.

Conclusion

Although image search engines do an adequate job of identifying relevant graphics for users to view and manipulate, developments that allow more precise searching are inevitable. But Web surfers shouldn't have any problem finding the images they want. The only problems that may arise will occur when trying to do something with the images they have found. Follow the *Kelly v. Arriba Soft* (Ditto.com) case for news on the legal perspective toward the use of images from the Web. Notwithstanding the outcome of Mr. Kelly's appeal, there are still plenty of terrific images out there to view and use.

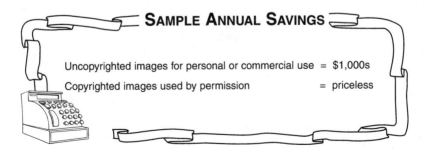

SAMPLE ANNUAL SAVINGS

Uncopyrighted images for personal or commercial use = $1,000s

Copyrighted images used by permission   = priceless

Additional Reading for Individuals Considering Images for Personal or Commercial Use

Scott Tambert. *How to Find Free and Low Cost Images.* Washington, DC: Scott Tambert. 2000.

Scott Tambert. *How to Use Images Legally.* Washington, DC: Scott Tambert. 1997.

Endnotes

1. Paula Berinstein. "The Big Picture." *Online.* May/June 1998. Volume 22. Issue 3. pp. 37–42.

2. Daniel Amor. *The E-business (r)evolution.* Upper Saddle River, NJ: Prentice Hall. 2000. p. 209.

3. Jodi B. Cohen. "Cyberspace is like wild west for copyright law." *Editor & Publisher.* December 21, 1996, Volume 129. Issue 51. p. 22.

4. "Web site held liable for offering photos copyrighted by Playboy." *Intellectual Property Litigation Reporter.* July 16, 1997. p. 8.

5. David Noack. "$3,500 to freelance photographer for image taken from Web." *Editor & Publisher.* June 13, 1998. Volume 13. Issue 24. p. 13.

6. Victoria Slind-Flor. "Thumbnail not even a tiny infringement." *National Law Journal.* December 6, 1999. Volume 22. Issue 15. p. B7.

7. Paula Berinstein. "Image Search Engines and Copyright." *Online.* November/December 1999. Volume 23. Issue 6. p. 91.

8. United States District Court of Appeals for the Ninth Circuit. Leslie A. Kelly vs. Arriba Soft Corporation. February 6, 2002. http://www.eff.org/IP/Linking/Kelly_v_Arriba_Soft/ 20020206_9th_cir_decision.pdf. June 4, 2002.

Chapter Seven

Pixels at an Exhibition

You know you can download free books and read all sorts of material from the Web, but you still stop in your favorite bookstore (where you, in person, occasionally purchase books and drink a cup of coffee). You take a break and read *The New Yorker* magazine. Besides the short fiction, cartoons, and film reviews, you like to see what's going on at some of the world's most famous museums. You discover that an exhibition called "Gauguin: The Lure of the Exotic" is starting at the Metropolitan Museum of Art and that the Guggenheim has just added 100 new works to its permanent collection.

Thumbing through *Boston Magazine* later, you notice in their "On the Town" column that an exciting exhibit of the work of 18th century romantic portraitist Thomas Gainsborough opens today at the Museum of Fine Arts. The *Washington Post* has a preview of a show at the Smithsonian American Art Museum featuring 400 paintings by George Caitlin, lawyer turned artist, a man who followed Lewis and Clark determined to accurately capture the customs of Native Americans in the 1830s. The *Guardian* says that the Australian

Museum in New South Wales has a splendid biodiversity exhibit. And you haven't revisited the British Museum nor seen the Rosetta Stone in years.

You want to get to some of these exhibitions. After all, money is no object and you love the arts and sciences. Let's just gas up the private jet and file flight plans to Sydney, D.C., Boston, London, and New York City. We're all set. Just one problem, you're sipping your latte in Singapore and your laptop says that the "perfect storm" is looming over the Pacific and the Doppler says it will last for days. Sigh ...

Exhibitions in the Physical World

Weather permitting, museum attendance runs high. According to a survey published in London's monthly *Art Newspaper*, approximately 8,000 people a day promenaded through the doors of New York's Metropolitan Museum of Art to see "Vermeer at the Delft School" for a total of 554,267 visitors during its two month run in 2001. Florence's Galleria degli Uffizi's exhibition of "The Medici and Science" eclipsed that figure attracting 861,865 visitors the same year.

The Museum of Modern Art (MoMA) was too late to submit its attendance figures to the *Art Newspaper* survey, but, according to the National Museum Director's Conference survey, MoMA alone averages 1.2 million visitors per year (getting about 10,000 per day during its Jackson Pollock retrospective in 1999). The Solomon R. Guggenheim Museum in Manhattan was not far behind with 1 million visitors.[1] Total attendance for the top 10 shows has been between 4 and 5 million every year in 1999, 2000, and 2001.[2]

Many institutions attract visitors to their on-site physical exhibitions. Reports have varied, yet even since the tragedy on September 11, 2001, museum attendance has remained strong, with 80 percent of responding art museum directors reporting attendance in spring 2002 as the same or higher than prior to the terrorist attacks.[3] Estimated revenue for museums and similar institutions in the United States was almost $8 billion.[4] If museums charge $15 to $20 a ticket for their hottest shows and have such great attendance, why do they choose the Web to play host to free online exhibitions? What do libraries possessing rare and interesting materials gain from displaying them in online special collections? What do their site visitors gain?

Online Collections, Galleries, and Exhibitions: The Raison d'Être

As with an abundance of other physical matter such as books, maps, recordings, magazines, and newspapers, the Web offers opportunities for individuals to enjoy materials on exhibition in museums, libraries, and other organizations. Individuals gain significant information and pleasure, in addition to other tangible and intangible benefits, by taking advantage of Web-based special collections and exhibitions.

INSIDER'S VIEWPOINT FROM YOUR WEB LIBRARY PROFESSIONAL: ALLEGRA BURNETTE, CREATIVE DIRECTOR OF DIGITAL PROJECTS, THE MUSEUM OF MODERN ART

The "Online Projects" page at the Museum of Modern Art in New York City, found at http://www.moma.org/onlineprojects, is a superior illustration of Web-based exhibitions. Allegra Burnette, Creative Director of Digital Projects for MoMA, shared her knowledge about online presentations and their value for both site visitors and institutions.

NT: According to the *Statistical Abstract 2001*, 32.5 million adults visit museums in the United States every year.[5] But when exhibitions are online and the institution is not charging for access to them, how does the museum benefit?

AB: I think it is part of the museum's goal of outreach and education. It's a way to make people aware of the museum so hopefully they actually come to the museum. So in terms of increased visitorship, increased membership, and just general information, online exhibitions are valid things that have either direct or indirect monetary impact. If more people are coming to the museum as a result of the information they are getting on the Web, the museum will benefit.

NT: Some of the exhibition sites I have viewed, and MoMA's "Online Projects" is an excellent example, seem to go far beyond a simple "taste of the collection" designed to attract people to the actual galleries. The MoMA site and its subsites are extremely robust and creative. They evidently have taken a great deal of imagination and effort to execute.

AB: Again, it's becoming another extension to doing exhibitions. What's the point of doing exhibitions? Well, we do exhibitions to give people access to the collection, give people information about the collection, and online exhibitions are pretty much the same thing. It is a continuation of what the museum does in a physical way. The goal of the museum is to bring the collection to the public and this is one form of doing that.

Taking on the Devil's Advocate

Having seen Vincent van Gogh's *The Starry Night* on a dozen prints, postcards, neckties, coffee mugs, umbrellas, and t-shirts, I finally made a pilgrimage to MoMA to see the masterpiece. Yet when I saw the mythical landscape at its permanent residence, I (a dilettante) concluded, "Hmmm. I thought it would have been larger." Which leads to the inverse argument: "Who wants to look at images when they can see the real thing?"

The most prominent criticism is that a virtual presentation must, of necessity, pale when contrasted with a physical exhibition. You might gain a refreshing perspective from the devil's advocate on this point. Such a critic asks a fair question: "Why would anyone bother with online exhibits when they can go to the library or museum and experience the exhibitions firsthand?" On the other hand: Why do people decorate their homes with prints of Kandinsky's and Dali's paintings? Why do people buy postcards of *The Scream*? Why would someone use a mousepad with Monet's *Water Lilies*? Why were the covers of *JAMA: The Journal of the American Medical Association* from the spring of 2002 adorned with fine art including reproductions of Romare Bearden, Thomas Hart Benton, Peter Paul Rubens, Arthur Armstrong, Childe Hassam, and Theodore Gericault?

Many individuals value art and science in all forms. The reason we enjoy a poster of *The Starry Night* or a coffee table book about white wolves or Andy Warhol's self-portrait on a postage stamp is that it interests us, engages us, challenges us to think about the subject, and satisfies or even dissatisfies us on some emotional or intellectual level.

Practically, often no physical parallel for a specific online exhibition exists or, perhaps, the online exhibition contains information, activities, or items not included in the physical exhibition. Several examples of online exhibitions illustrate these points. Although "The Artists of Brücke" (http://www.moma.org/brucke)—a robust and imaginative creation from the Museum of Modern Art in New York City—may be viewed on the Web, a physical counterpart was never on view at the museum. This is a case in which you could not walk through the exhibit (even if you wanted to); it didn't exist.

Similarly the National Gallery of Art in Washington maintains dozens of "In-Depth Study Tours" (http://www.nga.gov/online tours/onlinetr.htm) with content distilled for the site visitor, but having no physical equivalents at the museum. The "added content" concept is another consideration. Many institutions find that the Web allows more opportunity for interaction and straight information. For example, MoMA's Web site for "The Russian Avant-Garde Book 1910–1934" (http://www.moma.org/russian), a physical exhibition that premiered in the spring of 2002, contains research-oriented materials not presented in the gallery.

Behind the Scenes of MoMA's Online Exhibitions

For more information concerning the prevalence and composition of free online exhibitions, I continued my conversation with MoMA's Creative Director of Digital Projects, Allegra Burnette.

NT: I notice that most of the subsites linked to at the "Online Projects" page reflect actual exhibitions that have been mounted at the MoMA.

AB: Yes, for the most part that's correct. Almost all the Museum's actual exhibitions have some online form attached to them. It may be a more straightforward HTML site or it may be a more interactive Flash site. It will depend on the project, the time, the budget, the curator, the artist. For example, we've had artists who are not big fans of the Web and don't actually want their work to appear on the Web, so in those cases we will do a very straightforward site.

For "The Artists of Brücke," the curators wanted to do a project, but there was not an actual physical exhibition that was being done at the same time. So in a sense they created just a virtual exhibition. It does appear on stations in the Museum but there is not an exhibition surrounding it. The Russian Avant-Garde Books exhibition is something we produced online that *was* done in conjunction with a physical exhibition.

One of the things we are currently doing is redesigning and restructuring the Web site, because one of the things I think is actually confusing is that the Online Projects as defined there are actually different from online exhibitions. They are nonexhibition related projects.

For example, "What is a Print?" is not related to an exhibition. It was something the print department put together to explain a little bit more about the medium, but it was not done in connection with an exhibition.

NT: When you take material from an existing gallery exhibit, what limits how much you can put in the Web exhibit?

AB: In some cases we can actually put more online than is in the exhibition, but in other cases we are limited by rights or access to the images.

NT: What do statistics tell you about the popularity of your Online Projects? Do you have any idea of the number of computers that access the site?

AB: We get over half a million a month. It's between 500,000 and 700,000 a month right now.

NT: That's considerably more than actually come through the door at the Museum.

AB: Exactly. And it leads people to come in the door or become interested in some of the other programs that the museum is doing. The more information we can get out there and the more access we can give people to the collection over the Web, particularly when a museum is temporarily relocating, which ours will be to Queens until 2005, the better off we are.

NT: There is a wide variation in the exhibits at the Online Projects pages. For instance, there is a noticeable contrast between something like "What is a Print?" because it's a straightforward interactive exhibit and "The Artists of Brücke," which is completely unmediated.

AB: They're two different types of projects. "What is a Print?" is leading people through the print process and exploring that medium through stages. Whereas "The Artists of Brücke" is much more like an exhibition where you may have a path you would like people to go on, but you can never really constrain them to that. Some people will come in backwards and go through it the wrong way. One is a much more educational piece and the other is more like an exhibition. You have a layout but people can explore it in a more personal way.

NT: What drives all the ideas for MoMA's online exhibitions?

AB: Various things. Different departments will come to us with an idea for a project. The curators tend to come with particular exhibition-related projects or they might have an idea of something they want to do that is nonexhibition related. The education department will come to us with projects. In some cases we may think of something that we would like to do and try and find a way to do that by matching it up with a department. The ideas come from all different venues.

NT: How often are new exhibitions created?

AB: We try and match the exhibition schedule at the Museum as much as we possibly can. If we're doing a Web site that is about an exhibition, it will launch with the exhibition. New exhibitions here at the Museum tend to be every three months, so we generally have two projects launching every three months.

NT: I'm also trying to guide readers to resources that will help them find Web exhibitions on their own. Do you have any databases you check where you can get advanced notice of what is on at other institutions?

AB: Not in terms of Web sites. There are publications such as the American Associations of Museums' *Museum News* (http://www.aam-us.org). But I don't know that there is any source that is gathering information together that says, for example, "this month there are five different Web sites launching at these three museums." There's nothing quite that organized that I am aware of. The Whitney Museum hosts a site called the "Art Museum Network" that gathers some of that information together.

Online Collections, Galleries, and Exhibitions: The Distinctions

Online collections (or online galleries), incidentally, are simply digitized images of items from institutions' collections. In a gallery, no explicit thematic connection between the works need exist. An online exhibition should not only be aesthetically pleasing, but also try to bring the elements on display together conceptually. Martin R. Kalfatovic, Digital Projects Librarian at the Smithsonian Institution Libraries in his book *Creating a Winning Online Exhibition*, comprehensively distinguishes between digital collections (online galleries/online collections) and online exhibitions, writing: "It is very important to remember that a collection of objects does not make an exhibition. It is only when the objects are carefully chosen to illustrate a theme and tied together by a narrative or other relational threads that they become an exhibition." Kalfatovic continued by citing the Smithsonian's National Portrait Gallery as one illustration of his point. Although the Gallery maintains a database of 10,000 records, many including thumbnail surrogates in addition to cataloging information, it is not an exhibition.[6]

Online Collections: Two Exemplary Sites

Frick Collection Comprehensive List of Paintings
http://www.frick.org/html/pntgls1f.htm

Every painting in the New York City's Frick Collection Museum is listed at this site along with the artists' names, media, painting size, accession number, and status. Many, though not all, of the painting records come with thumbnail images, some of which you can enlarge. The thumbnails of paintings that include an enlargement also link to additional information about the painter and the work. Yet there is no explicit thematic union between the paintings on the list. It is a gallery; it is an online collection. It is not an exhibition.

Museum of Fine Arts, Boston
http://www.mfa.org/artemis/collections

Similarly, but on a larger scale, the MFA showcases its collections on the Web. While the Museum houses 350,000 objects, you can savor the essence of the collections by going to http://www.mfa.org/artemis/collections. On that page the "Guide to the Collections" breaks the Museum into nine sections. Choose "Art of Asia" and you can view seven pages of items from that collection. Within that collection, select an image and you can view a larger image and information including prior ownership, media, dimensions, title, and a paragraph discussing the piece. There are 500 objects in the "Guide," 50 of them accompanied by audio. You may also access the digitized collections through the "MFA Search the Collection" page at http://www/mfa.org/artemis/default.asp.

There are, however, several features of the MFA site that approach the status of online exhibitions. On the "Search the MFA Collection" page (which I just mentioned), you may choose to "Browse by Theme" and view a quasi-exhibition with images that have a common element. One such theme is "Dressing Up." Access "Dressing Up" and view 77 items and descriptions including silk robes, oak dressing tables, embroidered jackets from Elizabethan England, and an image from Monet's painting *La Japonaise* featuring his wife in a flamboyant robe holding a fan.

Although an online collection lacks the thematic cohesion of an online exhibition, bear in mind that viewing an online collection is still worthwhile. You might be unable to locate a current online exhibition of Joan Miro's paintings, for instance, but still visit several online museums that have his paintings in their online collections.

Online Exhibitions: Connecting Materials
Clockworks from the Sundial to the Atomic Second
http://www.britannica.com/clockworks/main.html

This Britannica.com Web site meets the criteria for a logically connected exhibition on the subject of keeping time. "Clockworks from the Sundial to the Atomic Second" takes the site visitor from sundial to astrolabe to the cesium atomic clock using drawings, animations, and textual information worthy of Britannica. The exhibition has so many features, including exploded drawings and QuickTime movies, that it probably requires several visits. Timely quotations (some lengthy) by Albert Einstein, Daniel Boorstin, Tennessee Williams, and others complement the factual information.

Previews (and Past Exhibitions)

To draw visitors to specific exhibitions, institutions often offer an example of highlights of their current exhibitions. Previews can range from very simple representations of the works that will await, for example a single representative image, to extended mini-exhibits with sound and video.

Similarly, pages labeled "Past Exhibitions" can transport the museum visitor who never viewed the exhibit or, having seen it, wishes to return to view featured and emphasized items. Additionally, some "Past Exhibitions" can be comprehensive online surrogates for physical shows.

Most online exhibitions do not display all the items from an actual exhibit venue, but rather offer a smattering of materials to provide the sense of the exhibit.

Previews of Current Exhibitions
(That May Be Viewed Past Tense)

Dangerous Curves: The Art of the Guitar
http://207.127.106.123/exhibitions/guitars/preview_launch.htm

If you did not make it to the Museum of Fine Arts in Boston during this exhibition, or if you attended but decided against buying the beautiful hardcover catalog ($45), or, worse yet, did not even know about the show that displayed 129 stringed instruments dating back to the 1600s, you can still appreciate "Dangerous Curves: The Art of the Guitar" through the preview site.

Audio clips featuring the dulcet voice of troubadour James Taylor accompany you through 28 of the items in the exhibit. You can zoom in on an 1810 lyre-guitar, see the excessive electric five-necked ax, or view the "Pikasso" reputed to have more strings (42) than any other guitar. This preview site is considerably more than the appetizer you might expect to encounter before an exhibition launches.

Past Exhibition: Recapturing and Edifying

Art of the Motorcycle

http://www.guggenheim.org/exhibitions/past_exhibitions/
motorcycle/motorcycle.html

This Solomon Guggenheim Museum's physical exhibition wound its way up and down the Frank Lloyd Wright structure between June and September 1998, garnering 301,037 visitors. A thorough summary of the exhibition resides at one of the Museum's "Past Exhibitions" pages. The online resume includes images and text, which are both informative and pleasing, to accompany the 130-year span covered by the exhibition, but it does not attempt to display all of the bikes.

Past Exhibition Comparable to Its Physical Counterpart

Hitchcock and Art: Fatal Coincidences

http://www.mbam.qc.ca/expopassees/a-hitchcock.html

This exhibition at the Montreal Museum of Fine Arts ran from November 2000 to April 2001. Though it's been de-installed, the surviving online exhibition features an interactive component, complete with script and suspenseful music from the films, which recreate the "three way," "split screen" effect achieved in the Museum's gallery. The main pages of this activity link to paintings and movie stills evoking the four themes discussed in the exhibition: terror, women, anxiety, and spectacle.

Uses of Online Exhibitions and Galleries

While we usually consider viewing exhibitions as a cultural but leisurely activity, online presentations tend to go beyond simply appealing to our eyes. Using the potential that technology affords, online exhibitions can expand to provide not only entertainment, but also information supporting research activities and educational objectives.

Education

In addition to appealing to our senses, many Web collections and exhibitions also appeal to our intellect. Some Web exhibitions can answer questions. These sites present facts and information, history and timelines, bibliographies, and teaching suggestions.

Not long ago I encountered a frustrated student. The student had spent an hour searching scientific, computing, and technology databases for information on early microprocessors (specifically the 8086). Unfortunately, since the student's search focused on material predating many of the subscription databases the library could offer, I could think of few valid recommendations.

One approach, I suggested, would be to scan the annual indexes bound in with early computing periodicals themselves; another might be to check appropriate periodical indexes that covered such journals. Neither strategy would necessarily provide her with a historical perspective on microprocessors.

The Intel Museum
http://www.intel.com/intel/intelis/museum/exhibits/ex_index.htm

How did the student solve the aforementioned problem? Working with the Google search engine, we entered the phrase "computer museums" exhibitions microprocessors (note the location of the quote marks).

To the student's delight, we located the site shown in Figure 7.1—the first site listed by Google . It provided information on the people who designed the first microprocessors and how the chips worked. The exhibit we found was based on a "real-life" exhibit at the Intel Museum in Santa Clara, California. Variations on the search strategy produced several informational sites.

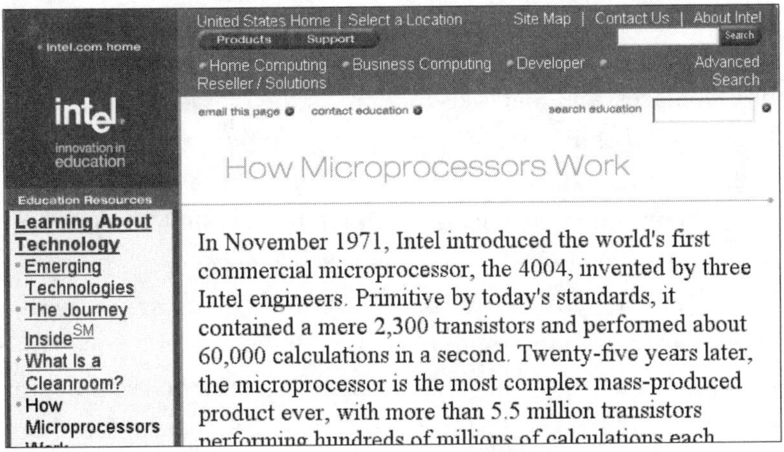

Figure 7.1   A Web exhibit explains "How Microprocessors Work." The Intel Museum. Courtesy Intel, copyright 2003.

Ocean Planet

http://seawifs.gsfc.nasa.gov/ocean_planet.html

Another case where a museum site answers questions is discussed in Selma Thomas and Ann Mintz's *The Virtual and the Real: Media in the Museum.* Chapter 11, called "Going Electronic: a Case Study of Ocean Planet and Its Online Counterpart," provides not only a great deal of background on the creation of a virtual exhibit, but also reveals an exquisite Web site for individuals to discover how environmental issues affect oceans.

Launched as the Smithsonian's first Web exhibition in April 1995, "Ocean Planet Online" succeeded in adapting a 6,000 square foot linear exhibition at the National Museum of Natural History that used space in five major adjacent galleries. Although the physical exhibit was viewed for free by the public, it cost thousands of dollars to create. However, due largely to a "tremendous level of cooperation and volunteerism" on the part of numerous professionals, chapter authors Judith Gradwohl and Gene Feldman tell us that the online counterpart was produced for only $1,200 (most of which was allocated to graphic designers who selected the colors, typefaces, and materials that reflect the themes as well as the look and feel of the original physical exhibition).

The site had already proved successful in 1997 when 400,000 unique computers had accessed the online exhibition. There are numerous ways to visit the exhibit. You may follow a floorplan (contemplating any part of the exhibit for as long as you wish), take a predetermined route hosted by the curator, or build your own tour. Gradwohl and Feldman stated that the online program contains all of the text, 80 percent of the images, most of the photo murals, sculpture, music, poetry, and 10 short video presentations that comprised the original exhibition. Regarding the additional information of scholarly value in the Web version, the authors noted the 400 footnote links added to the online version but unavailable for the physical exhibition.[7]

National Library of Medicine: Exhibitions in the History of Medicine http://www.nlm.nih.gov/exhibition/exhibition.html (Exhibitions home page) including Frankenstein: Penetrating the Secrets of Nature http://www.nlm.nih.gov/hmd/frankenstein/frank home.html

The Frankenstein exhibit required seven people working over 18 months to develop the content and mount the physical exhibit in 5,000 square feet of gallery space. The next logical step? Translate the physical exhibit to the Web. The trade-off, according to Patti Tuohy, Head of NLM's Exhibition Program, is that the online version is much smaller, mostly due to image availability, permissions to post on the Web, and expensive reproduction fees. The actual physical exhibit, scheduled to run until 2005, is making the rounds of 80 libraries in the United States. But don't worry if you can't catch it. You can learn about Mary Shelley's book; the Italian physician Luigi Galvani, who experimented with the relationship of electricity to nerve impulses; and explore some issues in bioethics by visiting the Web site that attracted 300,000 site visitors in 2001.

Art Renewal Center (ARC)
http://www.artrenewal.org

With approximately 800 sites pointing to it, the Art Renewal Center (ARC) has been online since November of 2000. It's a volunteer-run, nonprofit organization that hopes to advance the appreciation of realism while providing educational opportunities such as scholarships. ARC has become known as the focal point for those who want to hear responsible opposing views to the modernist bias of the current art establishment. But what the end-user, such as a student or an art teacher, will value most is its database of 20,000 paintings and sculptures representing the work of 2,100 artists.

Frederick Ross, curator and chairperson at ARC states that, "Certainly curators, museum directors, galleries, collectors, scholars, professors, students and art lovers of every stripe are all using our site. To my knowledge, we've been reviewed by the *Classical Realism Journal*, the *American Arts Quarterly*, the *Bulletin of the American Psychological Association*, *American Artist Magazine*, *The New Criterion*, and I'm sure others which I can't think of on the spur of the moment." He continues, "Many letters come from educators who ask permission to reprint articles [the site offers various technical documents and artists' biographies], or tell us how much they appreciate the site, which they use extensively as an educational resource. No other resource exists for viewing in such detail major works of art, and it could only be surpassed by traveling the world to hundreds of museums, and getting permission to climb up on a ladder to examine them."

According to Ross, ARC is happy to allow individuals to download its images for their own use.

Research

It is estimated that between 180 and 200 Gutenberg Bibles were printed, and only 48 have survived. It should not surprise you to learn that both the Old and New Testaments were auctioned together for $2.2 million in 1978. As with most treasures, their value increased: In 1987 a Tokyo book dealer bought only the Old Testament volume for $5.4 million at an auction held by Christie's in New York City.[8] While not all Web surfers will be entranced by the Gutenberg Bible, it is of extraordinary interest to scholars and the intellectually curious. The sites that have labored to offer the Bible are sound for scholarly work. Bearing the imprimaturs of the British Library and the Goettingen Library, these digital representatives of what has become known as the first printed book to be mass produced are proffered as penultimate artifacts recording a milestone in the progression of humanity.

The Gutenberg Bible: Digitized Images (The British Library)
http://prodigi.bl.uk/gutenbg/default.asp

Thanks to efforts at the British Library and its partners at Keio University in Tokyo, art historians, literary scholars, social and cultural historians, and the general public can inspect the pages of not just one, but two Gutenberg Bibles. The possibilities for comparison between the Grenville Copy (printed on vellum) and the King's Copy (printed on paper) seem limitless. The site goes well beyond making the 500-year-old copies available for viewing; it also offers detailed information on the copies and Gutenberg himself at http://prodigi.bl.uk/gutenbg/forste.htm.

Dr. Kristian Jensen, the Acting Head of Early Printed Collections at the British Library and curator of the collections, stated that individuals may download copies of pages for personal research use. Contrast this to the $50-a-leaf that Cooper Square Publishers asks for its facsimile pages (see http://www.gutenbergbible.net/bible-leaves/index.html), and you're saving a bundle. In an interview with the BBC, Jensen remarked that even though the books are quite strong, handling them too much will eventually destroy them. He added, "Of course, if you really need to look at the originals, you will get permission to do that, but a lot of the images are of such good quality that you'll be better off looking at them on the Internet. We've been able to magnify them to such an extent that you can see details that it's very difficult to see with the naked eye."[9]

The Gottingen Gutenberg Bible, Goettingen State and University Library, Gottingen, Germany
http://www.gutenbergdigital.de/gudi/start.htm

Johannes Gutenberg would have celebrated his 600th birthday in 2000. To commemorate this anniversary, an exhibition was presented in the Pauliner Church of Goettingen—a Gutenberg Bible, printed in 1454, was digitized and made available internationally just prior to the opening of the exhibition on June 23, 2000. The introduction to this research site tells us, "All 1,282 pages of the two volumes were scanned in at high resolution and processed for online presentation. This allows the public - in a digital 'hands-on' effect - on CD 1 [and also at the Web site] direct access to a priceless work which can normally only be stored in vaults or only a few pages can be shown at an exhibition."

An introductory quote tells site visitors that they may purchase Gottingen's digitized Bible on compact disc for 54 Euros ($50 U.S.). Harvard librarian Elizabeth McKeigue stated in *Library Journal*: "The total contents of this CD product are, in fact, fully presented on the Internet.... The Internet version does offer the advantage of including everything the CD does and more for free, but response time is not as good as on the CD. Even though Gutenberg Digital is available in its entirety on the Internet, biblical and printing scholars (and those libraries serving them) will want to pay the $50 for this disc and use it as it was intended, in tandem with the online version's [free Web version] additional features."[10]

Personally, if a value-added version exists for free on the Internet, I think I can endure the adversity of slower download response times.

The Gutenberg Bible at the Harry Ransom Humanities Research Center, University of Texas (Austin)
http://www.hrc.utexas.edu/exhibitions/permanent/gutenberg

Although the Ransom Center's Gutenberg Bible is not yet entirely online, the Web-based exhibition for the Center is well done and complements presentations from the other sites. For example, one section of the exhibition called "Anatomy of a Page" (http://www.hrc.utexas.edu/exhibitions/permanent/gutenberg/html/7.html) allows individuals, by passing the cursor over various sections of the page (e.g., the running headline or a scribe's note), to generously enlarge them for closer inspection. Additional text on the "Spread of Printing," and other topics, functions to further inform the reader.

Or Buy It—It's a Steal!
Library of Congress Rare Books and Special Collections Division/Octavo Digital Imaging
http://www.octavo.com/collections/projects/gtnbbl/index.html

Photographers from California's Octavo Digital Imaging spent four months during 2002 painstakingly capturing every page of the Gutenberg Bible owned by the Library of Congress. It was the company's eighth successful high-end digitization project (it has also digitized Chaucer, Milton, Blake, Shakespeare, and Sir Isaac

Newton). The camera used is rated at 130 megapixels and can produce 6 by 9 foot prints without loss of quality (compare this with my digital camera at home rated at 3 megapixels). Low resolution copies of each page were available during the project's working phase at the Octavo site, but when the company announced that the product was "ready for prime time" in June, 2003, the images disappeared from the Web. But now you can purchase the "Octavo Edition" on two compact discs for $65. It includes digital images of every page, cover to cover, in full color, presented as uncropped spreads and magnifiable to 200 percent of the original book's size.

If you are interested in these projects, you may also wish to visit National Public Radio, where you can listen to *All Things Considered* host Robert Siegel's report on "The Gutenberg Bible Goes Digital" from February 19, 2002: http://www.npr.org/programs/atc/features/2002/feb/gutenberg/020219.gutenberg.html

Additional Research Exhibitions Examples
Library of Congress American Memory Exhibits
http://memory.loc.gov/ammem/ammemhome.html

When it comes to research libraries, the Library of Congress is preeminent. With 121 million items in its collections (only a scant 17 million of them books), it is jammed with primary sources—the types of materials often required to sustain many important projects.

In addition to thousands of images drawn from "American Memory," the Online Exhibitions page at http://www.loc.gov/exhibits offers freely accessible information on a range of topics, for example: "John Bull & Uncle Sam: Four Centuries of British-American Relations" (a physical exhibit presented in 1999–2000 that holds up as a Web exhibition). With primary sources such as pages from the *Petition of First Continental Congress to the King* (a 1774 precursory note of caution to George III); Churchill's "Address to the Virginia General Assembly," March 9, 1946; and a 1941 letter to Orville Wright, the exhibition serves as not only an effective overview to the subject, but as a important point of discovery for researchers.

Some other online exhibitions on display at the Library of Congress:

Scrolls from the Dead Sea: The Ancient Library of Qumran and Modern Scholarship (with images of fragments from the scrolls).

Margaret Mead: Human Nature and the Power of Culture (with letters, notes, and diary entries from Mead's mother, teacher, and sister).

Chicago Historical Society: The Haymarket Affair Digital Collection
http://www.chicagohs.org/hadc

In 1886 violence between police and striking workers struck again at the McCormick Reaper Works in Chicago in 1886. This was the first "Red Scare" in America. After the initial melee a bomb thought to be thrown by an anarchist exploded in police ranks. The Chicago Historical Society has assembled numerous documents, artifacts, and other items that make it easy to research this incident so noteworthy to historians, politicians, sociologists, and students.

Divided into nine sections, the exhibit contains narratives, transcriptions of court information including testimony, indictments, jury selection, and exhibits from the trial; police reports; telegrams; broadsides; autobiographies; and other high quality images, including a "Declaration of Principles and County Platform of the Socialist Labor Party of Chicago. Adopted October 4, 1879." Many researchers would find this site beneficial.

Entertainment

Site visitors can learn something while enjoying numerous entertainment exhibitions on the Web. Celebrities, sports, cartoons, and the media are representative subjects.

National Baseball Hall of Fame
Online Exhibits Cooperstown, New York
http://www.baseballhalloffame.org/exhibits/online_exhibits/
index.htm

Aimed at the general public, not just baseball aficionados, the exhibits at the Hall of Fame are informational and visually engaging. Look at the "Baseball Enlists" exhibit, which recalls the American pastime's contributions to the war effort in the 1940s, including viewable artifacts ranging from autographed balls to team jackets. Many subsections offer vintage videos (http://www.baseballhalloffame.org/exhibits/online_exhibits/baseball_enlists/index.htm).

Life Magazine Cover Collection
http://www.life.com/Life/search/covers

Take a look at *Life*'s perspective of the world from 1936 to 1972 as you search nearly 2,000 covers.

Speak Softly and Carry a Beagle: The Art of Charles Schulz
http://www.nrm.org/exhibits/schulz/gallery

The Norman Rockwell Museum in Stockbridge, Massachusetts, offers this example of pure fun. This Web exhibition augments a physical exhibition on view in 2002. Biographies of the "Peanuts" characters, including their relationships with each other, are featured, and representative strips are included. To tour the site on your own, click on a subject from the "Peanuts Gallery" or just follow Woodstock for a guided tour.

Finding Online Collections, Galleries, and Exhibitions

Several Web sites provide directories of online exhibitions and galleries. Go to my page at http://library.ccsu.edu/library/tomaiuolon/theweblibrary.htm—there you will find links to the directories I discuss along with several online museum sites. If you desire to create your own list, I recommend that you make bookmarks for the following sites or add them to your own "favorites." These Web sites are excellent for locating museum pages, exhibition Web sites, and special library exhibits.

Archives & Museum Informatics
http://www.archimuse.com/mw2001/best/index.html
http://www.archimuse.com/mw2002/best/index.html
http://www.archimuse.com/mw2003/best/index.html
http://www.archimuse.com/mw2004/best/index.html

Archives & Museum Informatics in Pittsburgh, Pennsylvania, is a book publisher, conference organizer, and consultant to institutions including the American Antiquarian Society, the Association of Art Museum Directors, the Smithsonian Institution, the United Nations, and the World Bank to name a few. One of the conferences it organizes, called "Museums and the Web," has been an annual international meeting since 1997. Each year at the meeting, they hold a "Best of the Web" juried competition. Among the categories recognized are "Best Online Exhibition," "Best Museum Research Site," "Best Museum Website Supporting Educational Use," and "Best Overall Museum Site."

According to the A&MI site: "These sites excelled in presenting and interpreting museum collections and themes, providing a rich and meaningful virtual experience. They may have been a section of a larger museum web or a collaborative project between institutions and/or individuals and communities associated with museums. Entirely virtual museums were eligible to participate in this category as were exhibitions of web art and other 'born digital' collections."

Individuals may use this site to not only view the winners of the "Best of the Web" annual competitions, but also the Web sites of a long list of nominees.

Art Museum Network

http://www.artmuseumnetwork.org

The Whitney Museum of American Art located in New York City has been the home of the AMN since 1996. A link called "Excalendar" provides an official exhibition list of the world's leading museums and can serve as a guide to exhibition openings, including online exhibitions. The AMN page also links to an engine that searches the Art Museum Image Consortium (AMICO). The engine will help locate images in a database of over 100,000 items, which, in turn, can direct you to the appropriate museum collection or help you license the rights to a work.

Google Museum Directory

http://directory.google.com/Top/Reference/Museums

To browse geographically, select "By Region." Alternatively, you may begin by selecting a category such as "Children's Museums." A related link, exclusively for art museums, is http://directory.google.com/Top/ Reference/Museums/Arts_and_Entertainment/Art_Museums. You may select an area of the world to narrow your search.

Internet Public Library Exhibits

http://www.ipl.org/div/exhibit

There is a link to "Exhibits" from "Special Collections" on the Internet Public Library's home page, but the above URL will take you right there. The exhibits page lists a collection of current exhibitions and permanent exhibitions all originating at the IPL as a result of student projects at the University of Michigan School of Information. Recently, they added "Live @ IO," which covers the history of the Detroit music venue of the same name. The exhibit contains interviews, photography, and sound files.

To locate other Web exhibits throughout the Internet using the IPL, execute a search on the "Reference Center" at http://www.ipl. org/div/subject/browse/ref00.00.00. Change the search option from the default to "Search all of the IPL" and enter: exhibition exhibit exhibitions exhibits gallery galleries.

MuseumStuff.com

http://www.museumstuff.com/exhibits/index.html

This Web site posts featured virtual exhibitions and lists subject categories that help retrieve more virtual exhibits. The categories extend far beyond art to dolls, evolution, fossils, railroading, wax figures, and dozens of others.

WebExhibits.org

http://www.webexhibits.org

WebExhibits offers a manageable directory of Web exhibitions. The "Browse by Topic" option reaches just eight categories. Topic levels cover Creative Arts, Ancient World, Discovery & Expedition, Society & Culture, Health & Medicine, Environment, Science & Technology, and Academic Subjects. The eight categories are further subdivided, but the subdirectories are well-organized and easy to navigate. If you prefer a direct search, a search engine option appears on the home page as well as on the "Browse by Topic" page. Hundreds of exhibits are listed at the site, some of which WebExhibits produces, but including external sites too. Each listed site carries a concise review. Users can submit suggestions for exhibits they would like to see listed.

The "About" link states: "The exhibits on this site are produced by the WebExhibits project. We seek to improve cultural literacy by interesting the public in connections between art and science ... The exhibits are produced in collaboration with numerous educational, scientific and cultural institutions, including Brandeis University, Massachusetts; National Gallery of Art, Washington; and Museo Nacional del Prado, Madrid. Over the course of this project, it has been sponsored by numerous sponsors."

Explore the "Environment" heading, select the topic "Species & Biodiversity," and choose the subtopic "Odd Animals" to find seven exhibitions from various reputable organizations, including the universities of Hawaii and California (Berkeley), the National Geographic Society, the Carnegie Museum of Natural History, and the "Why Files" from the University of Wisconsin (Madison), with titles such as "The Feathered Dinosaurs," "Brave New Biosphere," and "Tusk, Tusk. Lifting the Ban on Ivory."

World Wide Web Virtual Library Museum Pages
http://www.icom.org/vlmp

This site claims to be the oldest catalog of the Web. Begin at http://www.icom.org/vlmp. If you select a country, you can view a list of museums with Web sites there. For a geographical approach to the WWWVLibrary's museums, you may also want to check http://vlmp.museophile.com/world.html.

To search by keyword, go to http://vlmp.museophile.com/find.html. There you may perform a search for collections that interest you. For instance, when I searched the word "Dali," the Museums Search engine found five Salvador Dali museums including one in Dali's homeland Catalia. It also found the Dali Museum in St. Petersburg, Florida, and another called the "Dali Virtual Museum of Art."

For another approach, select a category to retrieve a list of relevant museums. My favorite categories are "Art" and "Virtual Museums." Experimenting with other categories proved worthwhile also. Clicking on "Egyptology" retrieved, among others, the Egyptian Museum at Cairo. You may also view "All" museums on the list—but it is a long list and appears to have no structure.

Library and Archival Exhibitions on the Web
http://www.sil.si.edu/SILPublications/Online-Exhibitions

Diane Shaw, Special Collections Cataloger at the Smithsonian Institution Libraries and past chair (1999–2001) of the Exhibition Awards Committee of the Rare Books and Manuscripts Section (RBMS) of the Association of College & Research Libraries (a division of the American Library Association), maintains this alphabetical list. The site also offers a search utility linking to more than 2,000 online exhibitions from libraries, archives, and museums on the Internet. The Smithsonian's Library and Archival Exhibitions home page is shown in Figure 7.2.

This unparalleled aid for locating Web sites that educate and entertain includes exhibitions that "draw their inspiration and content primarily from library and archival materials, including, for example: printed books, book illustrations, manuscripts,

Figure 7.2   The Library and Archival Exhibitions home page. Sample exhibitions from all over the world by browsing or searching this database. Courtesy of the Smithsonian Institution Libraries.

photographs, printed ephemera, posters, archival audio and video recordings, artist's books, and the book arts (engraving, marbling, and bookbinding, etc.)."[11]

INSIDER'S VIEWPOINT FROM YOUR WEB LIBRARY PROFESSIONAL: DIANE SHAW, SPECIAL COLLECTIONS CATALOGER, SMITHSONIAN INSTITUTION LIBRARIES

NT: The Smithsonian's Library and Archival Exhibitions on the Web page provides links to over 1,600 exhibitions throughout the Web. It must require a considerable amount of time to maintain.

DS: When I first took the list on, it took a lot of my own time to try to get it in shape. Because it has become a very useful and highly visited part of the Smithsonian Libraries site, it is now one of my official responsibilities. I'm updating it quarterly at present.

NT: Have you considered how much time it would take to travel to each institution to see the parallel physical exhibitions, if they existed, or how much money it might cost if one were to attempt that type of road trip?

DS: Actually I hadn't really thought about it that way. When I first publicized on the ExLibris discussion list [*ExLibris is an electronic news and discussion group for those interested in rare books, manuscripts, and special collections, available at http:// palimpsest.stanford.edu/byform/mailing-lists/exlibris*] that I was taking this project on from the University of Houston, and I was asking for suggestions, I did have somebody write to me and say he hoped that if I had a search engine it would be able to show regions and geographic locations as well as title and subject. I was very surprised and I wrote back to him saying, "Why would you find that useful? Most of these shows have closed by the time I had them listed or maybe even never existed in real life." He told me, regardless of that, it still showed him what these libraries had, and if he was thinking of making a visit to a certain region, he might want to find out what were some of the libraries there that had special collections on certain topics. So it is interesting that people do apparently value a geographic way of accessing these too.

NT: People might even use the Web site to plan a trip?

DS: It sounded like he was planning to supplement travel plans. But I think there are a lot of armchair travelers, certainly I would say I am one, and I like being able to go and look at what the National Library of Australia has or the Bibliothèque Nationale— that sort of thing—that even though I may not ever get to those places, you learn more about their collections and what they think is important by looking at their Web exhibitions.

NT: What are some of the contrasts between special collections and exhibits that are Web-based and those that are physical?

DS: We've had some discussion even here at the museums as to whether there are certain advantages to Web exhibitions. Of course there will always be people who want to see the real thing. Nevertheless the nice thing about the Web exhibitions is that they are available 24 hours a day, 7 days a week, and you can access them from anywhere in the world as long as you've got an Internet connection. It's also viewed as a good way to supplement a physical exhibition because, of course, you can't re-create them exactly on the Internet as you can in the physical space but you can perhaps add more information, multimedia effects, and other things that you might not have been able to do in the physical exhibition. And the nice thing about it is that people can view it at their leisure. They can bookmark things; they can come back again and again. Another advantage to Web exhibitions is that oftentimes the contact information is much more clear. If you want to get in touch with the curator of the exhibition or the library that sponsored it, you can usually find a Web address or an e-mail address that you can use to get in touch with them. I wouldn't know how to get in touch with the people that put up most exhibitions that I go to in galleries.

NT: On my way to one of the reading rooms at the Library of Congress, I was impressed by the Gutenberg Bible on display in the Great Hall. A curator or librarian had turned it to an important set of pages, no doubt. But now the connected public may view two copies of every page of the Gutenberg Bible online from the British Library at http://prodigi.bl.uk/gutenbg/default.asp and two more at the Gottingen Gutenberg Bible site at http://www.gutenbergdigital.de/gudi/start.htm. I think this is an example of how a specimen in a special collection being made available for research online outdistances the actual specimen in every category except, perhaps, the "awe" factor.

DS: Here at the Smithsonian we've done some digitized editions of rare books as a similar thing. They're not exhibitions, but the curator has written an introduction and bibliographic description. Then we have high-quality photography of all the pages including the binding and end leaves. So that does serve as a surrogate for research.

NT: In that case although I would never be able to really see or physically turn the pages of that book, I could study it online?

DS: Yes. And if we had the book in the physical exhibition, of course, it would only be open to one place so you might be wondering what else is in that same book. When it's online it gives you a chance to really browse through it in a way that you certainly couldn't do if it was under glass in a gallery space.

NT: Can you give me an example from the Smithsonian Libraries?

DS: Go to Tycho Brahe's *Astronomi—Instaurat—Mechanica* from 1602 at http://www.sil.si.edu/DigitalCollections/HST/Brahe/brahe.htm. You can page forward or backward by clicking "back" or "next" on the page, or use the contents page and go directly to different sections of the book including the plates. The natural history books are also good examples because they have gorgeous illustrations.

NT: How do you acquire new sites for the list? Do the discussion lists play a role?

DS: Since I enjoy poking around, if somebody sends a message on a topic to one of the lists and includes a URL for their institution, I'll click on it and see what I can find. Sometimes if I've heard of an exhibition site, I'll go to that site directly. I also browse through college and university Web sites just to see if their libraries have any exhibitions online. This combination of strategies has proved useful.

When I first mentioned on the discussion lists that the University of Houston's listing of online library and archival exhibitions had moved to the Smithsonian, I received a number of URLs from people who'd read my note. And what surprises me is that even though I haven't, by any means, sent out this type of notification on a regular basis—there have only been a couple of times that I've mentioned the existence of this site on the discussion lists—there are still people who are very good about sending me new URLs for their shows or updates when they've made changes. I get about five new URLs per month sent to me.

The touching thing is that I've gotten requests from all over the world and I'm not sure how they heard about the site. But it's nice to hear from Northern Ireland or Brazil and these places that, before the Internet, you wouldn't have expected to have connections to; and they're asking me to add their shows.

NT: Please tell me more about the committee at ALA. Has it made awards for online exhibitions?

DS: Yes. The Rare Book and Manuscripts Section's "Katharine Kyes Leab & Daniel J. Leab *American Book Prices Current* Exhibition Awards" have presented awards for online exhibitions. These awards are given for "excellence in the publication of catalogs and brochures that accompany exhibitions of library and archival materials, as well as electronic exhibitions of such materials." Online exhibitions are recognized for Special Commendation awards, an outgrowth of the awards that the Rare Books and Manuscripts Section has been presenting since 1986 for printed exhibition catalogs. It is a reality that many places find it more practical to do an online exhibition than a printed exhibition catalog. The

RBMS Exhibition Awards Committee moved to recognize excellence in online exhibitions partly as an effort to level the playing field when evaluating what special collections libraries are doing to document their exhibitions. While the costs of doing printed catalogs can be prohibitive for some institutions, many special collections libraries have staff members with basic Web training who can put together a simple but effective Web exhibition. For better or worse, institutional administrators are often more willing these days to throw their support behind digital endeavors rather than printed catalogs.

One of the things I like about the "Library and Archival Exhibitions on the Web" list is that I've got some community colleges, even boarding schools represented, as well as national libraries. Depending on the amount of effort and creativity that has been put into the project, online exhibitions from smaller or lesser-known libraries can be as good as those from larger or better-funded institutions.

NT: When I find a good Web site, and your list is a great one, I begin to be apprehensive concerning the site's longevity. Will the project endure?

DS: Certainly. I feel it is worthwhile and looked upon as a great service.

NT: I agree. Initially the site was only accessible through an alphabetical list. You added a search engine in the summer of 2002. The ability to search for exhibits is the site's crowning glory in terms of functionality. I enjoy portrait painting, so it's easy to locate what I would find interesting without looking through a long list.

DS: It's an exciting development. I keep an Access database record for each exhibition. As I add exhibitions to the list I assign descriptors and geographic location to every record. I'd been doing this in anticipation of eventually adding the search engine.

NT: How do you know people are using the list?

DS: Well we know that many sites link into it. Also, when I go to conferences, people will approach me and say, "I teach a library school class and we like to use your list as a way of showing what other libraries are doing, or showing examples of what Web exhibitions can be."

NT: The list facilitates research, but what are some other ways you imagine it is being used?

DS: In some ways it's just a nice way to spend some time browsing around on the Internet. There's a lot of serendipity involved. Some of the topics are just so different that I think some of it is just pure enjoyment. And I think people in special collections like to look and see what other institutions have done, what kinds of styles of exhibitions are out there. Sometimes places will do Web exhibitions that are on the same topic and so they want to see what sort of treatment the person or subject they are focusing on has been given at other special collections Web sites.

NT: Do you have any personal favorites?

DS: That's a hard question. In 1995–1996 I was involved as a co-curator with a physical gallery exhibition here at the Smithsonian that I liked called "Science and the Artist's Book" (http://www.sil.si.edu/Exhibitions/Science-and-the-Artists-Book). Martin Kalfatovic translated it into a Web exhibit.

I also like the online exhibitions that were selected for the "Special Commendation" category of the RBMS Leab Awards in 2001: "Nabokov Under Glass" from the New York Public Library (http://www.nypl.org/research/chss/epo/nabokov) and one about bridges in the San Francisco and Oakland Bay area called "Bridging the Bay, Bridging the Campus" from the University of California at Berkeley (http://www.lib.berkeley.edu/Exhibits/ Bridge).

On Your Own: Other Strategies for Locating Online Exhibitions

Because no search engine exists to specifically root out online exhibitions, you need to ferret them out using Web searches. Fortunately, plenty of search engines exist and all are free. You will have little difficulty if you employ these simple search suggestions:

Using Google, enter these keywords including the quotation marks as shown:

"online exhibitions" museum

"online exhibitions" museums

"online exhibits" museum

"online exhibits" museums

"virtual exhibitions" museum

"virtual exhibitions" museums

"virtual exhibits" museum

"virtual exhibits" museums

You may want to try the singular form of "exhibitions" and "exhibits" in all these combinations, too. Using these and similar strategies, you will find a profusion of museum, library, and corporate pages to visit. You'll be amazed at the variety of information and images.

A Little Nonsense Now and Then

Here's something that would have made Lewis Carroll exclaim, "Frabjous!" At the Fine Arts Museums of San Francisco site visitors may create their own "Virtual Gallery." Although the Museum does not state how long the user-created galleries remain on its server (my "gallery" has been up for over a year), it invites you to choose from its 82,000 images. Simply find the pictures you want and hang them on the virtual walls—then e-mail your admirers and have an opening. As I've browsed through the galleries I've seen quite a few that bear names referring to art appreciation classes and elementary school projects, as well as many homages.

To get started, go to the Museum's home page at http://www.thinker.org and click "Create Your Own Gallery Online." While you're there, have a look at my gallery entitled "A Restoration Project," which features portraits of Charles II, his queen, and John Dryden.

Taking Full Advantage of Online Collections, Galleries, and Exhibitions

To gain the full benefit of many of the exhibitions, you will need "plug-ins" such as QuickTime, Flash, Shockwave, and RealOne Player. Check Chapter Eight, Software Keys to the Web Library, for information and Web addresses for these utilities.

Conclusion

Not everyone will be interested in the Gutenberg Bible, the Haymarket Affair, the history of the microprocessor, or Charles

Schulz and Snoopy. The sites I have chosen to illustrate the research aspects, education applications, and enjoyment possibilities offered by online exhibitions simply serve as examples. Readers may pursue their own interests. And cost to you is "zip."

Visitors to online galleries and exhibitions also escape subsidizing that pays the institution's overhead, which must be high, incurred by the physical exhibit. Even at free exhibitions, viewers must endure travel and queues; a hurry-up-and-wait mentality prevails or the attendees make other sacrifices. At the Web site, attendees may contemplate an item without peering around the cognoscenti and may return any number of times.

Yet even if you argue that there is no substitute for seeing the real exhibitions (assuming they actually exist in a physical format and you can arrange to visit them), you might concede that since online exhibitions have emerged, at least the viewer has a choice. And while not every venue has an exhaustive Web site, the money you save on some exhibitions will allow you to visit some of the more singular collections that aren't entirely represented on the Web.

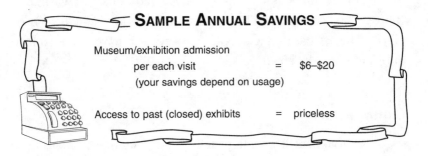

SAMPLE ANNUAL SAVINGS

Museum/exhibition admission
per each visit   = $6–$20
(your savings depend on usage)

Access to past (closed) exhibits   =   priceless

Endnotes

1. "Facts and Figures" London: National Museum Director's Conference. http://www.nationalmuseums.org.uk/news/facts.html. May 15, 2002.

2. "World-wide Exhibition Attendance Figures for 2001." *The Art Newspaper*. February 1, 2002. http://www.theartnewspaper. com/news/article.asp?idart=8716. May 22, 2002.

3. "Report Shows No Slump for Most U.S. Museums: Expansion Plans Go Ahead for 99% of U.S. Museums." *The Art Newspaper*. February 1, 2002. http://www.theartnewspaper.com/news/article.asp?idart= 8712. May 22, 2002.

4. U.S. Census Bureau. "Arts, Entertainment, and Recreation Services - Estimated Revenue: 1998 and 1999." Table 1231. *Statistical Abstract of the United States 2001*.

5. U.S. Census Bureau. "Adult Participation in Selected Leisure Activities by Frequency: 1999." Table 1243. *Statistical Abstract of the United States 2001*.

6. Martin R. Kalkatovic, *Creating a Winning Exhibition: A Guide for Libraries, Archives, and Museums*. Chicago: American Library Association, 2002.

7. Judith Gradwohl and Gene Feldman, "Going Electronic: A Case Study of "Ocean Planet" and Its Online Counterpart." In Selma Thomas and Ann Mintz (eds.), *The Virtual and the Real: Media in the Museum*. Washington, DC: American Association of Museums. 1998.

8. "Gutenberg Bible Sells for Record Price." *New York Times*. October 23, 1987. Section C. p. 31.

9. Christine McGourty, "Gutenberg Bible Goes Online." BBC News. November 22, 2000. http://news.bbc.co.uk/1/hi/uk/1035014.st. October 8, 2003.

10. Elizabeth McKeigue, "Gutenberg Digital." *Library Journal*. February 1, 2001. Volume 126. Issue 2. p.134.

11. Diane Shaw, "Introduction: Library and Archival Exhibitions on the Web." *Library and Archival Exhibitions on the Web*. Washington, DC: Smithsonian Institution. http://www.sil.si.edu/SILPublications/ Online-Exhibitions/online-exhibitions-intro.htm. May 28, 2002.

Chapter Eight

Software Keys
to the Web Library

Previous chapters have shown Web users the vast range of high-quality content that valuable free sites have to offer. Experts from publishing, librarianship, journalism, museums, and digital information distribution have shared their knowledge. Among other discoveries, we have found digitized versions of rare books, free magazines, free databases, thousands of free books, and image search utilities, and we virtually visited museums and libraries we may never actually see. We have learned that librarians and other information professionals will accompany and assist us on our information quests, dispense advice, and share ideas. So we don't lose sight of what we've gained, let's explore some particulars that will help us get the most out of our Web Library.

This chapter is designed to help you:

1. Locate plug-ins and helper applications to ensure you are able to hear, see, and read everything in your growing Web Library.

2. Consider toolbars to maximize Web navigation and install the ones you find useful.

3. Create your own free Web page and use it as a portal to the sites you consider most valuable.

Basic Plug-Ins

New computers possess remarkable features. We usually take the advances in hardware and preinstalled software for granted. However, it's unlikely your computer will come out of the box with every program you'll want or need. Intermittently, it may become necessary to locate and install software "on the fly" to view and manipulate items in the Web Library.

For example, to read the facsimile version of a free journal article from the 2000 volume of *Academic Medicine* (this publication is available through HighWire Press; see page 20), you need Adobe Reader. If the article you need to read appears at Britannica.com, FindArticles, or any of the many sites that simply display text, there's no problem—you can simply read it on the computer monitor without doing any extra work. But if your article only appears in Portable Document Format (PDF), you need to download Abode Reader to your computer. The advantage of PDF files is that they appear exactly like the original printed documents, with formatting, graphics, and fonts intact.

- Adobe Reader is available for free downloading at http://www.adobe.com/products/acrobat/readstep2.html

- David Moynihan's Blackmask Online (http://www.blackmask.com) carries nearly 10,000 e-books. If you wish to read some of Saki's satire, you will need Adobe

Reader or another e-book reader such as the free Microsoft Reader. The download takes 20 minutes with a 57K modem and you must register to activate the software on your PC, but it's worth it.

- There are 1,800 beautiful e-books at the University of Virginia's E-Book Library (http://etext.lib.virginia.edu/ebooks/ebooklist.html) just for the Microsoft Reader.

- The Microsoft Reader is available for free downloading at http://www.microsoft.com/reader/downloads/pc.asp.

More Software for Books and Other Documents

Because full-text documents are lengthy, providers often compress (zip) the files. To take advantage of many texts available on the Web, install software that will unzip zipped files. For example, if you want a free, albeit scary, romance novel, Project Gutenberg (http://www.promo.net/pg) offers a zipped version of Emily Brontë's *Wuthering Heights*. A popular program for handling zipped files is WinZip (http://www.winzip.com). WinZip has always allowed users to download a free "Evaluation Version" of its latest WinZip software. The download takes about five minutes over a modem. Once you have saved the program on your computer, you run its setup program. Then you can retrieve and save a zipped file and open it using the evaluation version.

For another example, look at Eric Lease Morgan's Alex Catalogue of Electronic Texts at http://www.infomotions.com/alex. It offers a large collection in an array of e-book formats. To use the collection and to prepare for other documents you will inevitably find, be sure you have installed the appropriate software (e.g., Adobe Reader, Palm Reader software) in the correct version for your computer or handheld device.

Additional free download sites:

Palm Reader for Windows, Palm Reader for Macintosh, Palm Reader for Pocket PC, and Palm Reader for Palm OS
http://www.peanutpress.com/product/reader/browse/free

AportisDoc Reader for Palm Powered Devices
http://www.aportis.com/tryme/download/AportisDoc/aportisdocreader.html

MobiPocket Reader
http://www.mobipocket.com/en/HomePage/default.asp

Multimedia Plug-Ins

The World Wide Web has encouraged people to produce all sorts of multimedia pages. But during its relatively short history, the Web has been navigable by only a handful or so of Web browsers. The most popular browsers for the majority of Web surfers are Netscape and Microsoft's Internet Explorer. Instead of reconfiguring the browsers and reissuing them every time a new type of multimedia appears, plug-ins are developed. These small pieces of software download quickly and work with the browser to play or read certain types of files.

Several major plug-ins exist for playing video and audio. Windows Media Player, RealNetwork's RealOne Player, and Apple's Quick Time are often needed when you go to Web sites that contain news reports (e.g., a video report by CBS News by Charlie Rose about open heart surgery on CBSNews.com), interviews, music and speech (e.g., James Taylor describing a guitar at MFA.org's "Dangerous Curves" exhibition), or animations. Some files that you will encounter are in the MPEG format (the acronym for the Moving Picture Experts Group). MPEG files are generally smaller than other video and audio files and can be handled by the Windows Media Player or RealOne Player. RealOne Player can also easily handle MP3 audio files. If you are interested in MP3 audio, go to MP3.com (http://www.mp3.com) to sample free music.

Other Web sites we may visit such as the Museum of Modern Art's "Artists of Brücke" (http://www.moma.org/brucke) or its interactive "What is a Print?" (http://www.moma.org/exhibitions/2001/whatisaprint/flash.html) employ more sophisticated multimedia software to enhance presentations. To enjoy the effects included in these exhibitions as well as other related Web sites, we often need to install Shockwave and Flash. Though similar, Shockwave and Flash, both products from Macromedia, do have differences. Tom Harris at "How Stuff Works" explains:

- Flash files load more quickly than Shockwave files.

- Shockwave is more versatile. You can create more complex games, more elaborate interactivity, and more detailed animation.

- You can use more types of files with Shockwave. You could, for example, import a Flash file into a Shockwave movie, but it won't work the other way around.

- Flash is more universal. More than 90 percent of Web users have the Flash plug-in installed, while a little less than 60 percent have the Shockwave plug-in.[1]

You also need a plug-in to enjoy Scaleable Vector Graphics (SVG), one of the newer graphical formats. Even after you have downloaded new browser software, you will occasionally need to install updated plug-ins. I recently downloaded version 7.1 of Netscape's browser, but as soon as I tried to listen to a newscast, the system prompted me to install a later plug-in, RealOne Player.

These free plug-ins are currently available on the Web:

Adobe SVG Viewer
http://www.adobe.com/svg/viewer/install/main.html

Apple Quick Time
http://www.apple.com/quicktime/download

Macromedia Flash and Macromedia Shockwave
http://www.macromedia.com/software/downloads

RealOne Player
http://www.real.com (Note: Be sure to select the free version.)

Windows Media Player
http://www.microsoft.com/windows/windowsmedia/download/
default.asp

To find additional plug-ins for Internet Explorer and Netscape consult:

Netscape's Plug-in Finder
http://wp.netscape.com/plugins/index.html

Yahoo's Plug-in Directory
http://dir.yahoo.com/Computers_and_Internet/Software/Internet/
World_Wide_Web/Browsers/Plug_Ins

C/Net's Shareware
http://shareware.cnet.com

The next level of Web graphics is 3-D animation. In traditional Web graphics, you see a flat 2-D rendering, but in 3-D you can actually turn the graphic around and otherwise control the display. I can imagine museum sites that will offer a new tier of interactive online exhibits. And to access the 3-D objects, you will need another plug-in. How will you know where to get the plug-in for the latest media? Perform a simple Google search! For example, my search on Google for "3D animation plug-in" took me directly to the Netscape "Browser plug-in—3D and Animation" page. There I had a choice of 26 3D plug-ins from "AXEL Player" to "WildTangent."

Toolbars—Coolbars

Web site authority and credibility are always issues. Throughout this book I have often mentioned site popularity or "rank" or the number of links that point toward a site. In some cases I have referred to site longevity. These factors are ways to arrive at an overall impression of a particular site's authority and credibility and, hence, its usefulness. Prior to using a site and, more importantly, before recommending it to readers, I take a close look at how it compares with similar Web sites. Besides applying common sense, what other tools can we use to learn more about a site? Do other tools exist that will streamline our Web Library? One attractive and free utility is a toolbar.

A toolbar's purpose is to put frequently used operations at the computer user's fingertips. There are many toolbars individuals may add to their computers. Some toolbars launch applications, others eject DVDs and CDs. For Web browsers such as Internet Explorer, one example is the Ask Jeeves toolbar (http://sp.ask.com/docs/toolbar). The Jeeves toolbar allows the user to search for news, weather, a dictionary, local events, and stock quotes without going to a search engine or typing addresses. It even offers a "zoom" tool that can enlarge the display on the computer screen up to 200 percent. This could be helpful at a conference in a large room or for the visually impaired. (For Internet Explorer only.)

Teoma, a popular search engine owned by Ask Jeeves, offers the "Teoma Search Bar" for free download. The toolbar's basic functions include highlighting your search terms on retrieved pages, a button that helps you e-mail a page to friends, and a dictionary search. Visit http://sp.ask.com/docs/teoma/toolbar for a complete description. (For Internet Explorer only.)

VPOP Technologies' "Ultrabar," available for free at http://www.ultrabar.com, is different because it allows the user to choose the search engine to be deployed from the toolbar. If your favorite search engine is All the Web (http://www.alltheweb.com) or if you frequently search for software from Tucows (http://www.tucows.com) you can set Ultrabar to use that resource. Over a dozen default search engines are built into Ultrabar, including the blog-searching Daypop. A "customize search engine" feature lets the user add any desired site. (For Internet Explorer only.)

All toolbars aim at increasing the user's efficiency, but the Yahoo! Companion (http://companion.yahoo.com) is the most fun to use. Available toolbar searches include news, finance, sports, entertainment, games, maps, and local movie times to name a few. "Reference" is also available, and the button leads to a collection of heavily used free online resources including books at Bartleby.com. Yahoo! Companion works with Internet Explorer and Netscape 4.x.

For serious Web surfers, however, the toolbars with the most functionality come from Alexa and Google. Both are versatile and can reveal information about Web sites that users can synthesize to make judgments regarding site content and validity.

The Alexa Toolbar

The Alexa Toolbar
http://www.alexa.com

How can you quickly learn what company or person is responsible for a Web site? Can you get an idea of when the site was launched? What sites are related to the site you are visiting? How much traffic does the site get? How many other Web sites link to the site you are looking at? These are important questions to consider when you surf the Web.

The Alexa Toolbar is a free utility offered by Alexa Internet, a company owned by Amazon.com. It's only available for Internet Explorer, but it has many features and uses, plus a related solution that serves people who prefer Netscape. The Alexa toolbar is shown in Figure 8.1.

Figure 8.1   The Alexa toolbar, for Internet Explorer, allows users to gather information about a Web site including its rank, number of sites that link to it, contact information, and archived pages. Courtesy Alexa Internet, copyright 2003.

General Features

Like Teoma's search bar, Alexa facilitates Web searches (and uses Google to do it). Dictionary and thesaurus searches use the Merriam-Webster Web site. Other handy searches include stocks and news (via Dogpile Newscrawler and Fast News Search). There is also an excellent "Site Search" that becomes useful when you encounter a site that does not have its own search function. Even when I've happened upon sites with their own search functions, Alexa's site search outperformed the native search tools. For example, a professor asked me to locate the number of full-time equivalent students at a specific university; the site search at the university's Web site was useless, but Alexa found the nugget.

Qualitative Features

Among the valuable information Alexa renders is "Site Info"— that is, a contact person or address for the site, when the site was launched, and how many sites link to the site you are visiting. Alexa takes this information from various domain name registry services such as InterNIC and Register.com.

Contact information is important when a site lacks any indication of who is responsible for the content. Furthermore, even when a clear statement of responsibility is present, contact information may be difficult to locate. Using the contact information from the Alexa toolbar I was able to reach several Web site sponsors to discuss their pages while I was preparing this book.

The number of "backward links" (sites that link into a site) is often regarded as a benchmark of site usefulness/popularity. Detractors of this axiom submit that sites with numerous backward links still may not necessarily be valid sites, and while many sites may be linked into for all the wrong reasons, it would certainly be preferable to reference a site with 10,000 backward links than to one with only 10.

"Online since" is another component of Alexa's "Site info" that helps users draw conclusions concerning a site's durability, longevity, and validity. One motto of information professionals when discussing the Web is *"panta rei"*—everything changes—but when you discover that a site has been online for a few years, there is at least some basis for judging it as reliable.

"Traffic rank" statistics help users determine the number of people on the Web that visit a site; a site with a higher traffic rank is garnering more visits. Alexa allows you to compare the traffic for two sites by going to one site's traffic rank details graph and then typing in another address. For example, at the height of the 2003 conflict in Iraq, the conservative Web magazine *The National Review Online* was outpacing the more liberal Web publication *The Nation*. Traffic rank also indicates whether a site has gained or lost popularity.

The concept of "Related Sites" is nothing new, but the Alexa toolbar offers this as well. It's an easy way to get to Web sites that may share similar content and themes with the one the user is currently browsing.

The Wayback Machine

This utility is super. Alexa has been taking "snapshots" of the Web since 1996 and archiving them in its Wayback Machine. The archive is impressive—so impressive that when Alexa's creator, Brewster Kahle, donated the Wayback's contents to the Library of Congress in October 1998, the LC Information Bulletin quoted Winston Tabb, its Associate Librarian for Library Services, as saying, "Alexa Internet's donation of the Web enhances the Library's holdings and ensures that one of the most significant collections of human thought and expression born of a new medium is preserved in the national collections." Because the Library of Congress is committed to collecting information in all its forms, Alexa's contribution was a most significant event in the context of digital information preservation.

Take Me *Way* Back!

These archived snapshots can play an important role for researchers, students, librarians, and the just plain curious! If we perceive the real-time Web as an invaluable resource, consider the staggering and interesting information its pages from the past can render.

How could we use this virtual scrapbook? Anytime we reach a page that no longer exists (or displays a "404 Page Not Found" message) we can just click the Wayback button on the Alexa Toolbar and view the page as it looked when Alexa grabbed it. What did the *New York Times* home page look like on the morning of 9/11? The Wayback Machine lists all the archived pages for that URL (http://www.nyt.com) since 1996. Simply choose the date you wish to see. Multiple snapshots are often listed for a date so the user can study a page's evolution.

Among other uses, I have deployed the Wayback tool when helping students locate items at existing URLs even when the specific items they seek have long disappeared. When faculty instruct students to consult obsolete links, the Wayback is the solution! Not only does Alexa archive a snapshot of a site's main page, but it also frequently archives other pages from the same site. This means that you can not only access the home page, but the page's links, along with their content, are often available too.

Disclaimers

Although the Wayback Machine is phenomenal, a few limitations exist. In deference to page owners and Webmasters, Alexa will ignore specific sites on request. Don't try to find a snapshot until six months have elapsed. This is the period of time that Alexa allows before it makes an archived page publicly available in order to respect the target site's freshness. Lastly, when accessing the Wayback for a specific site, you may find 50 snapshots for a given time period—or just one or two. But we know the fabric of Web is transitory, so using the Wayback for Web sites is the next best thing to pulling an out-of-print book off a library shelf.

The snapshots of covered Web sites are also available at the Internet Archive (http://www.archive.org), though it's more efficient to find them using the button on the Alexa Toolbar.

Popup Manager

For good measure, Alexa offers a feature that squashes popup ads. Upon visiting a Web site, if Alexa detects a popup it will ask the user if he or she wants to "block" the ad. The user says "yes" and Alexa adds the Web address of the site to its list, ending the nuisance. To download the toolbar, go to the Alexa home page and click on "Download the Alexa Toolbar."

Google Toolbar
http://toolbar.google.com

This utility resembles the Alexa Toolbar in some ways, but it possesses special qualities that make searching the Web easy without constantly going to Google's home page.

The Google Toolbar (see Figure 8.2) provides page rank and site information, though not so detailed as Alexa's. Once you have accessed a Web site, you can use the toolbar's "Search Site" function to find what you are really looking for using your keywords. For example, you go to the Frick Museum's site at http://www.frick. org looking for any information about Picasso. Type "picasso" into the Google toolbar search box and click "Search Site." Google then performs a search of the Frick's Web pages for your keyword.

Figure 8.2   The Google toolbar for Internet Explorer allows site searches and provides site information and page rank. Courtesy of Google, copyright 2003.

Moreover, as Figure 8.3 shows, you can use the Google toolbar to search for your keywords among images, Usenet groups, Google news, and the Google directory. Of course, Google explains all of this more eloquently than I can. If you desire additional information, go to http://toolbar.google.com/help.html. In 2003, Google released a new version of its toolbar (version 2.0). Like Alexa's, it has a built in popup manager, plus it displays an icon that allows bloggers (perhaps you?) to "Blog This"—or reference the page they are viewing—in their own blogs if hosted by Blogger.com (which is owned by Google).

Figure 8.3   The Google toolbar ready for deployment—Web searching at a
keystroke and a mouse click. Courtesy of Google, copyright 2003.

Two (Maybe Three?) Toolbars
Are Better than One

Each toolbar provides some unique properties, so I have
installed both Alexa's and Google's on my computer to run with
Internet Explorer version 6.0. I also like Ultrabar's features, so I
have that toolbar running as well.

Privacy Concerns

Some individuals may have misgivings about the Alexa and
Google toolbars because in order for the toolbars to offer site information ("Rank" in Alexa and "Page Rank" in Google), the software
has to collect information about the site you are visiting. You can
disable this feature on the Google toolbar, but you won't get the
"Page Rank" information if you do. The Alexa privacy policy states
that, "Although Alexa does not attempt to analyze web usage data

to determine the identity of any Alexa user, some information collected by the toolbar service is personally identifiable...."[2] While I am not personally concerned with this issue, readers should be aware of it. Incidentally, neither toolbar works with America Online's proprietary browser. (AOL subscribers may use AOL to connect to the Internet, but should download or use a generic version of Internet Explorer if they wish to install the toolbars.)

Alternative Solutions for Netscape Users

What's Related

Although the Alexa and Google toolbars only work with Internet Explorer, Mozilla Development offer its "Googlebar," which emulates almost all of the Google toolbar's functions (and even adds some "Special Searches" such as "College Search" and "Uncle Sam Search" that Google's toolbar does not yet support). It's available for free at http://googlebar.mozdev.org. Netscape users also have a built-in browser feature that they can deploy. Most of the Alexa Toolbar features for the Internet Explorer browser are available within Netscape, but not so obviously. When using Netscape, look for the "What's Related" panel. On older versions of Netscape, it appears right on the Netscape Toolbar. In new versions of Netscape, it appears to the left of the screen as a "Tab" that you can add to "My Sidebar" (see Figure 8.4). Using this feature, you can see (and access with a mouse click) sites related to the Web site you are visiting. In Figure 8.4 Alexa has listed the Merriam-Webster Online Dictionary, The Quotation Database, and the University of Pennsylvania's Digital Book Collection as related to Bartleby.com. You also receive information on the owner of the site, the date the site was established, its popularity in terms of traffic, the number of pages on the site, and the number of links to the site. For the newest versions of Netscape, the Alexa information may not appear at all, but there is an easy

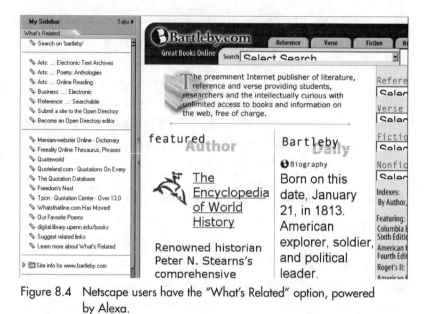

Figure 8.4   Netscape users have the "What's Related" option, powered by Alexa.

"fix" for this. I found it by searching the keywords "do you miss what's related" at Google Groups (http://groups.google.com). You can find it there as well, or you can refer to my Web page for the link to the fix.

Alexa Snapshot

While the Alexa Toolbar is incompatible with Netscape, the Alexa Snapshot can be downloaded quickly to Netscape. It provides most of the same Web site information that is available for Internet Explorer users through the toolbar. If you're on a Mac, or you're using Netscape, America Online's browser, or any other browser, get the Snapshot at http://pages.alexa.com/prod_serv/snapshot.html.

Your Personal Web Library Portal

In the preceding seven chapters, we have discussed hundreds of Web sites. If you explored the sites as you read about them, perhaps you have bookmarked some using Netscape Communicator or alternatively added them to your "Favorites" using Internet Explorer. Either approach will work until your Bookmark or Favorite lists become unmanageable. Creating your own Web page can help you keep track of your most useful Web Library links. And it's free.

A number of Internet services will allow individuals to create free home pages. Lycos offers the Angelfire service (http://angelfire.lycos.com) and Tripod (http://www.tripod.lycos.com/host/free.html). Either will give you 20 megabytes of free space for your pages. For reviews of various free Web page hosts consult "The Free Pages Page" at http://freepages.taronga.com.

Similarly, many Internet service providers (ISPs, the companies that you pay for your own connection to the Web) offer individuals the option of creating free Web pages. AT&T WorldNet gives subscribers 10 megabytes of space to create and publish free Web pages. America Online's AOL Hometown feature allows its subscribers to build pages as well. You may want to see if your ISP offers this advantage. On a slightly more advanced level you may use Netscape's Composer function, but you will need to upload it to a service that will host your page.

Many Web surfers have their own pages, and they are by no means all professors and techies. Teachers, students, rock bands, hobbyists, camp counselors, and others create and publish pages. Having no preference for any specific Web page host, providing that the service was free, I chose Yahoo!'s Geocities (http://geocities.yahoo.com) to create a sample page.

Using Geocities Free Web Pages

On your first trip to Geocities, you encounter a start page that offers various types of paid Web page building options. But if you look to the left of your computer screen you will notice "Try Geocities For Free." That's the option I suggest. You need to register, but that is also free.

Geocities allows 15 megabytes of free space to compose your Web page. The quickest and easiest method to create a Geocities page is to select "Page Builder." Once it is loaded on your computer, you simply click on various parts of the sample page to add your own text and links. The links added consist of the Web addresses of the resources you found most useful. Geocities even allows you to upload pictures and sounds. To upload a sound file or image from your own computer, click "File" and select "Upload Files and Images." You can then browse your own computer for an appropriate file.

Page Builder is graphical. If you want to add a link, simply type in some text to represent the link, highlight it, and click the icon of a chain on the toolbar. Add the URL for the link, and it's created. Save your work frequently; if your phone line drops the connection, for example, you won't have to begin all over. During subsequent visits to Geocities, you should sign in and then click "File Manager" in the "Advanced Toolbox" to edit your pages.

The sample page I created required three hours at the keyboard. It is accessible at http://www.geocities.com/weblibraryforfree/web libraryforfree.html and it is shown in Figure 8.5. (Please note that this is not the address for the comprehensive page that lists all the links mentioned in this book.) I created this page on Geocities to illustrate to readers how easily it can be done. You'll notice I uploaded one image. When uploading an image, be sure you own it or have no problem with someone else's copyright. The image on my sample page comes from a book about monastic libraries in the Middle Ages published in 1890. The image, therefore, is in the public domain. Since it is not a digital image, I needed to scan it, save it as a file, and then upload it. Similarly, try to get permission to link to sites. You almost always get a positive response and it's good "Netiquette."

The Web Library for free resources

Links compiled by Nicholas Tomaiuolo, MLS (page copyrighted 2003)

This page is a portal to free resources on the World Wide Web that parallel collections and resources found in traditional "bricks and

Figure 8.5   Easily create your own, free portal to your favorite resources.

And While You're At It

Having discovered Weblogs in Chapter Two, you may be interested in not only reading them, but also in creating one of your own. It is astoundingly simple—and it's free! Remember, blogs are vehicles of personal expression, but they may also be used collaboratively in a business setting (to get news out to coworkers) or by families (to keep one another updated about every day/significant events). The scope and content of your blog is only limited by your imagination.

Get going by visiting Blogger.com at http://www.blogger.com. That's where you will create your blog. Blogger is a generous service; it will even host your page for free. Give yourself a username and password, name your blog, give it a catchy Web address, and start publishing. Blogger streamlines the process with some natty templates, and you don't need to know anything about writing hypertext. You will be delighted by the speed of the process; your blog will be on the Web in minutes! Please visit my blogs (http://theweblibrary.blog spot.com and http://webtut.blogspot.com) while you're logged in.

Conclusion

If this book has accomplished its main objective, you now know about hundreds of valuable Web sites where you can find free information, documents, and images 24 hours per day, seven days per week, 365 days per year. Don't type an address every time you want to visit one of them: Create an attractive Web Library page that you can share and use whenever you want.

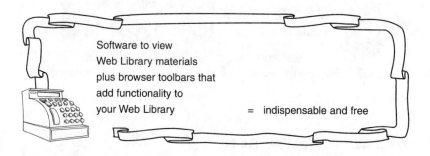

Software to view
Web Library materials
plus browser toolbars that
add functionality to
your Web Library   = indispensable and free

Endnotes

1. Tom Harris. "How Web Animation Works." How Stuff Works. http://www.howstuffworks.com/web-animation6.htm. August 22, 2002.

2. Alexa Internet. Privacy Policy. Updated March 17, 2003. http://pages.alexa.com/help/privacy.html. September 26, 2003.

Chapter Nine

Final Considerations

Free resources on the Web are a win–win proposition for everyone. Searchers almost always perceive the Web only as a source of information. By finding the desired information, they gain. But what about the other side of the proposition? What about the information providers, the entities that place these valuable resources on the Web? I believe they also profit, sometimes tangibly as in revenue, but sometimes, depending upon the providers' perspectives and business models, less evidently. Whether providers offer free or low-cost content to drive traffic to their sites where they can sell other content, or to bring site visitors who click on banner ads, or to make a better world, they are operating on a reward system. Although it may sometimes seem inexplicable, many free resources do exist, and individuals and librarians should look for them and use them.

What Have You Gained?

We know we may not only access, but also save to our computers, thousands of electronic documents in the public domain.

Thanks to the efforts of e-book pioneers such as Michael Hart and his volunteers at Project Gutenberg and allied document digitizers from all over the globe, this total is constantly increasing. Let's agree that you can easily fit 30,000 electronic texts on your computer from the public domain sites alone. Let's assume that using some of the ancillary sites and effectively searching for additional titles could add 5,000–10,000 to the total. At a nominal value of $2 per title, you have acquired $80,000 in books. And you didn't need to build an addition to your home to store them. Moreover these are searchable books. You can locate the text you desire by simply using the "Find" command. You can annotate these documents; frequently you can e-mail them. You may even wish to download two or three copies of the same title from different providers and analyze the editions.

Combine this value with the reference and factual information that is present at free Web sites. You may not be able to copy and save entire texts, but you can find updated information from trustworthy providers. Although not all of the reference information is quantifiable, full-text reference copyrighted texts such as *The Merck Manual, Roget's II: The New Thesaurus,* and 41 books at Xrefer are available. Library reference avatar and educator William Katz has predicted there is more to come.

Indexes, abstracts, and databases have always been key for finding what has been said about a subject and who has said it. For years librarians and their clientele have been dependent on proprietary services such as Wilson (for *The Reader's Guide to Periodical Literature, The Humanities Index,* and dozens of others) and database aggregators such as SilverPlatter (for MEDLINE, ERIC, PsycLit, and dozens of others) to provide access to what is written. If an individual enters a library and accesses a database, someone is paying for it. If a database is not available and a print resource is consulted, someone is paying for it. If the same individual accesses the free Web databases I described in Chapter One (i.e., ERIC, Ingenta, PubMed), they can accomplish the same objective free of charge.

Don't forget free journals and magazines: Remember that the FindArticles collection of 500 titles has the potential to save a voracious reader at least $20,000 per year on subscriptions. The alert Web surfer can locate innumerable articles that would cost a significant amount of money at the bookstore, newsstand, or by subscription. In most cases database vendors and content aggregators charge customers for almost every article located and read. Of course, the virtual articles aren't palpable—unless we print them— so we can't read them in the doctor's office or the barber's chair. But given time and handheld devices, we won't pine for the paper copies. In the interim, knowing where you can get the free articles and reading them when appropriate shouldn't be too hard to take.

Web-based chat reference with a librarian has many economic implications. Librarians are rising to the challenge of meeting the information needs of the public around the clock. They usually have relatively modest financial resources. To plan for and execute this type of service is an astonishing achievement. Library consortia are creating a solution for what individual libraries cannot do. When an individual connects with a librarian through a virtual reference environment, the cost may be transparent, but each answer has value.

It's Not Always About Money

Some of the value you accrue from the Web sites in this book will be intangible. How much is it worth to get a free breaking news e-mail that you can forward to an interested friend or colleague? How much is it worth for a patient to read about a treatment from a free medical preprint on the Web and have a physician decide it might be worth investigating? We cannot put a price on what we gain from accessing a multimedia presentation from a museum thousands of miles away. Perhaps we can revisit a gallery exhibition that we attended several years ago, but we can't really say we saved the $20 admission fee, only that we reinforced the impressions that we acquired when we enjoyed the real thing. These are things we cannot put a price on, but they have value.

What May Never Be in the Web Library

If a company or a person has the legal right to charge for something or has copyrighted something that otherwise could be digitized and made freely available, chances are it isn't something you will be able to view, download, or copy without paying (or breaking the law). The newest bestsellers—in fact, the majority of copyrighted books—are not going to be accessible without a fee. You may be able to locate promotional copies of books that you can download, but you'll never find all of the same titles that your public library displays on its "New Books" shelf. Conversely, there is still plenty to read that is free. If you started today, you'd have a big task ahead of you before you consumed it all.

Sensitive and proprietary business information is difficult to come by. It is true that you can access the annual reports of public companies, but judging from the recent stories of the bookkeeping practices of some top businesses, they may not always be of much help anyway.

Remain focused on the expanded capabilities of the Web. Sometimes your favorite magazine won't put the entire latest issue on the Web for a few weeks, but its Web site probably has far more in-depth information available that may include items that never appear in print. Perhaps you cannot view the entire newscast from PBS on the Web, but you can revisit important segments again and again.

Stay Tuned

While gathering information for this book, I encountered many people who communicated an ideal. They shared an excitement about making information available on the Web, for free, for everyone. This excitement and dedication is evident when we visit their Web sites. If there is information that can be legally digitized and put on the Web, there are people who will do it, often just on principle. Personally, I am waiting for an individual or institution to digitize Samuel Johnson's *Dictionary of the English Language*. It contains 114,000 illustrative quotations gathered by Dr. Johnson (they must be real "classics"). A digital version is available on CD-ROM for $295. But if someone can digitize the Gutenberg Bible, Johnson's *Dictionary* can't be far behind.

During our interview, Michael Hart of Project Gutenberg stated, "Drives keep driving, the Net keeps Netting." Raj Reddy, Herbert A. Simon professor of computer science and robotics at Carnegie Mellon University and internationally renowned scholar with a commitment to universally accessible digital libraries, reminded attendees at Georgia Tech's 10th Anniversary Convocation in April 2001 of "Moore's Law." Specifically, computational power doubles every 18 months for a 100-fold improvement over the next decade.[1] Dr. Reddy and colleagues from Carnegie Mellon, the National Science Foundation, the Massachusetts Institute of Technology, the Digital Library Federation, the Chinese Academy of Science, the Indian Institute of Science, and Beijing University (and others) have envisioned, planned, and begun work on the "Universal Library."[2] Their objective is to digitize all noncopyrighted works and any worthy copyrighted works that they are granted permission to digitize. The goal goes beyond books. Art, music, and video will also join the collection. Among many proposed components are "The Historical New York Times Project" (all *New York Times* issues in the public domain from 1851 to 1923) and "A Thousand Newspapers for a Thousand Years." They hope to offer one million books by 2005.[3] The Universal Library's current collection of books is available at its main URL (http://www.ul.cs. cmu.edu/html/index.html); its collection of multimedia and lectures is available at http://wean1.ulib.org/Lectures. "The Historical New York Times Project" is ongoing, and what has been loaded is exciting. View it at http://www.nyt.ulib.org.

Dr. Reddy told me that, "This is all going forward." He emphasized the need to perfectly execute the project, and cited several quality control issues that required addressing. For example, to be truly universal, the library must resolve language issues. Concerning the actual presentation of information, Dr. Reddy underscored the necessity of making certain that the data can be easily read and not default to quick and easy methods of uploading text.

Conclusion

As individuals take more control of their information needs, guided by librarians when appropriate, it becomes apparent that we've begun a revolutionary trek. Knowing about, linking to, reading from, and using the Web sites recommended in this book will provide immediate value; but we have only just achieved liftoff.

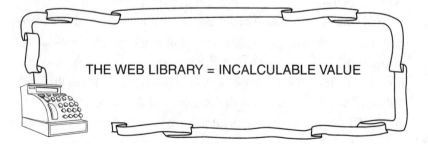

THE WEB LIBRARY = INCALCULABLE VALUE

Endnotes

1. Raj Reddy. "Computing: The Next Ten Years." April 6, 2001.
   http://www.cc.gatech.edu/external.affairs/anniversary/rajreddy.ppt.
   August 26, 2002.

2. Ruth Hammond. "The Ultimate Book Stacks: Universal Library
   Dwarfs Even Andy's Dream." *Carnegie Mellon Magazine*. Fall 2001.
   pp. 27–33. http://www.abbottdigital.com/more/univlib.pdf. August
   26, 2002.

3. Universal Library. Goals. http://ul.cs.cmu.edu. August 26, 2002.

Appendix:
Referenced Web Sites

Chapter One: Free Articles and Indexes

Free Articles

BioMed Central, http://www.biomedcentral.com

Dissertation Abstracts, http://wwwlib.umi.com/
dissertations/search

Electronic Journals from the Digital Library and Archives,
University Libraries, Virginia Polytechnic Institute and State
University, http://scholar.lib.vt.edu/ejournals

FindArticles, http://www.findarticles.com

HighWire Press, http://highwire.stanford.edu/lists/freeart.dtl

Internet Library of Early Journals, http://www.bodley.ox.ac.
uk/ilej

Making of America Journals at Cornell University,
http://cdl.library.cornell.edu/moa

Making of America Journals at University of Michigan,
http://www.hti.umich.edu/m/moajrnl

Portals to Free Articles

Online Books Serials Page, http://onlinebooks.library.upenn.
edu/serials.html

Resources for Research Periodicals, http://home.earthlink.net/
~ellengarvey/rsapresource1.html

Individual Magazines and Journals

Atlantic Unbound, http://www.theatlantic.com

Time Magazine, http://www.time.com

Other Individual Magazine Sites Through Google

http://directory.google.com/Top/Shopping/Publications/
Magazines

http://directory.google.com/Top/News/Magazines_and_
E-zines/E-zines/Directories

http://directory.google.com/Top/Arts/Online_Writing/
E-zines/Directories

http://directory.google.com/Top/News/Magazines_and_
E-zines/Directories

Other Individual Magazine Sites Through the Open Directory Project

http://search.dmoz.org/cgi-bin/search?search=magazines

Article Search from Magazine Sites/Links to Individual Magazines

Electronic Journal Miner, http://ejournal.coalliance.org,
http://ejournal.coalliance.org/info/other.html

Famous Magazines, http://magazineworld.spedia.net

Free Medical Journals Database, http://www.freemedical
journals.com

Headline Spot, http://www.headlinespot.com/type/magazines

Internet Public Library Serials, http://www.ipl.org/div/serials

Librarians' Index to the Internet: Magazines by Topic,
http://www.lii.org/search/file/magazines

Librarians' Index to the Internet: Periodicals,
http://www.lii.org/search?query=Periodicals;searchtype=
subject;view_all=Please

Magatopia, http://www.magatopia.com

Magazine Directory, http://magazine-directory.com

Magazines A to Z, http://www.magazinesatoz.com

magOmania, http://www.magomania.com

MagPortal.com, http://www.magportal.com

Newsdirectory List of Magazines, http://www.newsdirectory.
com/news/magazine

Primedia Business Magazines, http://industryclick.com/
icmagazines.asp

Free Indexes for Locating Bibliographic Information

Ask ERIC, http://www.askeric.org/Eric

Infotrieve, http://www4.infotrieve.com (DocSource and
MEDLINE only)

Ingenta, http://www.ingenta.com

MEDLINE/PubMed, http://www.ncbi.nlm.nih.gov/PubMed

National Criminal Justice Reference Service, http://www.ncjrs.
org/search.html

PubMed, http://www.ncbi.nlm.nih.gov/PubMed

Scientific Preprints

American Physical Society E-Prints, http://publish.aps.org/eprint

ARC: The Cross Archive Searching Service, http://arc.cs.odu.edu

CERN Document Server: Preprints, http://preprints.cern.ch

Chemical Physics Preprint Database, http://www.chem.brown.
edu/chem-ph.html

ChemWeb, http://www.chemweb.com

Clinmed Netprints, http://clinmed.netprints.org

E-Math, http://www.ams.org/preprints

e-Print Archive, http://xxx.arxiv.cornell.edu

NCSTRL (Networked Computer Science Technical Reference Library), http://www.ncstrl.org

PrePrint Network, http://www.osti.gov/preprint

SLAC SPIRES-HEP (Stanford Public Information Retrieval System —High Energy Physics), http://www-slac.slac.stanford.edu/find/spires.html

Social Science Research Network (SSRN), http://www.ssrn.com

Chapter Two: All the News that Fits and a Few Gigs More

Free Sites with High Standards

Hartford Courant, http://www.ctnow.com

Los Angeles Times, http://www.latimes.com

New York Times, http://www.nyt.com

Washington Post, http://www.washingtonpost.com

Links to News Sites

American Journalism Review, http://www.ajr.org/Newspapers.asp?MediaType=1

Google News Directory, http://directory.google.com/Top/News/Newspapers/Directories/NewsDirectory

News Directory, http://www.newsdirectory.com

NewsLink, http://www.newslink.org

Open Directory News, http://dmoz.org/News/Newspapers

RefDesk Newspaper Links, http://www.refdesk.com/paper.html

Yahoo! Newspapers, http://dir.yahoo.com/News_and_Media/Newspapers

News by Country or Region
Google Regional News, http://directory.google.com/Top/News/
Newspapers/Regional

Yahoo! News by Country, http://dir.yahoo.com/News_and_
Media/Newspapers/By_Region/Countries

Foreign Language News at MIT, http://libraries.mit.edu/
guides/types/flnews

Broadcast Journalism Sites
BBCi, http://news.bbc.co.uk

CBS News, http://www.cbsnews.com

C/NET: Tech News First, http://news.com.com

CNN, http://www.cnn.com

MSNBC, http://www.msnbc.com

National Public Radio, http://www.npr.org

Online Newshour with Jim Lehrer, http://www.pbs.org/
newshour

Alternative News
Ananova, http://www.ananova.com

Weblogs
Library & Information Science News, http://www.lisnews.com

Blogger, http://www.blogger.com

Blog Links and Search Engines
Blogdex MIT Media Lab, http://blogdex.net

Daypop, http://www.daypop.com

EatonWeb Portal, http://portal.eatonweb.com

Google Weblog Directory, http://directory.google.com/Top/
Computers/Internet/On_the_Web/Weblogs

Technorati, http://www.Technorati.com

Userland, http://www.weblogs.com

Archives of Older News

NewspaperArchive, http://www.newspaperarchive.com

U.S. News Archives of the Web, http://www.ibiblio.org/slanews/
internet/archives.html

News Search Engines

Google News, http://news.google.com

Ithaki News Metasearch, http://ithaki.net/news

Moreover Showcase News Portal, http://www.moreover.com/
cgi-local/page?o=portal

World News, http://www.worldnews.com

Breaking News and E-Mailed Alerts

ABCNews, http://www.abcnews.com

CNN's E-Mail Services, http://www.cnn.com/EMAIL

CNN Keyword Defined Alerts, http://www.cnn.com/youralerts

MSNBC, http://www.msnbc.com

Google's Customized News Alerts, http://www.google.com/
newsalerts

Sports Newsletters and Alerts

About.com, http://about.com/sports/newsletters.htm

CNNsi, http://www.cnnsi.com

Create Your Own News Portal

NewsIsFree, http://www.newsisfree.com

Chapter Three: Ready or Not?
Reference on the Web

Almanacs

African American Almanac, http://www.toptags.com/aama

Information Please Almanac, http://www.infoplease.com

Old Farmer's Almanac, http://www.almanac.com

World Almanac for Kids, http://www.worldalmanacforkids.com

Encyclopedias

Columbia Encyclopedia, http://www.bartleby.com/65

Encyclopedia.com, http://www.encyclopedia.com

Internet Public Library Music History 102: A Guide to Western Composers and Their Music from the Middle Ages to the Present, http://www.ipl.org/exhibit/mushist

Jewish Virtual Library, http://www.us-israel.org/jsource

King James Bible at the Electronic Text Center, Univ. of Virginia, http://etext.lib.virginia.edu/kjv.browse.html

Microsoft Network, http://encarta.msn.com/encnet/refpages/artcenter.aspx

New Advent Catholic Encyclopedia, http://www.newadvent.org/cathen

Nolo's Legal Encyclopedia, http://www.nolo.com/lawcenter/ency/index.cfm

University of Michigan Instrument Encyclopedia, http://www.si.umich.edu/chico/instrument

University of Michigan Instrument Encyclopedia, http://www.si.umich.edu/chico/instrument

Yahoo! Education, http://education.yahoo.com/reference/encyclopedia

Quotations

Bartleby.com, http://www.bartleby.com, includes:

- Bartlett's Familiar Quotations, 1919
  http://www.bartleby.com/100

- Columbia World of Quotations
  http://www.bartleby.com/66

- Simpson's Contemporary Quotations 1950–1988
  http://www.bartleby.com/63

Quoteland, http://www.quoteland.com

Yahoo! Graduation Speeches, http://dir.yahoo.com/Education/ Graduation/Speeches

Dictionaries/Language

Acronym Finder, http://www.acronymfinder.com

Allwords—With Crossword Solver, http://www.allwords.com

American Heritage Dictionary of the English Language, http://www.bartleby.com/61

American Verse Project, http://www.hti.umich.edu/a/amverse

Bartleby Verse, http://www.bartleby.com/verse

Chicago Manual of Style FAQ, http://www.press.uchicago.edu/ Misc/Chicago/cmosfaq.html

Dictionary of Difficult Words, http://www.tiscali.co.uk/ reference/dictionaries/difficultwords

Dictionary.com, http://www.dictionary.com

Merriam-Webster Online Language Center, http://www.m-w.com

Nolo's "Shark Talk" (Everybody's Legal Dictionary), http://www.nolo.com/lawcenter/dictionary/wordindex.cfm

OneLook Dictionaries—Search 738 online dictionaries at once, http://www.onelook.com

Roget's II: The New Thesaurus, 3rd ed. 1995., http://www. bartleby.com/62

University of Wisconsin, Madison: Writer's Handbook, http://www.wisc.edu/writing/Handbook/DocChicago.html

Your Dictionary, http://www.yourdictionary.com

Facts

Famous Firsts, http://www.corsinet.com/trivia/1-triv.html

Fast Facts: Almanacs/Factbooks/Statistical Reports & Related Reference Tools, http://www.freepint.com/gary/ handbook.htm

Guinness World Records, http://www.guinnessworldrecords.com

Health Information

American Medical Association Online Doctor Finder, http://www.ama-assn.org/aps/amahg.htm

Columbia Home Medical Guide (Columbia University College of Physicians and Surgeons), http://cpmcnet.columbia.edu/texts/guide

MayoClinic.com—Drug Information, http://www.mayoclinic.com/findinformation/druginformation/index.cfm

MEDLINEplus Directory of Dentists and Doctors, http://www.nlm.nih.gov/medlineplus/directories.html

MedlinePlus Drug Information, http://www.nlm.nih.gov/medlineplus/druginformation.html

MEDLINEplus Health Topics, http://www.nlm.nih.gov/medlineplus/healthtopics.html

MEDLINEplus Medical Dictionaries, http://www.nlm.nih.gov/medlineplus/dictionaries.html

MEDLINEplus Medical Encyclopedia, http://www.nlm.nih.gov/medlineplus/encyclopedia.html

Merck Manual Centennial Edition, http://www.merck.com/pubs/mmanual

Merck Manual of Medical Information, Home Edition, http://www.merck.com/pubs/mmanual_home/contents.htm

WebMD Drugs and Herbs, http://my.webmd.com/drugs

Geography

Columbia Gazetteer of North America, http://www.bartleby.com/69

Getty Thesaurus of Geographical Names, http://www.getty.edu/research/tools/vocabulary/tgn

United States Census Bureau, U.S. Gazetteer, http://www.
census.gov/cgi-bin/gazetteer

Worldwide Directory of Cities and Towns, http://www.calle.com/
world

World Sites Atlas, http://www.sitesatlas.com/Maps/index.htm

National Geographic Map Machine, http://plasma.national
geographic.com/mapmachine/index.html

MSN Maps & Directories, http://mappoint.msn.com

Yahoo! Maps, http://maps.yahoo.com

Biography

Academy of Achievement, http://www.achievement.org

Biographical Dictionary, http://www.s9.com/biography

Biography.com, http://www.biography.com

Librarians' Index to the Internet Individual Biography Sites,
http://www.lii.org/search?title=People;query=People;
subsearch=People;searchtype=subject

Art

Artcyclopedia, http://www.artcyclopedia.com

Metropolitan Museum of Art, http://www.metmuseum.org

Paris Pages Musee du Louvre, http://www.paris.org/
Musees/Louvre

Smithsonian Museums, http://www.si.edu/museums

Web Museum, http://www.ibiblio.org/wm

Book and Magazine Information

Amazon.com, http://www.amazon.com

Library of Congress Online Catalog, http://catalog.loc.gov

Bookfinder.com, http://www.bookfinder.com

Publist, http://www.publist.com

Business/Career

Dictionary of Occupational Titles (U.S. Department of Labor), http://www.oalj.dol.gov/libdot.htm

Hoover's Online, http://www.hoovers.com

North American Industry Classification System/Standard Industrial Classification Codes, http://www.census.gov/epcd/www/naics.html

Securities and Exchange Commission, http://www.sec.gov/edgar.shtml

Thomas Register, http://www.thomasregister.com

U.S. Department of Labor Occupational Outlook Handbook Online, http://www.bls.gov/oco/home.htm

Calculation and Conversion Tools

OnlineConversion.com—Convert Just About Anything to Anything Else, http://www.onlineconversion.com

Universal Currency Converter, http://www.xe.com/ucc

Colleges

Princeton Review: Best 331 College Rankings, http://www.review.com/college/rankings.cfm

Countries

Central Intelligence Agency: The World Factbook, http://www.cia.gov/cia/publications/factbook/

Library of Congress Country Studies, http://lcweb2.loc.gov/frd/cs/cshome.html

Lonely Planet, http://www.lonelyplanet.com

United States Department of State Background Notes, http://www.state.gov/r/pa/ei/bgn

World Factbook 2002, http://www.bartleby.com/151

Directory Information

AnyWho: Internet Directory Assistance, http://www.anywho. com/index.html

InfoSpace, http://www.infospace.com

Switchboard.com, http://www.switchboard.com

WhoWhere, http://www.whowhere.lycos.com

ZIP Code Lookup (United States Postal Service), http://www. usps.com/zip4/welcome.htm

Other Reference Sites

AdAccess, http://scriptorium.lib.duke.edu/adaccess

Adflip, http://www.adflip.com

All Classical Guide, http://allclassical.com

All Movie Guide, http://www.allmovie.com

All Music Guide, http://allmusic.com

AllRecipes.com, http://www.allrecipes.com

AltaVista's Babelfish, http://babelfish.altavista.com

American Advertising Museum, http://www.admuseum.org

Associations Central, http://www.associationcentral.com

Associations on the Net, http://www.ipl.org/div/aon

Boston Cooking School Cook Book (Fannie Farmer), http://www.bartleby.com/87

Botany.com, http://www.botany.com

Cemetery Transcription Library, http://www.interment.net

Constitution Society, http://www.constitution.org/rror/ rror--00.htm

Cyndi's List of Genealogy Sites on the Internet, http://www. cyndislist.com

Domania, http://www.domania.com

Emily Post Institute Etiquette Tips, http://www.emilypost.com/etiquette_index.htm

Encyclopedia of the Atmospheric Environment, http://www.doc.mmu.ac.uk/aric/eae/english.html

Eric Weisstein's World of Science, http://scienceworld.wolfram.com

Etiquette in Society, in Business, in Politics and at Home, by Emily Post, 1922, http://www.bartleby.com/95

Find a Grave, http://www.findagrave.com

FindLaw, http://www.findlaw.com

Free Translation.com, http://freetranslation.com

GourmetSpot, http://www.gourmetspot.com/recipes.htm

Internet Encyclopedia of Philosophy, http://www.utm.edu/research/iep

Internet Movie Database, http://www.imdb.com

Life Science Dictionary, http://biotech.icmb.utexas.edu/search/dict-search.html

NADA Appraisal Guides, http://www.nadaguides.com

Nolo—Law for All, http://www.nolo.com

Physics and Astronomy Online Education and Reference, http://www.physlink.com/Reference/Index.cfm

Realtor.com, http://www.realtor.com

Recipe Source, http://www.recipesource.com

Stanford Encyclopedia of Philosophy, http://plato.stanford.edu/contents.html

Virtual Bird Field Guide, http://birding.about.com/library/fg/blfg.htm

United States Census Data and Demographics

American FactFinder, http://factfinder.census.gov

CensusScope, http://www.censusscope.org/index.html

United States Census Bureau, http://www.census.gov/
statab/www

Sites Linking to Reference Materials

Internet Public Library Ready Reference, http://www.ipl.org/ref

Librarians' Index to the Internet, http://lii.org

LibrarySpot, http://www.libraryspot.com

RefDesk.com, http://www.refdesk.com

Virtual Reference Shelf: Selected Web Resources Compiled by the
Library of Congress, http://www.loc.gov/rr/askalib/
virtualref.html

Chapter Four: Reference Part II: Expert, AskA, and Digital Reference Services

AskA Services, General

Abuzz, http://www.abuzz.com

AllExperts, http://www.allexperts.com

Ask Jack, http://www.naysi.com/ask_jack/ask_jack.htm

Ask Jeeves, http://www.ask.com

Ask Joan of Art, http://nmaa-ryder.si.edu/study/nav-joan.html

Ask the Bird Expert, http://www.upatsix.com/ask-experts

AskERIC, http://ericir.syr.edu/About

Culinary.com, http://www.culinary.com

Ehow, http://www.ehow.com

FIND/SVP, http://www.findsvp.com

Google Answers, http://answers.google.com

Pitsco's Ask an Expert—the Kid Friendly Expert Site,
http://www.askanexpert.com

Usenet Groups via Google, http://www.google.com (click the "Groups" tab)

AskA Resources from Libraries

Bernie Sloan. A list of libraries offering e-mail reference, http://alexia.lis.uiuc.edu/~b-sloan/e-mail.html

Bernie Sloan. A list of collaborative live reference projects, http://www.lis.uiuc.edu/~b-sloan/collab.htm

Co-East (East of England), http://www.ask-a-librarian.org.uk

ELITE: Electronic Library, IT and Staff Education Project, http://www.le.ac.uk/li/distance/eliteproject/elib/chat.html

Gerry McKiernan. Registry of Real-Time Digital Reference Services, http://www.public.iastate.edu/~CYBERSTACKS/LiveRef.htm

Google directory, http://directory.google.com/Top/Reference/Ask_an_Expert/Libraries

Internet Public Library, http://www.ipl.org/div/askus

QuestionPoint at the Library of Congress, http://www.loc.gov/rr/askalib/chat-main.html

Links to Experts

AskA+ Locator, http://www.vrd.org/locator/subject.shtml

Canadian Learning Bank, http://www.cln.org/int_expert.html

Johnston Memorial School, http://www.geocities.com/johnstona1/know.html

RefDesk.com, http://www.refdesk.com/expert.html

Searchable Archive of Answers to Difficult Reference Questions

STUMPERS-L, http://listserv.dom.edu/archives/stumpers-l.html

Chapter Five: Books in the Web Library

Collections

Adelaide University Library E-Books, http://www.library.
adelaide.edu.au/etext

Alex Catalogue of Electronic Texts, http://www.infomotions.
com/alex

Bartleby.com: Great Books Online, http://www.bartleby.com

Bibliomania, http://www.bibliomania.com

Blackmask Online, http://www.blackmask.com

BookRags, http://www.bookrags.com

Eserver (formerly "The English Server"), http://eserver.org

Humanities Text Initiative, http://www.hti.umich.edu

Litrix Reading Room, http://www.litrix.com

Making of America Books, http://www.hti.umich.edu/m/
moa.new

Online Books Page, University of Pennsylvania, http://
onlinebooks.library.upenn.edu

Project Gutenberg, http://www.promo.net/pg

Renascence Editions, http://darkwing.uoregon.edu/~rbear/
ren.htm

University of Virginia's E-Book Library, http://etext.lib.virginia.
edu/ebooks/ebooklist.html

University of Virginia Electronic Texts, http://etext.lib.virginia.
edu

Web-Books.Com, http://www.web-books.com

Zeroland's Live Text Databases, Online Literature,
E-Libraries (New Zealand), http://www.zeroland.co.nz/
literature-etexts.html

Copyright Information

Extension of copyright explained, http://www.loc.gov/
copyright/circs/circ15t.pdf

New terms for copyright protection at, http://www.loc.gov/
copyright/slcirc15.pdf

Free Electronic Books from Commercial Sources

Adobe E-Book Store, http://bookstore.glassbook.com/store/
default.asp

Amazon.com eBooks Free Downloads, http://www.amazon.com/
exec/obidos/tg/browse/-/556968/104-7464443-1538330

EBookMall Free eBooks, http://www.ebookmall.com/
free-downloads.htm

Links to Electronic Books

CARRIE, http://www.ukans.edu/carrie

Electronic Texts on the Internet, http://www.refdesk.com/
factelec.html

Google Directory of Electronic Text Archives, http://directory.
google.com/alpha/Top/Arts/Literature/Electronic_Text_
Archives

Internet Public Library Book Collection, http://www.ipl.org/
div/books

Search Engine for Locating Electronic Books

SearcheBooks, http://www.searchebooks.com

Hypertext

Eastgate Systems "Serious Hypertext," http://www.eastgate.com

ELO—Electronic Literature Organization, http://www.
eliterature.org

Edward Picot's Independent Fiction, http://www.edwardpicot.
com/index.html including:

* Republic Pemberly, http://www.pemberley.com/janeinfo/
janeinfo.html

* Victorian Web, http://www.victorianweb.org

Chapter Six: When Image Is Everything

Image Search Engines

AltaVista Image Search, http://www.altavista.com/image/default

Big Search Engine Index to Images, http://www.
search-engine-index.co.uk/Images_Search

Ditto, http://www.ditto.com

Excite, http://www.excite.com

FAST Multimedia Search, http://multimedia.alltheweb.com

Google Image Search, http://www.google.com/advanced_
image_search

HotBot, http://hotbot.com

Ithaki Image and Photo Metasearch, http://www.ithaki.net/
images

IXQUICK, http://www.ixquick.com

Lycos Multimedia Search, http://multimedia.lycos.com

Picsearch, http://www.picsearch.com

Yahoo! Picture Gallery, http://gallery.yahoo.com

Examples of Image Collections

American Memory at the Library of Congress, http://memory.loc.
gov/ammem/amhome.html

Artcyclopedia, http://www.artcyclopedia.com

FreeFoto.com, http://www.freefoto.com

Free Images.com, http://www.freeimages.com

Free Images and Free Stock Photos, http://www.freeimages.co.uk

FreeStockPhotos.com, http://freestockphotos.com

Thinker Image Database, http://www.thinker.org

Public Domain Images, http://www.pdimages.com

Pay Services

Art Today, http://www.arttoday.com

Corbis, http://www.corbis.com

Getty Images, http://www.gettyimages.com

GoGraph, http://www.graphsearch.com

Imagestate, http://www.imagestate.com

TimePix, http://www.timepix.com

Copyright and Digital Watermarking

Digimarc, http://www.digimarc.com/products.htm

Blue Spike, http://www.bluespike.com/art.html

Digital Millennium Copyright Act Summary, http://www.loc.gov/
copyright/legislation/dmca.pdf

Net Copyright Law, http://netcopyrightlaw.com

Chapter Seven: Pixels at an Exhibition

Search Resources for Locating Online Special Collections/Exhibitions

Archives & Museum Informatics "Best of 2000-2002,"
http://www.archimuse.com/mw2001/best/index.html
http://www.archimuse.com/mw2002/best/index.html
http://www.archimuse.com/mw2003/best/index.html
http://www.archimuse.com/mw2004/best/index.html

Art Museum Network, http://www.artmuseumnetwork.org

Google Art Museums, http://directory.google.com/Top/
Reference/Museums/Arts_and_Entertainment/Art_Museums

Google Museum Directory, http://directory.google.com/Top/
Reference/Museums/Library

Archival Exhibitions on the Web, http://www.sil.si.edu/
SILPublications/Online-Exhibitions

MuseumStuff.com, http://www.museumstuff.com/exhibits/
index.html

WebExhibits.org, http://www.webexhibits.org

World Wide Web Virtual Library Museum Pages, http://www.
icom.org/vlmp

Exemplary Exhibitions

Art of the Motorcycle, http://www.guggenheim.org/exhibitions/
past_exhibitions/motorcycle/motorcycle.html

Artists of Brücke (MoMA), http://www.moma.org/brucke

Clockworks from the Sundial to the Atomic Second,
http://www.britannica.com/clockworks/main.html

Dangerous Curves: The Art of the Guitar, http://207.127.106.123/
exhibitions/guitars/preview_launch.htm

Frick Collection Comprehensive List of Paintings,
http://www.frick.org/html/pntgls1f.htm

Hitchcock and Art: Fatal Coincidences, http://www.mbam.
qc.ca/expopassees/a-hitchcock.html

Internet Public Library Exhibits, http://www.ipl.org/div/exhibit

Museum of Fine Arts, Boston, http://www.mfa.org/artemis/
collections

Museum of Modern Art Online Projects, http://www.moma.org/
onlineprojects

National Gallery of Art: "In-Depth Study Tours," http://www.nga.
gov/onlinetours/onlinetr.htm

Russian Avant-Garde Book 1910–1934 (MoMA), http://www.
moma.org/russian

Education (Examples)

Art Renewal Center, http://www.artrenewal.org

Frankenstein: Penetrating the Secrets of Nature, http://www.nlm.
nih.gov/hmd/frankenstein/frankhome.html

Intel Museum, http://www.intel.com/intel/intelis/museum/
exhibits/ex_index.htm

Ocean Planet, http://seawifs.gsfc.nasa.gov/ocean_planet.html

Entertainment (Examples)

Life Magazine Cover Collection, http://www.life.com/Life/
search/covers

National Baseball Hall of Fame Online Exhibits Cooperstown,
New York, http://www.baseballhalloffame.org/exhibits/
online_exhibits/index.htm

Speak Softly and Carry a Beagle: The Art of Charles Shulz,
http://www.nrm.org/exhibits/schulz/gallery

Special Research Collections (Examples)

Chicago Historical Society: The Haymarket Affair Digital
Collection, http://www.chicagohs.org/hadc

Gottingen Gutenberg Bible, http://www.gutenbergdigital.de/
gudi/start.htm

Gutenberg Bible: Digitized Images (The British Library),
http://prodigi.bl.uk/gutenbg/default.asp

Library of Congress American Memory Exhibits,
http://memory.loc.gov/ammem/ammemhome.html

Library of Congress Rare Books and Special Collections Division,
http://www.octavo.com/collections/projects/gtnbbl/
index.html

Do-It-Yourself Exhibit

Create Your Own Exhibit at the Fine Arts Museum of San Francisco's "Virtual Gallery," http://www.thinker.org

Chapter Eight: Software Keys to the Web Library

Basic Plug-Ins

Adobe Reader, http://www.adobe.com/products/acrobat/readstep2.html

Microsoft Reader, http://www.microsoft.com/reader/downloads/pc.asp

Winzip, http://www.winzip.com

E-Book and Document Software Downloads

AportisDoc Reader for Palm Powered Devices, http://www.aportis.com/tryme/download/AportisDoc/aportisdocreader.html

MobiPocket Reader, http://www.mobipocket.com/en/HomePage/default.asp

Palm Reader for Windows, Palm Reader for Macintosh, Palm Reader for Pocket PC, and Palm Reader for Palm OS, http://www.peanutpress.com/product/reader/browse/free

Multimedia Plug-Ins

Adobe SVG Viewer, http://www.adobe.com/svg/viewer/install/main.html

Apple Quick Time, http://www.apple.com/quicktime/download

Macromedia Flash and Macromedia Shockwave, http://www.macromedia.com/software/downloads

RealOne Player, http://www.real.com
(Note: Be sure to select the "free" version.)

Windows Media Player, http://www.microsoft.com/windows/windowsmedia/download/default.asp

Additional Plug-In Help

C/Net's Shareware, http://shareware.cnet.com

Netscape's Plug-in Finder, http://wp.netscape.com/
plugins/index.html

Yahoo's Plug-in Directory, http://dir.yahoo.com/Computers_and_
Internet/Software/Internet/World_Wide_Web/Browsers/Plug_
Ins

Toolbars

Alexa Toolbar, http://www.alexa.com

Ask Jeeves Toolbar, http://sp.ask.com/docs/toolbar

Google Toolbar, http://toolbar.google.com

Mozilla Googlebar, http://googlebar.mozdev.org

Teoma Search Bar, http://sp.ask.com/docs/teoma/toolbar

Ultrabar, http://ultrabar.com

Yahoo! Companion, http://companion.yahoo.com

Creating Your Personal Web Portal

Anglefire, http://angelfire.lycos.com

Tripod, http://www.tripod.lycos.com/host/free.html

Yahoo!'s Geocities, http://geocities.yahoo.com

Chapter Nine: Final Considerations

The Universal Library (Main URL and Book Collection),
http://www.ul.cs.cmu.edu/html/index.html

Universal Library Collection of Multimedia and Lectures,
http://wean1.ulib.org/Lectures

Universal Library "The Historical New York Times Project"
(ongoing), http://www.nyt.ulib.org

About the Author

Nicholas G. Tomaiuolo is a librarian and writer with a special interest in free Web content.

A native of Connecticut, Nick earned his graduate degree in library science from Southern Connecticut State University where he also merited introduction into Beta Phi Mu, the International Honor Society for Library Science. He earned a Bachelor of Science degree in Secondary English Education from the University of Connecticut and has also studied at Northeastern University and Trinity College (Hartford).

From 1988 to 1994 Nick worked as a clinical librarian and library education coordinator at the University of Connecticut Health Center. In July 1994 he began his current position as associate librarian in the reference department at the Elihu Burritt Library at Central Connecticut State University. His journal and magazine articles have appeared in *Searcher, Online, Computers in Libraries, Civilization: The Magazine of the Library of Congress,* and many others.

Aside from mining the Web, Nick enjoys being with his children, reading classic literature, and attending the theater.

About the Editor

After graduating library school in 1966, Barbara Quint went to work at the RAND Corporation, where she spent close to 20 years, almost all of it as head of Reference Services. In the course of that employment, she began her career as an online searcher. Her experience in founding the Southern California Online Users Group (SCOUG) led to her role as a consumer advocate for online searchers everywhere, a role that led her to leave familiar library work and become a leading writer and editor in the online trade press. In 1985, Barbara began editing *Database Searcher* for the Meckler Corporation, which led in 1993 to her current position as editor-in-chief of *Searcher* magazine for Information Today, Inc. She has also spoken often at national and international meetings, writes the "Quint's Online" column for *Information Today*, and operates her own information broker service, Quint and Associates.

Index

Page numbers in italics indicate figures, tables, and illustrations.

More Great Books from Information Today, Inc.

The Extreme Searcher's Internet Handbook

By Randolph Hock

The Extreme Searcher's Internet Handbook is the essential guide for anyone who uses the Internet for research—librarians, teachers, students, writers, business professionals, and others who need to search the Web proficiently. Award-winning writer and Internet trainer Randolph "Ran" Hock covers strategies and tools (including search engines, directories, and portals) for all major areas of Internet content.

There's something here for every Internet searcher. Readers with little to moderate searching experience will appreciate the helpful, easy-to-follow advice, while experienced searchers will discover a wealth of new ideas, techniques, and resources. Anyone who teaches the Internet will find this book indispensable.

As a reader bonus, the author maintains "The Extreme Searcher's Web Page" featuring links, updates, news, and much more. It's the ideal starting place for any Web search.

2004/296 pp/softbound/ISBN 0-910965-68-4 • $24.95

The Accidental Webmaster

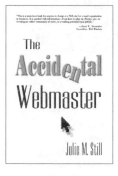

By Julie M. Still

Here is a lifeline for the individual who has not been trained as a Webmaster, but who—whether by choice or under duress—has become one nonetheless. While most Webmastering books focus on programming and related technical issues, *The Accidental Webmaster* helps readers deal with the full range of challenges they face on the job. Author, librarian, and accidental Webmaster Julie Still offers advice on getting started, setting policies, working with ISPs, designing home pages, selecting content, drawing site traffic, gaining user feedback, fundraising, avoiding copyright problems, and much more.

2003/208 pp/softbound/ISBN 1-57387-164-8 • $29.50

Business Statistics on the Web
Find Them Fast—At Little or No Cost

By Paula Berinstein

Statistics are a critical component of business and marketing plans, press releases, surveys, economic analyses, presentations, proposals, and more—yet good statistics are notoriously hard to find. This practical book by statistics guru Paula Berinstein shows readers how to use the Internet to find statistics about companies, markets, and industries, how to organize and present statistics, and how to evaluate them for reliability. Organized by topic, both general and specific, and by country/region, this helpful reference features easy-to-use tips and techniques for finding and using statistics when the pressure is on. In addition, dozens of extended and short case studies demonstrate the ins and outs of searching for specific numbers and maneuvering around obstacles to find the data you need.

2003/336 pp/softbound/ISBN: 0-910965-65-X • $29.95

The Skeptical Business Searcher
The *Information Advisor's* Guide to Evaluating Web Data, Sites, and Sources

By Robert Berkman
Foreword by Reva Basch

This is the experts' guide to finding high-quality company and industry data on the free Web. Information guru Robert Berkman offers business Internet users effective strategies for identifying and evaluating no-cost online information sources, emphasizing easy-to-use techniques for recognizing bias and misinformation. You'll learn where to go for company backgrounders, sales and earnings data, SEC filings and stockholder reports, public records, market research, competitive intelligence, staff directories, executive biographies, survey/poll data, news stories, and hard-to-find information about small businesses and niche markets. The author's unique table of "Internet Information Credibility Indicators" allows readers to systematically evaluate Web site reliability. Supported by a Web page.

2004/266 pp/softbound/ISBN 0-910965-66-8 • $29.95

Internet Prophets
Enlightened E-Business Strategies for Every Budget

By Mary Diffley

"A superb book ... full of insights into the Internet and ways to translate those insights into profits."

—Jay Conrad Levinson,
author of the *Guerilla Marketing* series

Since the bursting of the dot.com balloon, companies are approaching e-business with a new wariness— and rightly so, according to author and entrepreneur Mary Diffley. In *Internet Prophets*, Diffley speaks directly to the skeptics, serving up straightforward advice that will help even the most technophobic executive do more business on the Web. This readable, easy-to-use handbook is the first to detail the costs of proven e-commerce strategies, matching successful techniques with budgetary considerations for companies of all types and sizes. Unlike other books, *Internet Prophets* gets down to the nitty-gritty that every businessperson wants to know: "What's it going to cost?"

2002/366 pp/softbound/ISBN 0-910965-55-2 • $29.95

Super Searcher, Author, Scribe
Successful Writers Share Their Internet Research Secrets

By Loraine Page

Fifteen top writers share their Internet strategies and success stories. The impact of the Internet on the writing profession is unprecedented, even revolutionary. Wired writers of the 21st century rely on the Web to do research, to collaborate, to reach out to readers, and even to publish and sell their work.

Super Searcher, Author, Scribe illuminates the state of the art, bringing together a broad range of successful, Web-savvy writers to share their tips, techniques, sites, sources, and success stories. *Link-Up* editor Loraine Page combines a deft interviewing style and knowledge of the craft of writing to draw out gems of wisdom from fifteen leading journalists, book authors, writing instructors, and professional researchers in the literary field.

2002/216 pp/softbound/ISBN 0-910965-58-7 • $24.95

Web of Deception
Misinformation on the Internet

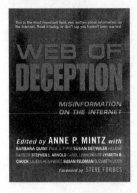

Edited by Anne P. Mintz
Foreword by Steve Forbes

"Experts here walk you through the risks and traps of the Web world and tell you how to avoid them or to fight back ... Anne Mintz and her collaborators have done us a geuine service"

—Steve Forbes, from the Foreword

Intentionally misleading or erroneous information on the Web can wreak havoc on your health, privacy, investments, business decisions, online purchases, legal affairs, and more. Until now, the breadth and significance of this growing problem for Internet users had yet to be fully explored. In *Web of Deception*, Anne P. Mintz (Director of Knowledge Management at Forbes, Inc.) brings together 10 information industry gurus to illuminate the issues and help you recognize and deal with the flood of deception and misinformation in a range of critical subject areas. A must-read for any Internet searcher who needs to evaluate online information sources and avoid Web traps.

2002/278 pp/softbound/ISBN 0-910965-60-9 • $24.95

Net Crimes & Misdemeanors
Outmaneuvering the Spammers, Swindlers, and Stalkers Who Are Targeting You Online

By J.A. Hitchcock
Edited by Loraine Page

Cyber crime expert J.A. Hitchcock helps individuals and business users of the Web protect themselves, their children, and their employees against online cheats and predators. Hitchcock details a broad range of abusive practices, shares victims' stories, and offers advice on how to handle junk e-mail, "flaming," privacy invasion, financial scams, cyberstalking, and indentity theft. She provides tips and techniques that can be put to immediate use and points to the laws, organizations, and Web resources that can aid victims and help them fight back. Supported by a Web site.

2002/384 pp/softbound/ISBN 0-910965-57-9 • $24.95

Electronic Democracy, 2nd Edition
Using the Internet to Transform American Politics

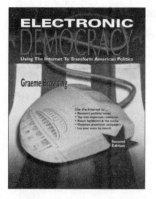

By Graeme Browning
Foreword by Adam Clayton Powell III

"By harnessing the power of the Internet to inform, organize, and advocate, Americans can use technology to broaden and deepen their role in our representative democracy. Combining political savvy with computer know-how, Graeme Browning shows us how."

—Bill Bradley

In this new edition of *Electronic Democracy*, award-winning journalist and author Graeme Browning details the colorful history of politics and the Net, describes key Web-based sources of political information, offers practical techniques for influencing legislation online, and provides a fascinating, realistic vision of the future.

2002/200 pp/softbound/ISBN 0-910965-49-8 • $19.95

Naked in Cyberspace, 2nd Edition
How to Find Personal Information Online

By Carole A. Lane
Foreword by Beth Givens

"Perfect for someone trying to trace a person with whom contact has been lost, or to build a profile of a potential business associate ... arguably the only essential manual for the work of today's private investigator."

—*The Electronic Library*

In this fully revised and updated second edition of her bestselling guide, author Carole A. Lane surveys the types of personal records that are available on the Internet and online services. Lane explains how researchers find and use personal data, identifies the most useful sources of information about people, and offers advice for readers with privacy concerns. You'll learn how to use online tools and databases to gain competitive intelligence, locate and investigate people, access public records, identify experts, find new customers, recruit employees, search for assets, uncover criminal records, conduct genealogical research, and much more. Supported by a Web page.

2002/586 pp/softbound/ISBN 0-910965-50-1 • $29.95

The Librarian's Internet Survival Guide
Strategies for the High-Tech Reference Desk

By Irene E. McDermott
Edited by Barbara Quint

"Finally—a comprehensive handbook written by a practitioner for practitioners. The Librarian's Internet Survival Guide *can be read cover to cover or one can cherry pick according to interest: biography, news, kids, health, privacy, it's all here."*

—Diane Kresh
Public Service Collections Library of Congress

In this authoritative and tremendously useful guide, Irene McDermott helps her fellow reference librarians succeed in the bold new world of the Web. *The Survival Guide* provides easy access to the information librarians need when the pressure is on: trouble-shooting tips and advice, Web resources for answering reference questions, and strategies for managing information and keeping current. In addition to helping librarians make the most of Web tools and resources, McDermott covers a full range of important issues including Internet training, privacy, child safety, helping patrons with special needs, building library Web pages, and much more.

2002/296 pp/softbound/ISBN 1-57387-129-X • $29.50

Net Effects
How Librarians Can Manage the Unintended Consequences of the Internet

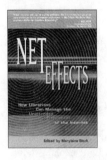

Edited by Marylaine Block

The Internet is a mixed blessing for libraries and librarians. On the one hand, it provides opportunities to add services and expand collections; on the other, it has increased user expectations and contributed to techno stress. Today, the Net is challenging librarians' ability to select, threatening the survival of the book, necessitating continuous retraining, presenting new problems of access and preservation, putting new demands on budgets, and embroiling information professionals in legal controversies.

In *Net Effects*, librarian, journalist, and Internet guru Marylaine Block examines the issues and brings together a wealth of insights, war stories, and solutions. Nearly 50 articles by dozens of imaginative librarians—expertly selected, annotated, and integrated by the editor—suggest practical and creative ways to deal with the range of Internet "side effects," regain control of the library, and avoid being blindsided by technology again.

2003/380 pp/softbound/ISBN 1-57387-171-0 • $39.50

Smart Services
Competitive Information Strategies, Solutions, and Success Stories for Service Businesses

By Deborah C. Sawyer

"Finally, a book that nails down what every service business needs to know about competition and competitive intelligence. Smart Services offers competitive information strategies that firms can put to immediate use."

—Andrew Garvin
CEO, FIND/SVP

Here is the first book to focus specifically on the competitive information needs of service-oriented firms. Author, entrepreneur, and business consultant Deborah C. Sawyer illuminates the many forms of competition in service businesses, identifies the most effective information resources for competitive intelligence (CI), and provides a practical framework for identifying and studying competitors in order to gain a competitive advantage. *Smart Services* is a roadmap for every service company owner, manager, or executive who expects to compete effectively in the Information Age.

2002/256 pp/softbound/ISBN 0-910965-56-0 • $29.95

Super Searchers on Competitive Intelligence
The Online and Offline Secrets of Top CI Researchers

By Margaret Metcalf Carr
Edited by Reva Basch

"Super Searchers on Competitive Intelligence features the insights and experiences of some of the best in the business. The referenced sites alone are worth the price of the book"

—Carolyn M. Vella, SCIP Meritorious Award Winner and author, *Bottom Line Competitive Intelligence*

Here are leading CI researchers in their own words, revealing their secrets for monitoring competitive forces and keeping on top of the trends, opportunities, and threats within their industries. Researcher and CI pro Margaret Metcalf Carr asked experts from 15 CI-savvy organizations to share tips, techniques, and models that can be successfully applied to any business intelligence project. Includes dozens of examples of CI research in action and a range of strategies that can help any organization stay several steps ahead of the competition.

2003/336 pp/softbound/ISBN 0-910965-64-1 • $24.95

Building & Running
a Successful Research Business
A Guide for the Independent Information Professional

By Mary Ellen Bates
Edited by Reva Basch

This is the handbook every aspiring independent
information professional needs to launch, manage,
and build a research business. Organized into four
sections, "Getting Started," "Running the Business,"
"Marketing," and "Researching," the book walks you
through every step of the process. Author and
long-time independent researcher Mary Ellen Bates
covers everything from "is this right for you?" to
closing the sale, managing clients, promoting your
business, and tapping into powerful information sources.

2003/360 pp/softbound/ISBN 0-910965-62-5 • $29.95

Super Searchers Make It on Their Own
Top Independent Information Professionals Share Their
Secrets for Starting and Running a Research Business

By Suzanne Sabroski
Edited by Reva Basch

If you want to start and run a successful Information Age
business, read this book. Here, for the first time
anywhere, 11 of the world's top research entrepreneurs
share their strategies for starting a business, developing a
niche, finding clients, doing the research, networking with
peers, and staying up-to-date with Web resources and
technologies. You'll learn how these super searchers use
the Internet to find, organize, analyze, and package
information for their clients. Most importantly, you'll discover their secrets for
building a profitable research business.

2002/336 pp/softbound/ISBN 0-910965-59-5 • $24.95